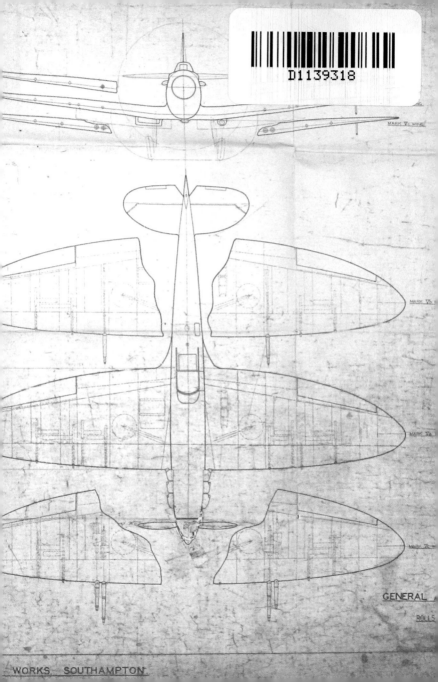

MARK Vc WING

MARK Vb

MARK Vb

MARK Vc

GENERAL

ROLLS

WORKS, SOUTHAMPTON

THE
SPITFIRE
POCKET MANUAL

COMPILED AND INTRODUCED BY MARTIN ROBSON

CONWAY

Acknowledgements

I owe a debt of gratitude to a number of people who helped me during the production of this book. At the National Archives Dr Edward Hampshire assisted me to get up to speed with the nuances of the Air Ministry classification system, thereby greatly aiding the identification of key documents. At the Air Historical Branch Dr Seb Ritchie provided reassurance that I was on the right track with my document selection. Fellow colleagues of King's College London, Defence Studies Department at the Joint Services Command and Staff College, Defence Academy of the UK, provide a constant source of intellectual inspiration. In particular, Dr Guy Finch's encyclopaedic knowledge of all things nuts and bolts greatly helped in the identification of key documents relating to the technical development of the Spitfire while Dr David Hall provided much interesting information on tactical developments. As my Editor at Conway, Alison Moss is, as ever, a judicious and patient taskmaster and her input into this work has been much valued. Any errors that remain in the text are entirely my own. Finally, Charlotte and Harry have provided much needed support, encouragement and enjoyment and it is to them that this work is dedicated.

Ide, June 2010

Dr Martin Robson, King's College London, Defence Studies Department at the Joint Services Command and Staff College, Defence Academy of the UK.

Publishers Note.

In this facsimile edition, references to material not included in the selected extract have been removed to avoid confusion, unless they are an integral part of a sentence. In these instances the note [not included here] has been added.

Contents

Introduction

'Here', I thought to myself, 'is a real lady'.
Jeffrey Quill, Spitfire Test Pilot

The Supermarine Spitfire. Legend. That is what the facts say. The only fighter in service on the first day and the last day of the war. Loved by its pilots, feared by its enemies – even one of the German Aces, Adolf Galland, is alleged to have retorted to *Generalfeldmarschall* of the *Luftwaffe* Hermann Göring that what he needed to win the Battle of Britain was a squadron of Spitfires. The Spitfire was, and still is, an emotive aircraft and with so many books published on the subject, and more coming in this the 70th anniversary year of the Battle of Britain, it would be easy to present a synthesis of ideas.

There is, however, the historian's requirement to bring something new to the story, and that is difficult given the vast literature available on the subject. Instead, there is much to be learned by revisiting the original sources and presenting those of interest in a single volume – it is hoped that this approach will do two things. First, it will assemble a body of evidence to support the arguments made here, not as to whether the Spitfire was or was not a superb aircraft, for of that there can be no doubt, but instead to explore some of the reasons, in particular the relationship between technical and tactical developments – in other words, the thinking through of problems to come up with solutions. Second, this approach allows the historian to make a case yet also provides freedom for the reader to make up their own mind.

Presenting an accessible collection of documents relating to the Spitfire poses some problems. Perhaps the obvious one is to slip into the well-trodden ground covered by historical narrative – for instance, readers hoping to find an exhaustive account of the role of the Spitfire in the Battle of Britain will be disappointed. Secondly, there is so much to choose from, hence I have decided to tie the documents into a technical and tactical framework.

Third, I want to present documents which are interesting to the historian as well as the general reader. Finally, I intend to present documents that relate directly to the Spitfire. For instance, an obvious choice would have been to plump for the pilot notes for the Mark I Spitfire, for it was this model which fought in the Battle of Britain. But some of its performance and handling can be gleaned from the documents presented relating to the origins and testing of K-

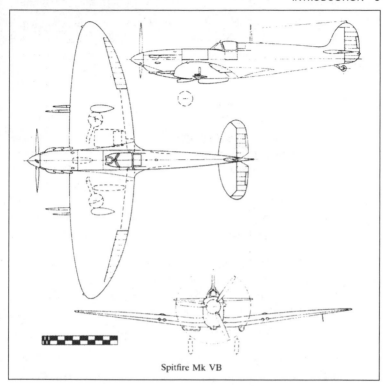

Spitfire Mk VB

5054 as can the experience of flying the Mark I in battle from David Crook's Flying Log. What might seem like other obvious omissions, such as 13 Group's 1941 publication 'Forget-Me-Nots for Fighters', has general tactical relevance beyond the Spitfire and again is not reproduced here (it is worth pointing out that on 1 August 1940 13 Group contained nine squadrons of Hurricanes compared with only five of Spitfires).

Bottom up development in tactical thinking was indicative of a period of reflection following the Battle of Britain when rigid RAF pre-war doctrine had been ripped up by the harsh realities of air fighting. One of the key issues facing such pilots as Crook was the RAF's tactical obsolescence in 1939. RAF doctrine instructed squadrons to fly in 'vic' formations – one aircraft forming the point of a 'V' with two wingmen, one each side, stationed slightly aft thereby forming the distinctive shape. The twelve aircraft of each squadron would replicate this, led by the squadron leader, to produce a tight and neat looking formation supposedly ideal for attacking enemy bombers. What had not been considered was the need to engage escorting enemy fighters, and 'vics' were an excellent target for them. The 'vic' was rigid and its application was stringently guided by doctrine in the form of the wholly impractical Fighting Area Attacks.

It took the realities of combat for those at the sharp end to realise the unsuitability of the 'vic' and to introduce looser formations, such as the 'finger-four' or *Schwarm* often used by the Luftwaffe, who had already spent many years fighting and learning stretching back to the Spanish Civil War. The 'finger-four' contained two elements of two aircraft and thereby provided greater tactical flexibility, as encapsulated in Adolf 'Sailor' Malan's 'Ten Rules for Air Fighting'. Malan flew with 74 Squadron (equipped with the Spitfire Mark I until September 1940 when it received the Mark IIA) and his rules were devised while flying the Spitfire and hence are highly relevant:

1. Wait until you see the whites of his eyes. Fire short bursts of one to two seconds only when your sights are definitely "ON".
2. Whilst shooting think of nothing else, brace the whole of your body: have both hands on the stick: concentrate on your ring sight.
3. Always keep a sharp lookout. "Keep your finger out".
4. Height gives you the initiative.
5. Always turn and face the attack.
6. Make your decisions promptly. It is better to act quickly even though your tactics are not the best.
7. Never fly straight and level for more than 30 seconds in the combat area.
8. When diving to attack always leave a proportion of your formation above to act as a top guard.
9. *INITIATIVE*, *AGGRESSION*, *AIR DISCIPLINE*, and *TEAMWORK* are words that MEAN something in Air Fighting.
10. Go in quickly – Punch hard – Get out!

One only has to compare the roles envisaged for fighters encapsulated in the document describing tactical trials between Spitfires and Blenheims from 1939 with Malan's approach outlined above. But this was a very personal approach and tactical dissemination of lessons learned within the RAF was ad hoc to say the least, and usually occurred at a squadron or group level. The advantage of this was that squadron leaders could ignore doctrine and implement more empirical knowledge, after all, they were at the sharp end and, generally, knew best (one exception to this was Douglas Bader's 'Big Wing', a return to a mass formation which was less than successful). As one would expect, tactical development continued throughout the war as the Spitfire was adapted to fill other requirements, such as those contained in the 2nd Tactical Air Force publications from 1944.

This tactical flexibility came from technical flexibility, and herein lies a problem. Many of the technical histories of the Spitfire are jam-packed with interesting data, statistics, facts and figures but are not particularly accessible or do not necessarily make for easy reading. Starting with the Air Ministry's requirements and specifications, I have used the development of the prototype K-5054 as the starting point for the technical side of the story.

Mutt Summers was the first to fly a Spitfire, the prototype K-5054 for around 15 minutes on 6 March 1936 at Eastleigh. His words upon landing – 'I don't want anything touched' – have often been repeated to prove the aircraft was already almost perfect. In fact there was much testing ahead and Summers' comment was probably to the ground crew not to fiddle with anything before he took to the air again later that day. Summers might have been the first to take to the air, but no one knew the aircraft better than Jeffrey Quill who served as the Spitfire's Test Pilot and flew K-5054 on 26 March 1936. He paints a vivid picture of the pilot's surroundings:

> The cockpit was narrow but not cramped. I sat in a natural and comfortable attitude, the rudder pedals were adjustable, the throttle and mixture controls were placed comfortably for the left hand, the seat was easily adjustable up or down. The retractable undercarriage selector lever and hydraulic pump were situated to the right of the seat. The instrument panel was tidy, symmetric and logically laid out. The windscreen was of curved Perspex which gave a good deal of optical distortion but it had a clear view glass panel (not yet armoured) for vision dead ahead in the line of the gunsight. The sliding canopy was straight sided and operated directly by hand with a latch which engaged the top of the windscreen. With the seat in the fully up position there was very little headroom, but at once I felt good in that cockpit.

Quill flew K-5054 twice that day and twice again the next day. On 26 May K-5054 went to the Aeroplane and Armament Experimental Establishment (AAEE) at Martlesham Heath for testing. It performed well, reaching a top speed of 349mph at 16,800 feet and climbed to 15,000 feet in 5 minutes 42 seconds. Speed and rate of climb were two key factors in air fighting – height was everything and the ability to reach a higher altitude than the enemy was to prove crucial during the summer of 1940.

Quill quickly became acquainted with some of the Spitfire design idiosyncrasies. A long nose obstructed the pilot's view ahead on take-off and landing and necessitated zig-zagging on taxying, the hand-operated hydraulic undercarriage lever was sometimes forgotten about while the undercarriage itself was damage prone. Yet, these were minor issues when compared to the performance and handling achieved by two absolutely key parts of the design.

The Spitfire had been designed to maximise performance and vital to that was the engine, a Rolls Royce Merlin III (though K-5054 had housed a Merlin II) – the length of which had necessitated that long nose. Though the Merlin III also powered the Hurricane, they were fundamentally different aircraft in one crucial area – wing design. Even more important than propulsion, it was the elliptical wing – a design classic from the drawing board of Reginald J. Mitchell – which truly set the Spitfire apart. Fighter wings were generally straight from fuselage to wing tip and relatively thick, like those on the Hurricane. The Spitfire's thinner wings and elliptical wing shape, curving, some might say in an almost sensual fashion, from fuselage to the wing tip, provided aerodynamic performance and aesthetic glamour.

There would be manufacturing problems; Mitchell's desire for performance had produced an engineering marvel but a production manager's nightmare. The Hurricane was constructed from a steel frame covered with wooden runners and fabric, ensuring relative ease of manufacture and thereby allowing the Air Ministry to order 1,000 by late 1938. The Spitfire, on the other hand, utilised Mitchell's Schneider Trophy* experience to produce an all metal wing and fuselage of some complexity requiring developments in manufacturing to meet the requirements of the Air Ministry's order. Compounding this, the British aviation industry was simply not set up for mass production and encountered problems throughout the process. In the end the Spitfire Mark I entered service late, but not too late, for it was the Mark I that took to the skies in the late summer of 1940.

---

*A competition for seaplanes (like all good yarns the Spitfire story really did begin at sea).

Both the Hurricane and the Spitfire wings provided ample room for fitting guns, though the Spitfire wing design necessitated a spread in her arrangement while those in the Hurricane were concentrated together making it easier and quicker for ground crew to reload. Mitchell was Chief Designer of the Supermarine Aviation Works and responsible for the design of three winners (S.5 in 1927, S.6 in 1929 and S.6B in 1931) of the Schneider Trophy. At a time when the RAF were still flying biplanes, Mitchell's monoplanes designs were at the cutting edge of aircraft development – and they served as the ideal blueprint for fast fighter aircraft. Diagnosed with rectal cancer in 1933, Mitchell, convinced that the storm clouds were gathering across Europe, responded with vigour throwing himself into his work. Responding to the Air Ministry's 1930 F.7/30 specification Mitchell produced two further designs, both of which failed.

Air Ministry specifications were issued to produce aircraft for a reason, in the case of F.7/30 to provide the RAF with a fighter to counter the growing threat from enemy bombers. Interwar air theorists were convinced that future conflict would be decided in the air by mass formations of enemy bombers who, according to many, 'would always get through' defences to drop their payloads on helpless civilian populations. In fact, there would be little point trying to stop them, hence for many efforts to build up a credible fighter force were a waste of time, money and resources. Instead, the main role for air power would be to strike back at Britain's likely enemy, France, and expanded after 1933 to include Germany, through offensive strategic bombing, the main proponent of which was Marshal of the RAF Sir Hugh Trenchard. It is no surprise that Bomber Command attracted the bulk of RAF resources.

There were a few dissenting voices, including Air-Vice Marshal Sir Hugh Dowding who had flown fighters in the First World War. Dowding was tasked with Air Ministry research and development, a position which gave plenty of opportunity to counter orthodox bomber theory through his influence over the issuing of fighter specifications. Two further specifications would have a major impact upon British fighter design. The first was F.37/34, issued in December 1934 and which had been formulated with one of Mitchell's F.7/30 failures in mind, the Type 300. While the Spitfire and its classic wing was built to F.37/34 it was F.10/35 of April 1935 which led to another design feature which was to have a major impact in 1940 – the incorporation of eight guns into the wing design.

The Spitfire entered production on 3 June 1936 with an Air Ministry order for 310 at £4,500 per aircraft. Testing of the design continued with Quill often at the controls of K-5054. Quill was also in the cockpit of the first production model, K-9787, which flew on 15 May 1938 – it is testament to the genius of the original design that Quill thought there was little difference between prototype and production version. Only three months later, on 4 August 1938, the Mark I Spitfire K-9789 was the first to enter service, with 19 Squadron Royal Air Force based at Duxford.

Mitchell did not live to see how successful his design was, he had died on 11 June 1937. Responsibility for the Spitfire design had passed onto Joseph Smith who oversaw the logical development of the design up to and during the Second World War. If one can judge success in numerical terms the fact that 22,759 Spitfires were built through 24 different marks and 52 different design variants to fulfil a number of roles including high-altitude photo reconnaissance, adaption for service in the Middle and Far East, and a navalised variant, the Seafire, for use at sea, it is beyond doubt that the Spitfire was a triumph. In all this performance remained key and continual improvements were made to the piston engine. The Rolls Royce Merlin III of the Mark I was superseded by a number of Merlin variants through to the Merlin 70 of the Mark XI, before the engine itself was completely replaced by the Rolls Royce Griffon used in the Spitfire Mark XII.

Right from the start, changes were made to the standard armament, for instance the classic Mark I housed eight .303 Browning machine guns, four in each wing, whereas the Mark IB housed only four .303 machine guns in total but carried added punch from the inclusion of two 20mm Hispano cannon. Three standard wing designs 'A', 'B' and 'C' provided for this mix of armaments again allowing the Spitfire to fulfil a number of roles whether attacking enemy fighters or bombers. The 'C' wing, containing four .303 machine guns and either two or four 20mm cannon, became the universal design due to its flexibility. Later Spitfire versions carried 500lb and then 1,000lb bombs. Clearly, as operational needs moved from the pure fighter role required for the air defence of Great Britain against *Luftwaffe* bombers and fighters in 1940 through the offensive use of fighters in gaining air superiority over Europe (and to show the Russians that the Western Powers were doing *something*) and then to the fighter-bomber role to provide close air support in 1944. In this latter role a Spitfire of 412 Squadron claimed a notable success on 17 July 1944 when strafing a staff car and wounding its occupant, *Generalfeldmarschall* Erwin Rommel. Clearly, the Spitfire design had met the challenges thrown up by war.

It was the very flexibility and adaptability of the design that ensured the Spitfire could fulfil a range of roles. The Mark V, for example, was built in larger numbers than any other Spitfire – 6,479 aircraft. So while the Mark I might be considered to be the classic design due to its participation in the Battle of Britain, from a technical and production point of view the Mark V might be considered the most successful design providing the backbone to the RAF's 'leaning into Europe' strategy during 1941–43. This involved the use of 'Rhubarbs' (small-scale fighter offensives searching for opportunity targets in France), 'Circuses' (short range bomber attacks with fighter escorts) and larger fighter sweeps. Unlike the Mark I, the Mark V was not limited to operations in Europe. From the deserts of North Africa, the Jungles of the Far East to a return to its spiritual home – flying off aircraft carriers – the Mark V saw action in all theatres of the Second World War. The Spitfire story is a truly international affair, for it was not just the preserve of British pilots. During the Battle of Britain many had been flown by non-British nationals including Poles, Canadians and New Zealanders – and 'Sailor' Malan was South African. Later in the war Spitfires were sent to the Air Forces of Russia, Portugal, Australia, India, South Africa and the USA.

A further catalyst for technical development was, of course, the enemy, and the appearance of the FW 190 in the skies above Europe in the late summer of 1940 was a sharp surprise. Until that date the Spitfire had generally the better of German fighters (for a number of reasons beyond technical superiority including the basic fact of fighting over home soil allowed for the recovery of many downed pilots, plus radar and better command and control systems). Its main opponents had been the single-seat Bf109, a more than capable design in the hands of an expert though which generally had mixed results over Britain, and the heavier and cumbersome Bf110, which suffered greatly at the hands of the RAF in 1940. In response came the interim Mark V clipped wing, which enhanced manoeuvrability, until the Mark IX came into service and, albeit narrowly, tipped the balance back towards the RAF. With the appearance of *Luftwaffe* high-altitude bombers flying at around 40,000ft the interim Mark VI and VII had been developed with pressure cabins and heating to meet the threat. Many variants followed but even in the last year of the war Spitfire Mark IXs provided a substantial number of the RAF's operational fighter airframes.

Of the later variants, it was the Mark XIV which truly stands out with its Griffon engine and five-bladed contra-propeller. It entered service in January 1944 and Quill thought it a quantum jump in performance – an opinion backed up by the Air Ministry who concluded it had the best all-round performance of any fighter then in service. With the war approaching a conclusion Spitfire production wound down; of the last variant, the Mark 24, only 81 were built.

On 20 February 1948, Spitfire VN496, a Mark 24, rolled off the production line as the last of the design to be produced. Jet engines were the future, and had in fact already entered service with the RAF in 1944 in the form of the Gloster Meteor with the de Haviland Vampire following suit two years later.

In the post-war period there were a few last hurrahs for the piston-engined Spitfire – rocket-armed Mark XVIII's were used for close air support and to strike at enemy ground targets in the Malayan Emergency with the last such attack taking place on January 1951. Predating this had been the last air-to-air combat for the Spitfire; it was also one of the most unusual for it was against itself. In January 1949 as part of the Arab-Israeli War, Israeli Mark IX Spitfires had engaged RAF Mark XVIII Spitfires.

Today the roar of a Merlin or Griffon engine can still be heard as part of the RAF's Battle of Britain Memorial Flight which contains five Spitfires, including the only flying survivor of the Battle of Britain, the Mark IIA Spitfire P7350.

There is one final detail which causes some puzzlement: why the Spitfire? The name appears first in the records in late June 1935. Mitchell did not name his design, it was Sir Robert McLean, the Chairman of Vickers, Supermarine's parent Company, who named it after his daughter Ann, who he thought of as a 'little spitfire'. This was a huge improvement on Vickers's original selection of the 'Shrew' – and perhaps the last word on that proposal is best left to Mitchell who commented it was 'just the sort of silly name they would give to it'.

Martin Robson

SPITFIRE AND SEAFIRE OPERATIONAL MARKS

[Source: Jeffrey Quill, *Spitfire: A Test Pilot's Story*, pp. 296–298]

SPITFIRES: FIGHTERS

Mk IA	1030 hp R.R. Merlin II, III	8 × .303 machine guns
Mk IB	1030 hp R.R. Merlin III	Armed initially with 2 x 20 mm cannon only; later 2 × 20 mm plus 4 rcmg
Mk IIA	1175 hp R.R. Merlin XII	Produced at Castle Bromwich
Mk IIA (L.R.)	1175 hp R.R. Merlin XII	Fitted with 30 gal. long range fuel tank under port wing

Mk IIB	1175 hp R.R. Merlin XII	Mk II with 'B' Wing – 2 × 20 mm plus 4 remg
Mk IIC	1175 hp R.R. Merlin XII	Later designated ASR II (Air Sea Rescue)
Mk VA	1470 hp R.R. Merlin XLV (45)	8 rcmg
F.Mk VB	1470 hp R.R. Merlin 45	'B' Wing
	1415 hp R.R. Merlin 46	Engine with higher rated altitude
L.F.Mk VB	1585 hp R.R. Merlin 45M	Lower altitude rating engine
F.Mk Vc	1470 hp R.R. Merlin 45, 50, 50A, 55, 56	'C' Universal wing
	1415 hp R.R. Merlin 46	
L.F.Mk Vc	1585 hp R.R. Merlin 45M, 50M, 55M	Lower altitude rating
Mk VI	1415 hp R.R. Merlin 47	Pressure cabin (PC)
Mk VII	1710 hp R.R. Merlin 64	PC & 2-speed, 2-stage Merlin
	1565 hp R.R. Merlin 61	
F.Mk VIII	1565 hp R.R. Merlin 61	
	1650 hp R.R. Merlin 63	
	1710 hp R.R. Merlin 63A	
L.F. Mk VIII	1580 hp R.R. Merlin 66	
H.F.Mk VIII	1475 hp R.R. Merlin 70	
F.Mk IXc	1565 hp R.R. Merlin 61	
	1650 hp R.R. Merlin 63	
	1710 hp R.R. Merlin 63A	
L.F.Mk IXc	1580 hp R.R. Merlin 66	
H.F.Mk IX	1475 hp R.R. Merlin 70	
F.Mk IXE	R.R. Merlin 61, 63, 63A	'B' Wing 2 × 20mm mgs + 2 × 0.5 in. mgs
L.F.Mk IXE	1580 hp R.R. Merlin 66	
H.F.Mk IXE	1475 hp R.R. Merlin 70	
Mk XII	1735 hp R.R. Griffon III, IV	
Mk XIVc	2035 hp R.R. Griffon 65	'C' Wing
F.Mk XIVE	2035 hp R.R. Griffon 65	'E' Wing

F.R.Mk XIVe	2035 hp R.R. Griffon 65	Rear-view fuselage. Oblique camera in rear fuselage
L.F.Mk XVI	1580 hp Packard R.R. Merlin 266	'C' Wing
L.F.Mk XVIe	1580 hp Packard R.R. Merlin 266	'F' Wing
Mk 21	2035 hp R.R. Griffon 61	

SPITFIRES: PHOTO RECONNAISSANCE

Type 'A'	1030 hp R.R. Merlin III	No extra fuel
Type 'B'	1030 hp R.R. Merlin III	Extra 30 gal. tank in fuselage behind pilot
Type 'C'	1030 hp R.R. Merlin III	As 'B' with additional 30 gal fuel tank under port wing
Type 'D'	1030 hp R.R. Merlin III	Special long range. Leading edge wing tank, + 30 gal. fuselage tank
{ Type 'F' (PR Mk VI)	1030 hp R.R. Merlin III 1470 hp R.R. Merlin 45	{ As 'B' with additional 30 gal. tank under each wing
{ Type 'G' 1(PR Mk VII)	1030 hp R.R. Merlin III 1470 hp R.R. Merlin 45	{ Armed low level PR Aircraft
P.R. Mk IV	1470 hp R.R. Merlin 45 1415 hp R.R. Merlin 46	Production version of Type D, fitted with Merlin 45/46
P.R. Mk X	1475 hp R.R. Merlin 77	P.C. 2-stage, 2-speed s/c
P.R. Mk XI	R.R. Merlin 61,63,63A, 70	
P.R. Mk XIII	1645 hp R.R. Merlin 32	Armed low level P.R. produced by conversion
P.R. Mk XIX 66 F.Mk VI (P.R.)	2035 hp R.R. Griffon 65, 1415 hp R.R. Merlin 47	All except first 22 with PC 6 Mk VI fighters sent to ME in 1942 for P.R. work

SEAFIRES

Mk IB	1470 hp R.R. Merlin 45	Produced by conversion
	1415 hp R.R. Merlin 46	from Spitfire VB
Mk IIC	1470 hp R.R. Merlin 45,	'C' Wing
	50A	
	1415 hp R.R. Merlin 46	
Mk L.IIC	1645 hp R.R. Merlin 32	
Mk L.R. IIC	1645 hp R.R. Merlin 32	F.R. version of L.IIC
Mk L.IIc (Hybrid)	1585 hp R.R. Merlin 55M	26 basic Mk IIIs produced
		by Westlands with fixed
		'C' Wing
Mk F.III	1470 hp R.R. Merlin 55	Folding 'C' Wings
Mk L.III	1585 hp R.R. Merlin 55M	
Mk F.R. III	1585 hp R.R. Merlin 55M	
Mk XV	1815 hp R.R. Griffon VI	
Mks F & FRXVII	1815 hp R.R. Griffon VI	
Mks F & FR 47	2145 hp R.R. Griffon 87	
	2350 hp R.R. Griffon 88	

NOTES

1 Spitfire Mk IIA (L.R.) is an unofficial designation, but is a convenient way of distinguishing the IIA with the extra under wing fuel tank from the standard IIA. Approximately 100 were produced.

2 Spitfires F & F.R. Mk XVIII and Mk 22 did not become operational in the Royal Air Force until after the cessation of hostilities.

3 Spitfire 'P.R. Type E': There was only one known example and I have omitted it from the list.

4 Spitfire F.Mk VI (P.R.). This again is an unofficial designation. These aircraft were soon relegated to communications duties, but two operational sorties took place with 680 (P.R.) Squadron in 1943: one in April to Crete, the other in May to Crete and Piraeus.

5 Seafire XV. This aircraft received its Service Release in April 1945.

6 The Seafires Mk XVII and 47 entered Squadron Service after the cessation of hostilities. The Mk 47 was operational in the Korean War.

CHAPTER I
Air Ministry Specifications

SPECIFICATION NO F. 7/30
1st OCTOBER 1931

Single Seater Day and Night Fighter

1. General Requirements

(a) The aircraft is to fulfil the duties of "Single Seater Fighter" for day and night flying. A satisfactory fighting view is essential and designers should consider the advantages offered in this respect by low wing monoplane or pusher.

The main requirements for the aircraft are:

(i) Highest possible rate of climb

(ii) Highest possible speed at 15,000 feet

(iii) Fighting view

(iv) Manoeuvrability

(v) Capability of easy and rapid production in quantity

(vi) Ease of maintenance.

(b) The aircraft must have a good degree of positive stability about all axes in flight and trimming gear must be fitted so that the tail incidence can be adjusted in flight to ensure that the aircraft will fly horizontally at all speeds within the flying range, without requiring attention from the pilot.

(c) When carrying the total load specified in paragraph 3, the aircraft must be fully controllable at all flying speeds, especially near the stall and during a steep dive, when there must be no tendency for the aircraft to hunt.

(d) The aircraft must have a high degree of manoeuvrability. It must answer all controls quickly and must not be tiring to fly. The control must be adequate to stop an incipient spin when the aircraft is stalled.

An approved type of slot control, or other means which will ensure adequate lateral control and stability, at and below stalling speed, is to be embodied.

The design of the aileron control is to be such that operation of the ailerons in flight will produce the minimum of adverse yawing effect on the aircraft.

(e) The aircraft is to be designed to accommodate the equipment listed in paragraph 6 and scheduled in detail in the Appendix "A" [not included here] to this Specification.

(f) The crew, armament and equipment are to be arranged as specified in paragraph 7 of this Specification.

(g) The arrangements for alighting and taking off must be as specified in paragraph 8 of this Specification.

(h) The aircraft and all parts thereof are to be designed and constructed in conformity with the requirements of the Director of Technical Development, Air Ministry.

A "Type Record" for the aircraft, including all drawings and a complete set of strength calculations and weight estimates must be submitted to the Director of Technical Development or his authorised representative for acceptance. The contractor, pending acceptance, may proceed with construction if he so desires, but the Director of Technical Development reserves the right to reject any part or parts so made if subsequently found to be under strength or otherwise unsuitable for H. M. Service.

Two copies of fully-dimensioned General Arrangement drawing to the aircraft as actually built, together with a General Arrangement drawing showing the layout of the complete equipment, are to be supplied to the Director of Technical Development (R.D.A3) immediately on the completion of the first aircraft. Similarly in the case of any subsequent aircraft if differing from the first.

(i) The aircraft is to be constructed throughout in metal and is to be constructed and protected as to adequately withstand sudden changes in temperature and humidity such as are experienced in semi-tropical climates. Streamline wires, tie-rods and other parts not of stainless steel are to be coated with cadmium or zinc by an approved process. Aluminium and aluminium alloy parts are to be anodically treated.

(j) As soon as possible after the mock-up conference the contractor is to supply to the Director of Technical Development (R.D.4) a General Arrangement Drawing of the engine installation (including fuel, oil and water systems, tankage and engine controls). (See also paragraph 10).

(k) On the completion of the first aircraft off the contract the contractor shall supply to the Director of Technical Development such details of the equipment and its accessories and the detail weights, length and quantities thereof as will enable the Appendix "A" Schedule of Equipment to be completed.

This information is to be supplied by amending a copy of the current Appendix "A" to agree with the approved aircraft, in conformity with the current master schedule.

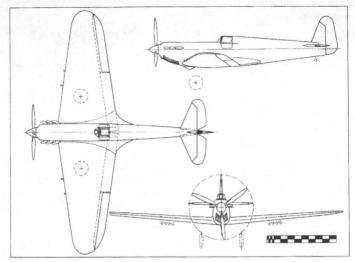

F.7/30 development

Similarly, on the delivery of the last aircraft off the contract, if alterations have been made to the equipment, a suitable amended copy of the current Appendix "A" is to be supplied to the Director of Technical Development.

(l) All materials used must, where possible, be to B.E.S.A. or other standard Specifications as approved by the Director of Technical Development.

All materials quoted under approved Specifications are to be to the latest issue of the Specification. A list of approved Specifications showing the latest issue numbers may be obtained on application in writing to the Director of Technical Development.

Similarly, all A.G.S. parts incorporated in the aircraft are to be to the latest approved issue of the appropriate drawings but the issue number should not be quoted on the aircraft drawing. Where the contractor proposes to use materials for which standard approved Specifications are not available, the contractor is required to notify the Director of Technical Development, in writing, of his intention, and to supply such information and test pieces of the materials proposed as the Director of Technical Development may deem necessary, to enable adequate tests of the materials to be carried out.

(m) Two copies of rigging and maintenance notes are to be supplied to the Director of Technical Development (R.T.P.) not later than the date on which the first aircraft is delivered to the experimental establishment.

In order to facilitate further reproduction of any diagrams contained in the notes, tracings thereof are to be supplied also.

The note should anticipate any difficulty likely to be encountered by the Service Unit during the development of a new type and are to include:-

(i) leading particulars, principal dimensions, and the capacities of fuel and oil tanks in tabular form;

(ii) complete and detailed instructions for rigging the aircraft;

(iii) any unusual features (including non-standard equipment) from the point of view of maintenance;

(iv) lubrication instructions;

(v) description of the engine mounting and installation in so far as they are peculiar to the particular aircraft;

(vi) three-view general arrangement drawings (showing the horizontal datum line on the side view) and diagrams of the petrol and oil systems;

(vii) the approved equipment layout drawings as called for in paragraph 10 (d).

It is to be observed that these notes are required only for a preliminary guide for those who will be responsible for maintaining the aircraft in its early stages and it will suffice if they are written on the lines of a works instruction.

In the event of the aircraft being adopted for use in the Royal Air Force the contractor will be required to prepare notes and drawings covering the repair of the aircraft by Service Units.

2. Power Unit

(a) Any approved British engine may be used. It is to be noted that, when an engine is in process of development, provision is to be made in the aircraft design for a possible increase in engine weight.

(b) The installation of the engine is to be so arranged that the engine is capable of being rapidly and easily removed from the aircraft.

Supports and footholds are to be provided to facilitate minor repairs and adjustments to be the engine installation.

(c) The whole of the cowling is to be designed to facilitate rapid and easy removal and replacement and is to be sufficiently robust to withstand frequent removal and constant handling; wire skewers are not to be used.

(d) The cowling is to be finished in an approved manner so as to give adequate protection against corrosion and to prevent the reflection of light which might betray the presence of the aircraft or dazzle the crew.

(e) Before drawings relative to the engine installation can be accepted the engine, fuel, oil and water systems, and the accessories and piping therefore, must be fitted in the first experimental aircraft and put in proper running order, so that the installation as a whole may be examined and, if satisfactory, approved by the Director of Technical Development, or his authorised representative.

(f) The airscrew is preferably to be of metal construction, and is to be designed in accordance with the required performance of the aircraft as specified in paragraph 4 of this Specification, but no airscrew will be accepted which allows the maximum permissible r.p.m. to be exceeded in full throttle horizontal flight at the supercharged altitude of the engine, or the normal r.p.m. to be exceeded in full throttle climbing flight at the best rate of climb above this altitude.

A standard engine instruction plate is to be fitted in a position where it will be clearly visible to the pilot.

2. (A) Tankage including gravity tanks to be provided for the endurance specified in paragraph 3.

(a) Adequate air space is to be provided in the oil tank: at least 1 gallon for air-cooled engines and 2 gallons for water-cooled engines.

(b) A gravity fuel tank is to be provided sufficient for at least 20 minutes at full throttle at ground level.

(c) The fuel tanks are to be adequately protected from deterioration in a manner approved by the Director of Technical Development and may be either:-

(i) Carried inside the fuselage

or

(ii) Carried inside the main planes. In this case the construction of the portions of the main planes containing the fuel tanks and the installation of the fuel tanks therein must be such that there can be no possibility of escaping fuel or fuel vapour from a damaged tank spreading to any inflammable portions of the aircraft structure

or

(iii) Carried externally in such a position that if damaged the escaping fuel will be blown clear of all parts of the aircraft structure when in flight.

(d) All tanks are to be provided with readily removable sumps or with approved means of removing all dirt and foreign matter from the interior of the tank.

(e) The delivery from the tank to the piping system is to be so arranged as to prevent as far as is practicable the passage of foreign matter from the tank into the piping system.

Means are to be provided, under the control of a member of the crew, for stopping and restarting the flow from any of the fuel tanks at each outlet from which the fuel would otherwise escape if the pipe line or balance pipe connected therewith were to break.

(f) Arrangements are to be made for the rapid and easy draining of the tanks, and rapid and easy filling with standard filler nozzles.

(g) All tanks are to be designed to be readily removable from and replaceable in position in the aircraft, with a minimum of disturbance to the aircraft structure and to other installations.

2. (B) Fuel and Oil Systems

(a) The fuel and oil systems shall be in general accordance with the requirements of Specification No 18 (Misc)

(b) All pipe joints are to be of approved metallic type, and together with all cocks, plugs, etc., are to be locked in accordance with A.G.S. Mod 157.

(c) The bore of the main fuel pipes must be such that the flow of fuel sufficient to maintain full power on the ground is exceeded by 100 per cent when the carburetter unions are uncoupled and the supply is in the condition of minimum head with the aircraft set at the appropriate angle so defined hereunder in clause (d) (i).

The last section of the delivery pipe to the carburetters is to be of the approved flexible type.

(d) The fuel feed may be either:-

(i) By approved fuel pumps from the main tanks direct to the carburetters with a by-pass to a gravity tank, so situated that, when the aircraft is flying at its maximum climbing angle, or when the aircraft is tail down on the ground, whichever condition gives the greatest inclination of the aircraft axis to the horizontal, the minimum effective head above the jet level of the highest carburetter when the gravity tank is practically empty is not less than the minimum specified for the type of carburetter used.

In calculating the minimum effective head due allowance must be made for any effect due to acceleration when the aircraft is in motion.

The delivery from the pumps to the carburetter must be via an approved release or reducing valve to a distributer cock or cocks so arranged that the following selections can be made.

(1) Pumps to carburetters and gravity tanks

(2) Pumps to carburetters direct

(3) Gravity tanks to carburetters

(4) Off

Wind driven pumps are not to be used.

An overflow pipe of sufficient bore to deal with all excess fuel must be provided from the gravity tank to the main tank or to some other approved point in the fuel system.

A prismatic flow indicator visible to the pilot is to be fitted in the overflow pipe

or

(ii) By gravity tanks alone feeding direct to the carburetter. Such gravity tanks must conform to the requirements laid down in (i) above.

(e) A diagram of the fuel system is to be affixed in an approved position in the aircraft.

(f) An approved type of petrol filter is to be fitted so that the whole of the fuel passes through it before reaching the carburetter. The filter must be disposed so that it will be accessible for cleaning.

2. (C) Cooling Systems

(a) Provision is to be made for adequate oil cooling and a thermometer registering in a position visible to the pilot is to be fitted in such a position as to indicate the temperature of the oil supplied to the engine.

In addition, on the first aircraft, an oil thermometer registering in a position visible to the pilot, is to be fitted in the return pipe from the engine between the scavenger pump and the oil cooler.

(b) If a water or evaporating engine is used, the cooling system, which is to be installed in accordance with the requirements of D.T.D., is to be designed to fulfil English summer requirements, with provision for changing to a system fulfilling Tropical summer requirements, with a minimum of alteration. If water indicators are used they are to be fitted with shutters or other approved means of temperature control.

(c) In addition to the thermometer fittings and thermometers normally required on radiators for production aircraft, the experimental aircraft is to be provided with approved thermometer fittings in the outlet header tanks or each radiator or auxiliary radiator.

2. (D) Engine Starting and Silencing

(a) The exhaust manifold of approved type supplied with the engine is to be fitted in such a manner as to provide adequately for silencing, and for flame-damping during night flying.

(b) Provision is to be made on the aircraft by the installation of the requisite approved fittings for the installation of an R.A.E. Mark II Starter and for the rapid and easy attachment of a compressor type engine starter carried on a separate trolley.

(c) Provision is to be made for rapidly warming the engine oil. It must be possible to take off within 2½ minutes from a cold start.

3. Load to be carried

In addition to any stowages and mountings necessitated by the requirements of paragraphs 6 and 7 and by alternative loads, the following load is to be carried during the acceptance flights:-

	Removable	Fixed	Total
Crew (1)	180	—	180 lb
Oxygen	15	8	23
Instruments	1	25	26
R/T Apparatus	46	6	52
Electrical Equipment	41	17	58
Parachute and belt	20	3	23
Armament			
4 guns and C.C. gcar*	120	20	140
Gun sights	—	5	5
200 rounds S.A.A.	145	—	145
Signal Pistol & Cartridges	7	1	8
Military Load;	575	85	660 lb

*This item will be adjusted to the actual gun installation adopted

Fuel	For ½ hour at full throttle at
Oil	ground level, plus 2.0 hours at full
Water (if required).	throttle at 15,000',
	Oil—ditto plus 50% excess.
	Water—ditto.

4. Contract Performance

The performance of the aircraft, as ascertained during the official type trials when carrying the total load specified in paragraph 3 and with an airscrew satisfying the requirements of paragraph 2 (e) shall be:-

Horizontal speed at 15,000 ft not less than 195 mph

alighting speed not to exceed 60 mph

Service ceiling not less than 28,000 ft

Time to 15,000 ft not more than 8½ mins

The specified alighting speed must not be exceeded, but may be obtained by variable camber or equivalent devices provided that control and manoeuvrability are not adversely affected.

5. Structural Strength

(a) The strength of the main structure when carrying the load specified in paragraph 3, plus 100 lb shall not be less than as defined hereunder:-

Load factor throughout the structure with the centre of pressure in the most forward position: 9.0

Load factor for wing structure with the centre of pressure in its most backward position in horizontal flight: 6.0

Load factor in a terminal nose dive: 1.75

Inverted Flight

(1) Load factor at incidence corresponding to the inverted stall and with C.P. at 1/3 of the chord: 4.5

(2) Load factor at incidence appropriate to steady horizontal inverted flight and at the maximum speed of horizontal normal flight: 4.5

(b) The alighting gear must be able to withstand an impact at a vertical velocity of 10 feet per second and at this velocity the load on the alighting gear must not exceed three times the fully loaded weight of the aircraft.

(c) When subject to the impact forces on alighting, as specified above, the load factor for the alighting gear must not be less than 1–1/3, and for the remainder of the structure not less than 1–1/2. The load factor for the structure and the attachment fittings of the alighting gear must always be greater than that for the alighting gear itself by the margin indicated above.

(d) The maximum weight per wheel of the aircraft in pounds must not exceed 12 times the product of the wheel and tyre diameters in inches with the aircraft carrying the full load specified above.

(e) The above factors are to be determined by the approved official methods as published by the Directorate of Technical Development and the detail requirements given in A.P. 970 are also to be satisfied. With a view to minimising the risk of flutter, attention should be given to the recommendations of R. & M. 1177, particularly as regards the static balance of ailerons.

(f) The wing is to be sufficiently rigid to withstand satisfactorily any torsional or other loads which may be encountered during service operations.

(g) Ribs (both main plane and tail unit) are required to develop, on test, factors 20 per cent greater than those specified for the aircraft as a whole.

6. Equipment

The equipment as listed hereunder and as scheduled in detail in the Appendix "A" to this Specification [not included here] is to be provided for and the contractor will be required to supply and fit all parts necessary for its installation; in the case of R/T panels, etc., etc., the position for all instruments and the identities of plugs and leads must be indicated by fixed labels.

It is to be noted that the weights of various items of fixed equipment listed hereunder and scheduled in detail in the Appendix "A", but not quoted in paragraph 3, are to be allowed for in design.

Diagrams of the wiring and piping for all equipment installations are to be provided, for carrying in a canvas bag fitted in an approved position on the aircraft.

All equipment is to be installed in accordance with the requirements of the Director of Technical Development.

(a) Armament

Reflector sight (To be installed in
Ring and Bead Sight accordance with
Signal Pistol and 8 cartridges Specification
4 x 20 lb bombs No G.E. 126)

2 x .303" Vickers guns installed in the cockpit under the control of the pilot with C.C. gear as necessary. and either:-

    (i) 2 x .303" Vickers guns installed in the cockpit or wings. If in the cockpit and synchronised an additional C.C. gear reservoir is to be fitted for them. If in the wings adequate locating arrangements are essential.

or:-

    (ii) 2 x .303" Lewis guns installed so that synchronisation is unnecessary. These guns do not require heating. 2000 rounds of ammunition for the above guns with links or drums as necessary. The minimum supply to be forwarded for any gun is 400 rounds. 400 round drums will be available for Lewis guns.

(b) Electrical Equipment

Services are to be provided for: (To be installed in accordance with Specification No G.E. 164)

Navigation and Identification Lights

Gun Heaters

(as necessary for outboardguns)

Wing tip flares

(on concealed brackets)

Instrument Lighting

(c) Instruments and General Equipment

The following instruments (of luminous pattern, where available) are to be fitted in the cockpit in accordance with the requirements of the Director of Technical Development:-

1 Air Speed Indicator

1 Altimeter

1 Revolution Indicator

1 Oil Pressure Gauge

Fuel Contents Gauge (1 per main tank)

1 Oil Thermometer (An extra oil thermometer is required on the first aircraft).

1 Radiator Thermometer (if required). An extra water thermometer is required on the first aircraft.

Boost Gauge (if required)

1 Watch and Holder

1 Compass

1 Pilot's Fighting Harness (Sutton Type)

Oxygen Apparatus

1 Map Case

1 Turn Indicator

(d) Wireless Equipment

Earth System, Bonding and Screening in accordance with Specification G.E. 125.

R/T Apparatus (Two-way)

R/T Box

Fixed Aerial.

(e) Parachute Equipment

1 Irving type Parachute

7. Disposition of Crew, Armament and Equipment

(a) The Pilot's view is to conform as closely as possible to that obtainable in "pusher" aircraft. The following requirements indicate the ideal view which is considered to be necessary, and the aircraft should be designed to conform as closely to them as is possible in practice.

(b) The pilot must have a clear view forward and upward for formation work and manoeuvring, and particular care is needed to prevent his view of hostile aircraft being blanketed out by top planes and centre sections when manoeuvring to attack. Planes should be so disposed as not to obstruct the pilot's view of other aircraft, when his own is pointing within 60° of their direction.

The direction in which obstruction by planes is least serious is in the backward and downward directions.

(c) For landing a good view forward and downward is necessary, and the pilot must be able to see within 17° from the vertical over the side when wearing the Sutton harness.

The point on the ground on which the pilot desires to land should not be obstructed by planes during the gliding approach. This applies especially to normal landing manoeuvres such as banked turns and side slips.

The windscreen should be sufficiently high to enable the pilot to have a clear view forward through the screen. When taxying with the tail down the pilot, with minimum movement of his head, should be able to see directly in front of his aircraft, while with tail up for taking off he should be able to see the ground 50 feet ahead over the centre line of the aircraft, with his seat in the normal flying position. The top fuselage coaming, on either side of the windscreen, should be as narrow and tapered as possible consistent with adequate protection from the slipstream.

(d) For gun aiming purposes the pilot should have an unobstructed view forward over as wide a cone as possible the sight being the axis of that cone with his eye the apex.

(e) The pilot is to be provided with 4 guns, and stowage for 2000 rounds of ammunition as detailed in paragraph 6(a).

Provision is to be made for fitting of a G.3 camera gun complete with firing and cocking controls. The mounting and controls must be quickly removable and must not interfere with the guns and sights in any way. This provision is secondary and must not influence the design of the aircraft in any way.

(f) The pilot is to be provided with a map case, and stowage for knee-type writing pad mounted in a convenient position.

(g) The relative positions of the pilot's seat and rudder bar are to be designed to be adjustable both vertically and horizontally to suit pilots of different trunk length and leg reach.

(h) The design of the cockpit must be such as to provide the comfort necessary for the pilot to fulfil his various duties efficiently, and must allow complete freedom of movement, particularly in an emergency that obliges the pilot to take to his parachute.

The cockpit is to be adequately screened from the wind but the windscreen must not interfere with the satisfactory use of sights, one of which should be on the centre line of the aircraft, the sights being interchangeable in position.

The cockpit is to be painted internally with an approved grey-green paint. This instruction does not apply to the instrument board.

The cockpit padding and other upholstery is to be rendered fireproof to the satisfaction of the Director of Technical Development.

(i) Standard clips are to be provided under the wings for the carrying of one standard bomb rack for 4 x 20 lb bombs.

Room is to be provided to enable the bomb release gear for these bombs to be fitted inside on the port side of the cockpit.

The arrangement of the bomb carrier installation must be such that sufficient clearance is provided to enable the bombs to be released even when the aircraft is in a very steep dive.

(j) Arrangements are to be made to provide adequate cockpit heating without resort to electrical appliances.

(k) The dynamo for the electrical equipment is to be stowed internally and driven from the engine. The aircraft designer must agree the details of the drive with the engine designer.

8. Arrangements for alighting and taking off

(a) The aircraft is to be designed to pull up quickly on alighting and wheel brakes of an approved type are to be fitted.

The brake controls shall be such that the brakes can be applied together or independently. It is essential that the pilot shall not be obliged to abandon the aircraft or engine controls when applying the brakes. Means are to be provided for locking the brakes in the "on" position so that the wheel chocks may be dispensed with if so desired. The whole of the braking system is to be capable of rapid and easy removal when not required.

(b) The aircraft is to be suitable for operation from small, rough-surfaced and enclosed aerodromes.

(c) The alighting gear is to be of oleo or equivalent type in which the use of rubber in tension is eliminated.

(d) The wheel track of the alighting gear must be such as to provide stable taxying conditions in any direction in a wind of 20 mph without any tendency for the aircraft to capsize.

(e) The wheels of the alighting gear are to be provided with approved means for lubricating the wheel bearings, which are to be designed so that no wear takes place on the axle.

(f) The design and disposition of the alighting gear are to be such as to allow of the aircraft being readily and securely supported without the use of elaborate jacking, trestling or slinging during and subsequent to the removal of the alighting gear or the wheels of the alighting gear. If necessary, special arrangements are to be made in the design of the aircraft structure to permit of such support being readily given and the points of support so specially provided must be clearly marked on the aircraft.

9. Miscellaneous

(a) The aircraft is to be constructed in quickly detachable units for ease of transport and storage.

(b) Means are to be provided for locking the slats in the closed position and maintaining the controls in a central position when the aircraft is left unattended on the ground. The means so provided must preclude the possibility of the pilot attempting to take-off with the slats and/or the controls locked.

(c) Suitable holding-down rings are to be provided under the bottom planes.

(d) The aircraft is to be provided with all necessary handgrips and other facilities for ease of handling on the ground.

(e) Provision is to be made in the design for the protection of all moving parts against the destructive effects of sand and, as far as may be possible, for their lubrication by grease gun from a central point.

(f) Detachable covers of approved type are to be supplied for the engine and cockpit as a protection against deterioration when the aircraft is pegged down in the open.

(g) The attachment points for the pilot's fighting harness together with those parts of the aircraft to which the belt loads are transmitted are to be capable of withstanding the failing load of the belt or harness.

(h) The design of the structure in the vicinity of the cockpit is to be such as to afford the pilot as much protection as possible in the event of a heavy landing, or crash or overturning.

Such structure should be appreciably stronger than the adjacent parts so that these latter may absorb some of the shock by deformation before the former yields.

(i) The design of the aircraft is to be such that standard Service equipment can be used for ground operations such as fuelling, rigging, manhandling, etc. Particulars of service ground equipment can be obtained on application in writing to the Director of Technical Development (R.D.A.5.).

(j) The design and layout of the aircraft is to be such as to offer every facility for rapid and easy inspection and maintenance in service and, in general, is to permit of maintenance operations being performed with standard Service equipment. Special equipment (including tools) shall be provided with the aircraft if an essential supply, but the introduction of non-standard articles is to be avoided whenever possible.

(k) Parts that require to be frequently replaced or inspected are to be easily accessible, and fully visible to a mechanic working on them.

(l) Control cables are to be arranged so that the deterioration due to wear is a minimum. Means are to be provided to facilitate the fitting of new cable and its rapid threading through fairleads. The splicing of the cable in place is prohibited.

(m) Positive-locking devices shall be provided for all joints and fastenings; such devices are to be rapidly and easily adjustable.

(n) Adequate facilities are to be provided for inspecting the fuselage interior and working parts, particularly those of the tail skid and tail plane adjusting gear.

(o) Arrangements are to be made for defining the position of the centre of gravity in accordance with Aircraft Design Memorandum No 205.

10. Provision of Mock-up

(a) In order that the proposed disposition of the crew, armament etc., may be properly examined and approved by the Director of Technical Development before construction is commenced the contractor is required to provide suitable "mock-up" of the aircraft at his works. The "mock-up" so provided must include all parts and components which are likely to interfere with the all-round view from the cockpit and must shew the internal arrangements of the cockpit and such details of the engine installation as the arrangements for engine-starting and the positions of cocks, pumps, etc.

(b) The "mock-up" must be erected full size and must be constructed true to scale and all instruments and equipment must be represented full size.

(c) The "mock-up" must be capable of being inclined at angels corresponding to the cruising and alighting attitudes of the aircraft and to this end must be constructed to the correct height from the ground.

(d) Within 10 days of the mock-up conference the contractor is to submit to the Director of Technical Development (R.D.A.4.) two copies of provisional drawings of the layout as decided at the mock-up.

Four copies of the layout drawings as finally approved are to be supplied to the Director of Technical Development (R.D.A.4).

These equipment layout drawings are to be a $1/8^{th}$ scale and are to consist of skeleton views of the fuselage and other pertinent structure shewing views of all equipment:

(1) positioned on the starboard side of the aircraft, viewed from the inside;

(2) positioned on the port side, viewed from inside;

(3) positioned in plan, together with

(4) full views of instrument boards, W/T panels, etc. and

(5) a schedule of equipment indexed to correspond to "balloon" pointers (a spare column is to be provided for notes or alterations).

Each of the drawings is to shew also seats, tanks, controls, etc. appropriate to each view.

In accordance with the procedure laid down in Aircraft Design Memorandum No 135 the contractor is to supply a bare W/T panel as and when required.

11. Test Specimens

(a) The Contractor will be required to supply and ordinarily test (see clause (d)) such specimens of parts of the aircraft as the Director of Technical Development may consider should be tested in order to ensure that the design and construction of the aircraft will be satisfactory.

(b) Tenders for the supply of aircraft in accordance with this specification are to include a Schedule of the specimens and tests considered sufficient to meet the requirements of clause (a) and are to cover the cost of supplying and testing the specimens. Any schedule that is considered by the Director of Technical Development to be inadequate will be returned to the firm concerned for amendment.

(c) The specimens and tests that will generally be essential are indicated hereunder:

Complete ribs. The specimens are to be tested under the conditions of normal flight and, when appropriate, inverted flight. Metal ribs will be required to undergo, in addition, a vibration test.

Metal spars. The specimens will be submitted to the standard test, if applicable, and otherwise to such test as the Director of Technical Development may require.

(d) Except as provided for hereafter, the testing shall be done by the Contractor, or he shall arrange for it to be done at some approved Testing Establishment; in either case, due notice of the time and place of the tests shall be given to the Director of Technical Development so that he may arrange for a representative to witness them; the conditions governing the tests are to be in accordance with the requirements of the Director of Technical Development and the tests are to be performed to his satisfaction; reports on the tests are to be supplied to the Director of Technical Development in duplicate. If neither of the aforementioned arrangements is possible, the tests will be done at the Royal Aircraft Establishment, at the Contractor's expense.

(e) The Director of Technical Development reserves the right to call for specimens and tests additional to those referred to in the Contractor's Schedule, should he at any time after the placing of the contract consider them to be necessary.

(f) No specimen of any part of the aircraft shall be submitted for testing without it being previously certified by the Inspector-in-Charge at the Contractor's works, that the specimen is typical, as regards materials, dimensions, limits and workmanship of the actual part.

(g) A thin coat of oil or Vaseline may be applied to metal specimens to prevent corrosion. Varnish, enamel or similar substances must not be used for this purpose.

12. Provision of Drawings for a Model

If at any time the Director of Technical Development shall so desire, the contractor shall supply the drawings and data necessary for the construction of a true-to-scale model of the complete aircraft suitable for aerodynamic trials in a wind tunnel; such drawings, if required, would form the subject of an amendment to contract.

13. Publication of Test Results

The Director of Technical Development reserves the right to publish data contained in reports of any wind tunnel or other tests relating to the design of the aircraft which may be undertaken on his behalf.

14. Pre-acceptance Test Flights

(a) Prior to the delivery of the aircraft to the Departmental Establishment at which the Type Trials are to take place it shall have been certified to the Director of Technical Development:

(i) That the aircraft has been subjected to the contractor's pilot to the flight tests referred to in the "Statement of Special Contract Conditions' accompanying the contract and

(ii) that these tests have shewn that the aircraft is safe to be flown by pilots of the Royal Air Force.

(b) The tests referred to in (a) shall include:-

(i) A demonstration that the aircraft may be spun, both to the right and to the left, without undue risk when loaded in accordance with paragraph (3) of the Specification, and with the Centre of Gravity at the aft authorised limit. For this purpose it is required that the aircraft, after being put into a spin, shall be allowed to complete not less than eight turns before the pilot sets his controls for recovery. The aircraft will be deemed satisfactory as regards its behaviour in a spin if the height loss in recovery does not exceed 1500 feet. This height loss is to be reckoned from when the pilot sets his controls for recovery until the aircraft "flattens out" from the landing dive.

(ii) A dive to the terminal velocity.

(iii) A demonstration of satisfactory behaviour during normal aerobatics such as the loop, roll, stalled turns, etc.

AIR MINISTRY
Directorate of Technical Development

SPECIFICATION F.37/34
3rd JANUARY 1935

Experimental High Speed Single Seat Fighter
(Supermarine Aviation Works)

1. General

This specification is intended to cover the design and construction of an experimental high speed single seat fighter substantially as described in the Supermarine Specification No 425a and drawing No 30000 Sheet 13, except that an improvement in the pilot's view is desirable. The aircraft shall conform to all the requirements stated in Specification F.7/30 and all corrigenda thereto, except as stated hereunder.

2. Power Unit

(a) The engine to be installed shall be the Rolls Royce P.V.XII

(b) The airscrew shall be of wooden construction. The Provisions of Para 2(f) of Specification F.7/30 as regards the provision for the effect of a metal airscrew on weight and C. of G. movement can be ignored.

(c) The fuel system shall be in accordance with DTD Specification No DTD 1004. A duplicate engine-driven system may be used.

(d) A cooling system is to be of the evaporative cooling type, using wing condensers in association with an auxiliary radiator.

(e) Hand starting gear only is provided for engine starting.

3. Load to be Carried

The service load shall be as defined in Specification F.7/30, except for departures which may subsequently be agreed between the contractor and the Director of Technical Development. The fuel load to be carried is to be 94 gallons with oil appropriate to the endurance implied by this fuel.

4. Equipment and Miscellaneous

(a) Non-standard navigation lights of the type approved by DTD may be fitted, and will be supplied by the contractor.

(b) The requirement for Para 8(a) of Specification F.7/30 that the braking system is to be capable of rapid and easy removal is to be deleted.

(c) The reference to the hand holds or other aids to the handling at the wing

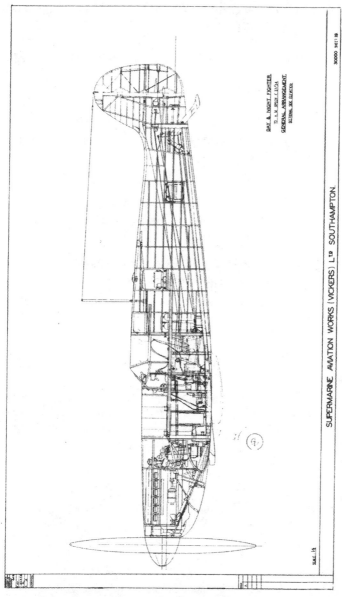

DAY & NIGHT FIGHTER
TO A.M. SPEC F.37/34
GENERAL ARRANGEMENT
SHOWING SKIN STRUCTURE

SUPERMARINE AVIATION WORKS (VICKERS) L^{TD} SOUTHAMPTON.

Supermarine drawing of the Spitfire Mk I, showing fuselage structure, engine installation and controls

tips of Para 9(d) of Specification F.7/30 is to be altered to read: "Internal provision is to be made for taking holding-down guys at the wing tips. Hand holds or grips will not be necessary."

(d) The requirement for Para 6 as regards gun installation is modified. All four guns may be installed outside the airscrew disc.

(e) Tail wheel is to be fitted if practicable.

5. Structural Strength

(a) Para 5(d) of Specification F.7/30 is to be altered to read: "The alighting gear must be able to withstand an impact at a vertical velocity of 10 feet per second, and at this velocity the load on the alighting gear must not exceed 4½ times the fully-loaded weight of the aircraft."

(b) Wheels not conforming with Para 5(d) of Specification F.7/30 will be accepted, but the actual size and type proposed must be approved by the Director of Technical Development.

REQUIREMENTS FOR SINGLE-ENGINE SINGLE-SEATER DAY AND NIGHT FIGHTER (F.10/35) APRIL 1935

1. General

The Air Staff require a single-engine single-seater day and night fighter which can fulfil the following conditions:-

(a) Have a speed in excess of the contemporary bomber of at least 40 mph at 15,000 ft.

(b) Have a number of forward firing machine guns that can produce the maximum hitting power possible in the short space of time available for one attack. To attain this object it is proposed to mount as many guns as possible and it is considered that eight guns should be provided. The requirements are given in more detail below.

2. Performance

(a) Speed. The maximum possible and not less than 310 mph at 15,000 ft at maximum power with the highest speed possible between 5,000 and 15,000 ft.

(b) Climb. The best possible to 20,000 ft but secondary to speed and hitting power.

(c) Service Ceiling. Not less than 30,000 ft is desirable.

(d) Endurance. ¼ hour at maximum power at sea level plus 1 hour at maximum power at which engine can be run continuously at 15,000 ft. This should provide ½ hour at maximum power at which engine can be run continuously (for climb etc.), plus 1 hour at most economic speed at 15,000 ft (for patrol), plus ¼ hour at maximum power at 15,000 ft (for attack). To allow for possible increase in engine power during the life of this aircraft, tankage is to be provided to cover ¼ hour at maximum power at sea level plus 1¼ hours at maximum power at which engine can be run continuously at 15,000 ft.

(e) Taking off and landing. The aircraft to be capable of taking off and landing over a 50 ft barrier in a distance of 500 yards.

3. Armament

Not less than 6 guns, but 8 guns are desirable. These should be located outside the airscrew disc. Re-loading in the air is not required and the guns should be fired by electrical or means other than Bowden wire.

It is contemplated that some or all of these guns should be mounted to permit of a degree of elevation and traverse with some form of control from the pilot's seat. Though it is not at present possible to give details, it is desirable that designers should be aware of the possibility of this development, which should not, however, be allowed to delay matters at this stage.

4. Ammunition

300 rounds per gun if eight guns are provided and 400 rounds per gun if only six guns are installed.

5. View

(a) The upper hemisphere must be, so far as possible, unobstructed to the view of the pilot to facilitate search and attack. A good view for formation flying is required, both for formation leader and flank aircraft and for night landing.

(b) A field of view of about 10° downwards from the horizontal line of sight over the nose is required for locating the target.

6. Handling

(a) A high degree of manoeuvrability at high speeds is not required but good control at low speeds is essential.

(b) A minimum alteration of tail trim with variations of throttle settings is required.

(c) The aircraft must be a steady firing platform.

7. Special Features and Equipment

(a) Enclosed cockpit

(b) Cockpit heating

(c) Night flying equipment.

(d) R/T.

(e) Oxygen for 2½ hours.

(f) Guns to be easily accessible on the ground for loading and maintenance.

(g) Retractable undercarriage and tailwheel permissible.

(h) Wheel brakes.

(j) Engine starting. If an electric starter is provided a ground accumulator will be used with a plug-in point on the aircraft—an accumulator for this purpose is not required to be carried in the aircraft. The actual starting must be under control of the pilot. In addition hand turning gear is required.

CHAPTER II
Handling Trials of the Spitfire K-5054

Aeroplane and Armament Experimental Establishment, Martlesham Heath, September 1936

A.M. Ref:-431708/35/R.D.A.1.
A.&A.E.E. Ref:-M/4493/20—A.S.56

Handling trials were done at a total weight of 5332 lb, the centre of gravity was 9.7 inches aft of the datum point.

Limits 8.25"–9.9" aft—extended by .01 chord to 10.8 inches aft.

CONTROLS

Ailerons

On the ground the aileron control works freely and without play. Full movement of the control column can be obtained when the pilot is in the cockpit.

In the air the ailerons are light to handle when climbing and on the glide they become heavier with increase in speed, but by no more than is required to impart good "feel".

The aeroplane was dived to 380 mph A.S.I. and up to that speed the ailerons were not unduly heavy, and gave adequate response.

The ailerons are effective down to the stall and give adequate control when landing and taking off. The response is quick under all conditions of flight, and during all manoeuvres required from a fighting aeroplane.

There was no snatch or aileron vibration at any speed, and in general the aileron control is excellent for a high speed fighting aeroplane.

Rudder

On the ground the rudder control operates freely and without play. There is an excellent adjustment for the position of the rudder bar. In the air it is moderately light and extremely effective. The rudder becomes heavier with increase of speed, but by no more than is necessary in a high speed aeroplane, and at the highest speeds it is still effective.

The aeroplane responds easily and quickly to the rudder under all conditions of flight.

Although the rudder is heavier than the ailerons, yet it should not be made lighter as with a very light rudder the pilot might overload the aeroplane at high speeds.

Rudder Bias Gear

The rudder bias control was quick and easy to operate, it is effective and gives adequate range.

Elevators

On the ground full movement of the elevators can be obtained. Operation is light and there is no play.

In the air the elevator control is light and very effective down to the stall.

Heaviness increases with speed, but by no more than is necessary. In the dive the aeroplane is steady. The elevators give rapid response with a small movement of the control column. When landing the control column need not be fully back.

The control is satisfactory as regards "feel" and response, but would be improved if the movement of the control column for a given movement of the elevators was slightly greater. A small movement of the control column produces so large an effect that an unskilled pilot might pull the nose of the aeroplane up too much when landing; however, a change to alter the gearing between control column and elevator is not considered advisable until spinning trials show it to be safe.

Tail Trimming Gear

The tail trimming gear, which is of the trimmer tab type, is easy to operate and very effective. A very small movement of the lever has a powerful effect, and a lower gearing would be an advantage. There is adequate range for trim for all conditions of flight, in fact, only half the available movement of the lever is required.

Engine Controls

Engine controls are well placed in the cockpit. They work easily and without play and do not slip.

Flaps

The flaps are operated pneumatically and move down through an angle of 60°. Control is by a switch moved one way for "down" and the other way for "up". The system worked well and gave no trouble in maintenance.

When the flaps are down they reduce the stalling speed by about 12 mph

A.S.I. (Uncorrected) and the aileron control is better at the stall with the flaps down than with them up. Putting the flaps down caused a noticeable change in trim, which can easily be taken up on the trimming gear or on the elevators.

Although these flaps appreciably reduce the flatness of glide, yet this aeroplane would be easier to bring in if the flaps were made more effective either by putting the angle up to 90° or increasing their area.

Since this aeroplane was first flown at this Establishment the pilots have had experience of very high drag flaps on several aeroplanes, and they are unanimous in their opinion that higher drag flaps on the Spitfire would improve its characteristics in the approach, and make it easier for the unskilled pilot to get into a small aerodrome.

If the flaps are modified to give higher drag, two "down" positions should be provided (say 60° and 90°) because a very high drag flap, although suitable for use in day time, involves too sudden a change of attitude when flattening out during a landing at night.

The ideal system of operation is a smaller lever by which the flaps can be set to any position as required, but failing this, a system of operation to allow of two settings for the flaps at 60° and 90° is essential.

Brakes

The brakes are hand operated with differential control on the rudder. They are smooth, progressive, easy to operate and effective. They do not tend to tip the aeroplane up at the end of the landing run.

FLYING CONTROLS

Stability

Laterally the aeroplane is stable. If one wing is depressed and the control column released the aeroplane will return to a level keel in a reasonable time. Directionally the aeroplane is stable under all conditions of flight, engine on or off. Longitudinally the aeroplane is neutrally stable with engine on and stable in the glide. The aeroplane is unstable in the glide with flaps and undercarriage down.

In general the stability characteristics are satisfactory for a fighting aeroplane and give a reasonable compromise between controllability and steadiness as a gun platform.

Characteristics at the stall

As the elevator control is very powerful the aeroplane will stall long before the control column is moved right back. The stall is normal. There is no vice nor snatch on the controls. In tight turns, giving approximately 3g as registered on the accelerometer, at speeds from 140 mph A.S.I. downwards there was a distinct juddering on the whole aeroplane. Under these conditions the aeroplane is probably in a semi-stalled condition and this juddering effect may be due to slight buffeting on the tail. This can be stopped at once if the control column is eased forward.

Tests according to A.D.M. [aircraft design memorandum] 293 were done with the following results:-

On No 1 test with the undercarriage and flaps up it is difficult to keep the aeroplane steady when the control column is right back. It wallows from side to side and there is snatch on the control column from the elevators. With the undercarriage and flaps down the aeroplane is steadier in the stalled glide and there is no snatch.

In Test No 2 with the undercarriage and flaps down it was possible to pull the wing up when ailerons were applied to unbank, but in turns both to the left and to the right, the aeroplane tends to take charge at the stall and cannot be said to comply with these tests when the control column is pulled right back.

In the third test with the undercarriage and flaps up, the wing can be pulled up, but in this test again the aeroplane takes charge to such an extent that the pilot found it almost impossible to make sure of centralising the rudder. With the undercarriage and flaps down the aeroplane's behaviour was much the same.

In tests Nos 2 and 3 the movements of the aeroplane are more violent to the right than to the left after applying the controls. No spin resulted in either of these two tests.

This aeroplane, in common with other fighters tested at this Establishment, cannot be said to comply fully with tests Nos 2 and 3, as its behaviour depends so much on the way the pilot uses his controls. Its behaviour in test No 1 indicates that there is sufficient lateral control at the stall for a heavily loaded high speed aeroplane of this type.

Aerobatics

Loops, half rolls off loops, slow rolls and stall turns have been done. The aeroplane is very easy and pleasant to handle in all aerobatics.

Landing and take-off

The aeroplane is easy and normal to take-off. There is a slight tendency to swing, but this is not so pronounced as on a Fury and is automatically and easily corrected by the pilot. The aeroplane is simple and easy to land, but requires very little movement of the control column as the elevator control is so powerful, and it is not necessary to have the control column fully back.

If the engine is opened up with the flaps and undercarriage down, the aeroplane can be easily held by the control column. The aeroplane does not swing when landing.

Sideslipping

The aeroplane does not sideslip readily.

Ground handling

The ground handling is exceptionally good. The aeroplane is easy to turn and taxi in fairly strong winds. It is a more satisfactory aircraft for operating in high winds than the normal biplane fighter.

UNDERCARRIAGE

The undercarriage has excellent shock absorbing qualities, and good rebound damping.

The controls for the hydraulically retracting mechanism are simple and well arranged. The undercarriage can be raised in about 10 seconds and lowered in about 15 seconds, without undue effort. The indicators were satisfactory. The wheels cannot be seen, but when the undercarriage is lowered two small rods project through the wings to show its position.

When the undercarriage is fully up or down, the hand lever of the oil pump can no longer be moved, and this is a useful additional indication that the undercarriage is in the required position.

A Klaxon to warn the pilot that the undercarriage is up works when the throttle is pulled back beyond two thirds, but is not loud enough to be heard by him with the cockpit open and the engine on.

FLYING VIEW

View forwards is fair and upwards is good. View to the rear is fair for a covered cockpit.

The present windscreen gives great distortion. If a curved windscreen of this shape cannot be made in either moulded glass or in suitable material to give no distortion, it is considered that it should be replaced by a flat-sided type, even though this might involve a slight reduction in performance.

With the cover open, the cockpit is remarkably free from draught, and it is possible to land and take-off with the cockpit cover open without using goggles.

COCKPIT COMFORT

The cockpit is comfortable and there is plenty of room, even for a big pilot. The head room is somewhat cramped for a tall pilot. It is not unduly noisy and the instruments and controls are well arranged. The cockpit is easy to enter and leave when the aeroplane is on the ground and foot steps on the wing are not considered necessary.

At speeds over 300 mph A.S.I. the cockpit cover is very difficult to open, although it has been opened at 320 mph A.S.I., and will stay open. Attention should be given to this question, as it is most important that the pilot should be able to get out of the aeroplane at the very highest speeds without difficulty. A small air flap operated by the handles on the sliding cover might make it easier to open at high speeds.

Although no heating is provided the cockpit was kept warm by heat from the engine and exhaust at 25,000 ft. Gloves were not necessary.

INSTRUMENTS

All instruments are well arranged and are clearly visible to the pilot. The compass is steady at all speeds.

SUMMARY OF FLYING QUALITIES

The aeroplane is simple and easy to fly and has no vices. All controls are entirely satisfactory for this type and no modification to them is required, except that the elevator control might be improved by reducing the gear ratio between the control column and elevator. The controls are well harmonised and appear to give an excellent compromise between manoeuvrability and steadiness for shooting. Take-off and landing are straightforward and easy.

The aeroplane has rather a flat glide, even when the undercarriage and flaps are down and has a considerable float if the approach is made a little too fast. This defect could be remedied by fitting higher drag flaps.

In general the handling of this aeroplane is such that it can be flown without risk by the average fully trained service fighter pilot, but there can be no doubt that it would be improved by having flaps giving a higher drag.

CHAPTER III
Spitfire Mark I Performance Trials

SPITFIRE N.3171. MERLIN III – ROTOL CONSTANT SPEED AIRSCREW. COMPARATIVE PERFORMANCE TRIALS.

Aeroplane and Armament Experimental Establishment Boscombe Down, 19th March, 1940.
A. & A.E.E. Ref:– 4493/44 – A.S.56/8.
A.M.Ref:– B.8242/39/A.D./R.D.L.

In accordance with Air Ministry letter, reference B.9242/39/A.D./R.D.L. dated 4th November 1939, performance trials have been carried out to compare this aeroplane with the standard Spitfire I fitted with a 2-pitch airscrew.

1.0 Comments on Trials.

As delivered, this aeroplane was fitted with a bullet proof windscreen, armour plating over the fuel tank, and a domed top on the sliding hood to allow of more headroom for the pilot. None of these modifications had been made to K.9793 fitted with a two-pitch metal airscrew the performance of which is given in Part of Report M.692,b dated 12th July, 1939. Consequently changes in performance, particularly in level speed cannot be attributed solely to the change in airscrew.

2.0 Take-Off.

The take-off run in zero wind and under standard atmospheric conditions is better than that of the 2-pitch airscrew Spitfire. The accompanying table gives the take-off for the 3-types of airscrews.

Airscrew	Take-off run (yards)	Distance to clear 50' screen (yards
Rotol	225	370
2-Pitch Metal	320	490
Wooden Fixed Pitch	420	790

3.0 Climb

It was found that the best climbing speed as determined from partial climbs was not suitable owing to the instability, uncomfortably steep attitude, and poor view obtaining at this speed. This climbing speed was increased by 22 m.p.h. to a more suitable speed which improved the handling qualities of the aeroplane on the climb.

The following table gives comparative times in minutes to reach various heights for the best climbing speed and the recommended climbing speed. Also included are the times to height for Spitfires with 2-Pitch and fixed pitch airscrews.

Airscrew	Time to Height (Feet.)				
	10,000	15,000	20,000	25,000	30,000
Rotol Best Climb	3.4	5.3	7.7	11.1	16.1
Rotol Recommended	3.5	5.4	7.7	11.0	16.4
2-Pitch Metal	5.5	8	11.3	15.9	23.8
Wooden Fixed Pitch	4.4	6.6	9.4	13.8	22.4

Best climbing speed:- 140 m.p.h. A.S.I. to 12,000' thereafter decreasing by 1 m.p.h. per 1000 feet.

Recommended climbing speed:- 162 m.p.h. A.S.I. to 12,000' thereafter decreasing by 2½ m.p.h. per 1000 feet.

4.0 Level Speeds.

In addition to the routine speed tests on this aeroplane as it was delivered, subsidiary tests were made to determine the effect of the bullet proof windscreen, and engine r.p.m. on the top level speed.

4.1 Windscreen test.

The bullet proof windscreen was replaced by the prototype Spitfire pattern of windscreen.

As delivered the aeroplane was fitted with a bullet proof windscreen which has a flat front panel protruding about 1½ inches beyond the framework. After level speed tests had been completed this was replaced by the prototype pattern of windscreen. This consists of a windscreen with a curved front panel and is perhaps slightly better aerodynamically than the production pattern which has a flat, though flush-fitting front panel. Photographs are included at the end of this report showing both bullet-proof and prototype windscreens. As shown in Fig.2 [not included here] the loss of speed resulting from the projecting bullet proof windscreen is 6 m.p.h.

4.2 Controlling R.P.M.

Speed tests were made at three heights below full throttle height with the boost pressure maintained constant at 6¼ lb. per sq.inch whilst the R.P.M. was varied over a range from 2600 to 3000.

The results show that the maximum level speed is reached with the airscrew controlling at 2800 engine r.p.m. On increasing the r.p.m. to 3000 the speed was reduced, on the average by 4 m.p.h.

For the particular engine fitted there is a reduction of 17 b.h.p. at constant boost (+6¼ lb) when the r.p.m. are increased from 2800 to 3000. The loss of speed is therefore probably due to the loss of power accompanied by a slight decrease in airscrew efficiency. The matter is being further investigated by Messrs.Rolls-Royce and Messrs.Rotols. It will be noted that reducing the R.P.M. from 3000 to 2800 lowers the full throttle height by 2000 feet.

4.3 Engine Power.

The engine installed in the aeroplane develops slightly less power under test bed conditions than that in K.9793, the aeroplane fitted with the 2-pitch airscrew. This could have the effect of reducing the top level speed by about 2 m.p.h.

SUMMARY OF TRIALS

AEROPLANE	Spitfire I		No. N.3171
SPEC. NO.	16/36		
CONTRACTOR	Vickers-Armstrong (Supermarine) Ltd.		
TYPE	Landplane	DUTY	Single Seater Fighter.
ENGINES.	Merlin III	Normal B.H.P	950/990 at
			Rated Altitude 12,250 ft

At 2,600 R.P.M. at rated boost pressure +6¼ lb/sq.in. boost

	lb.
Tare weight	4713.0
Weight light	4476.5
Fixed military load	236.5
Service Load	657.5
Fuel 84 gallons*	630.0
Oil 5½	49.5
Flying weight on trials.	6050

* Based on 7.5 lb. per gallon.

At Full Throttle			
Height Feet	Top Speed M.P.H.	Time To Climb Mins.	Rate of Climb Ft./Min.
S.L.	–	–	–
2,000	–	0.7	2820
5,000	–	1.8	2850
10,000	320.5	3.5	2895
15,000	339	5.3	2430
20,000	353.5	7.7	1840
25,000	345	10.9	1250
30,000	319	16.4	660

Service Ceiling   34,700 ft.   Landing speed   - M.P.H.

Take off run   225 yds. Time - secs. Distance from rest to clear

                                      50 ft. screen   370 yards

Stalling speed

        flaps up 78 M.P.H.   Gliding in A.S.I.   87 M.P.H.

       "- Down 68 M.P.H.

Best landing A.S.I. 66 M.P.H.

Landing and take off tests corrected to zero wind and standard atmosphere.

             AIRCRAFT.   Spitfire I.   N-3171

             ENGINE   Merlin III.

                          Airscrews

Position	Centre
Variable Pitch airscrew	Rotol
Type	Merlin.
Serial No.	2572.
Makers No.	–
Diameter	10'-9"
No. of Blades	3.
Direction of Blades	Rt.Hd.
A.M. Serial Nos. Hub	2572.
A.M. Serial Nos. Blade 1	A-4184.
A.M. Serial Nos. Blade 2	A-4185.
A.M. Serial Nos. Blade 3	A-4136.

Basic Pitch Setting	–
Pitch Range.	35° 0'
High Pitch Setting	58° 20' (estimated)
Low Pitch Setting	23° 20'

CLIMBING TRIALS
Spitfire N.3171

Height in Standard Atmosphere Feet	Time From Start Min.	Rate of Climb Ft/Min.	True Air Speed M.P.H.	A.S.I. M.P.H.	P.E.C.	Comp.	R.P.M.	Boost lb.sq.in.
Sea Level	0							
1,000	0.4	2810	163	161	-0.7	-.1		6.4
2,000	0.7	2820	165	161	-0.7	-.1		6.4
3,000	1.1	2830	167.5	161	-0.7	-.2		6.4
5,000	1.8	2850	172.5	161	-0.7	-.2		6.4
6,500	2.3	2860	176.5	161	-0.7	-.3		6.4
10,000	3.5	2895	186.5	161	-0.7	-0.4		6.4
11,000	3.9	2905	189	161	-0.7	-.5	Controlled	6.4
13,000	4.6	2665	193.5	159.5	-0.4	-0.7	at	5.2
15,000	5.3	2460	195.5	155.5	+.2	-0.7	2600	3.9
16,500	6.0	2250	197.0	152.5	+.7	-0.8		3.1
18,000	6.7	2075	198.5	149.5	+1.2	-0.8		2.2
20,000	7.7	1840	201.0	146	+1.8	-0.9		1.0
23,000	9.5	1480	205.0	140	+2.9	-1.0		-0.8
26,000	11.8	1130	209.0	134.5	+3.9	-1.0		-2.5
28,000	13.8	895	212.0	130.5	+4.7	-1.1		-3.6
30,000	16.4	660	214.0	126.5	+5.4	-1.1		-4.7

Estimated absolute ceiling   35,600   Greatest height reached   30,000

R.P.M. stationary on ground 2850   Boost pressure lb./sq.in.   +6½

*Full throttle height

Service ceiling   34,700 feet

SPEED TRIALS

at 3000 R.P.M. and 6¼ lbs.per sq.inch boost (nominal)

Spitfire N.3171

Height in Standard Atmosphere Feet	True Air Speed M.P.H.	A.S.I. M.P.H.	Compressibility and Position Error Correction M.P.H.		R.P.M.	Boost lb/sq.in.
			P.E.	C.E.		
Sea Level					Controlling at 3000 R.P.M.	
1,000						
2,000						
3,000						
5,000						
6,500						
10,000	320.5	286	-8.5	-2.1		+6.1
13,000	332	283.5	-8.5	-2.9		+6.1
15,000	339	280.5	-8.5	-3.4		+6.1
16,500	345	279	-8.5	-3.8		+6.1
18,000	350.5	277.5	-8.5	-4.2		+6.1
20,000	353.5	271	-8.5	-4.6		+5.25
23,000	350	255.5	-8.4	4.8		+3.15
26,000	341.5	237.5	-8.0	-4.7		+1.1
28,000	332	222.5	-7.4	-4.5		-0.3
30,000	319	205	-6.3	-4.0		-
18,900	354	276	-8.5	-4.4		+6.1

Landing and take off tests corrected to zero wind and standard atmosphere.

Take off run   225

Distance from rest to clear   50   foot screen   370 yds.

Gliding in A.S.I.   87   M.P.H.   Stalling speed   -

Best landing A.S.I.   66   M.P.H.

Distance to rest (with brakes) after passing over 50 ft. screen   -   yds.

Landing run with brakes   310   yds.   Landing run without brakes   -   yds.

<u>T.O. and Landing Runs</u> under actual conditions of tests, i.e:- wind 4 m.p.h., Temp. +8°C., Press. 30.0" Hg

T.O. Run 195 yds. in 9.1 secs.
Distance to 50' screen 335 yds.
Landing run 265 yds. in 16.7 secs.

*Full throttle height

Conclusions.

1.   This aeroplane has a much better take-off and climbs faster than other Spitfires fitted with wooden fixed pitch or metal two pitch airscrews.

2.   There is a drop of 13 m.p.h in maximum level speed compared with the 2-pitch airscrew aeroplane but of this, 8 m.p.h. can be attributed to sources other than the airscrew.

3.   Below full throttle height an increase in speed of about 4 m.p.h. can be attained by controlling the engine R.P.M. at 2800 instead of 3000.

4.   The limiting diving speed can be reached much more rapidly with this aeroplane than with Spitfires fitted with fixed pitch wooden and 2-pitch metal airscrews.

CHAPTER IV
Fighting Tactics for Squadron Formations of Fighters and Bombers

Air Fighting Development Establishment, R.A.F. Station, Northolt, 1939
  Ref:- FC/S. 17154/Air Trg.
  Date:- 22nd July 1939.

1.   The enclosed extract from A.F.D.E. Report No.12 is forwarded for the information of all concerned.

TRIALS WITH SPITFIRES V BLENHEIMS.
PART I – INTRODUCTION.

At the 16th Meeting of the Air Fighting Committee, (para.83 of the minutes), it was decided that experiments should be arranged by No.12 Group and Bomber Command to determine the Air Fighting Tactics applicable to formations up to the strength of complete squadrons of fighters and bombers. The programme was to be drawn up by A.F.D.E. which was also to supervise the experiments.

2.   In particular, it was desired to determine how far:-

  (i) Two boxes of Blenheims could protect each other, especially against the Climbing Attack,

  (ii) A complete squadron of Spitfires could carry out synchronised attacks against 12 Blenheims.

Consideration of the two problems shows that it would be unrealistic for the bombers continually to maintain a single rigid formation in all circumstances, or for the fighters to approach and attack in any one way, whatever the bomber formation or their own relative position to it on sighting might be.

3.   The problems were therefore set out for the participants as follows:-

  (i) <u>Fighters – Approach</u>. To close 12 Fighters on to a formation of 12 Bombers in:-

    (a) the Flat Astern attack,
    (b) the Climbing attack,

  so as to achieve maximum concentration of fire.

  (ii) <u>Bombers – Prevention of Surprise, and Defence by Mutual support</u>.
  To avoid surprise and concentration of fire and to provide supporting

fire by formation manoeuvres.

The investigation should also show whether by any manoeuvre early in the fighter approach, the bombers can delay the closing for such a distance as to improve materially the chances of reaching their objective intact.

4.   In order further to clarify the problems, some primary and secondary questions were formulated to indicate the lines of the investigation, with the intention that they should, if necessary, be added to as it proceeded. Two additional primary questions introducing considerations of search as affecting the fighters' approach were subsequently indicated and explored.

PART II – METHOD OF INVESTIGATION.

5.   The trials were carried out by No.19 Squadron at Duxford and No.114 Squadron, assisted by aircraft of No.139 Squadron, at Wyton, between the beginning of April and the beginning of June. Since the attached officer from Bomber Command to A.F.D.E. (recommended by para.80 (vi) of Minutes of 16th Meeting, Air Fighting Committee) was not forthcoming and the single A.F.D.E. Staff Officer was fully employed in the conduct of both day and night trials at Northolt, the day to day conduct of these trials was left to the Unit Commanders with the guidance of general instructions and a detailed programme which were drawn up here. Close contact, however, was maintained throughout between this Establishment and the Unit Commanders, whose collaborations was excellent. Frequent visits were also paid from here to watch key trials both from a back seat of the Bomber formation and from an independent Hurricane.

6.   A photographer and projector were lent to Wyton, Duxford having a private projector, and as many cine guns as possible were also provided. Sufficient were available to equip the majority of the aircraft taking part by the time that full numbers were engaged.

Films were shown to personnel to check their ideas of their shooting, but much value for the fighters was lost by delay in having films developed at Wyton (which often allowed other tests to intervene before the first were available for projection) and by lack of any previous experience of their use.

7.   Representative films were examined and assessed here to ensure that they compared with the measurements of aiming in smaller formations which had been

made in previous trials. Detailed measurement was found to be unnecessary.

8.   The programme, which is attached together with the general instructions at Annexure 'B' [not included here], was drawn up so as to train the personnel in small formations in Part 1 to produce consistent answers when full numbers were involved in Part 2.

The 12 fighters could not attempt to attack together against some of the more difficult forms of bomber evasion detailed, but the full number was shown in each item to ensure that means of concentrating the maximum feasible should not be overlooked. The extent to which concentration was possible is summarised in para. 28 below.

9.   The Blenheims flew at heights varying from 6,000 feet to 16,000 feet and at a normal cruising speed of approximately 230m.p.h.

10.   In clear air the Blenheims flew along the Bedford Rivers between St. IVES and DOWNHAM MARKET.

To start a series of attacks, the Spitfires passed them and then turned about. The Blenheims continued on to the end of the run and turned about in the opposite direction, whilst the Spitfires did the same at the opposite end to bring the two formations head-on. Similar turns were made between each attack.

To work above clouds, the Spitfires went up quickly to form a focal point on which the sections of Blenheims could rally in order to start a similar procedure.

11.   The head-on and slightly beneath approach was used by the fighters because it presented to them the most difficult problem of conforming rapidly to the bombers' formation during the approach, besides providing a well defined relative position (when the combatants passed each other in opposite directions) from which comparative times for the complete attack could be measured for varying speeds of the target formation etc. This head-on approach reduced stern chasing to a minimum and so gave the bombers the most difficult problem in avoiding surprise.

12.   In view of the great speed superiority of the Spitfire over the Blenheim, it appeared possible that results obtained might not be applicable with a reduced speed margin. The Hurricanes of No.111 Squadron were therefore used as targets in place of the Blenheims in a single test comprising three flat astern attacks on a Vic of nine, whilst their Commanding Officer watched the Spitfires attacking. He then led his own Hurricanes in the same attack on the Blenheims. Finally, three Spitfires of No. 66 Squadron were used to represent three bomber

section leaders for the whole of No. 19 Squadron to deliver similar attacks. (See para. 31 below).

13.   Reports from Unit Commanders were called for urgently by the Headquarters of their own Groups, in one case even before the trials were completed, and have therefore been prepared without full co-ordination. There is, however, some value in this lack of co-ordination since it ensures that their ideas have been expressed free of any preconceived ideas at this Establishment which might well have tainted them otherwise. The two reports are attached herewith, that by Officer Commanding No.114 Squadron at Annexure 'C' [not included here], and by Officer Commanding No.19 Squadron at Annexure 'D' [not included here]. In the circumstances some repetition is inevitable and the reports include matter arising from the preliminary practices with small formations, which, though valuable, is not directly concerned with the particular problems in hand. This matter is not being dealt with in this report, but it will be taken up in the forthcoming report on the Hampden trials still in progress here.

14.   The whole of this report has been agreed to by the Officers Commanding Nos. 19 and 114 Squadrons as representative of their views.

PART III – FLYING RESULTS.

Bombers.

15.   <u>Boxes</u> – The best position in relation to a box of Blenheims in which a second box can keep station is about 300 yards to the flank, 75 yards behind and 100 feet above. On this width of front the two can assist each other by keeping watch below, but they are both susceptible to surprise by A.A. fire. They cannot close laterally enough to afford useful supporting fire to each other, and each is best occupied in defending itself. If, however, the situation demanded delaying action, one box could afford indirect protection to the other by falling in below and behind it or crossing its track below and behind. If the leading box had been armed to fire downwards, it might then be able to fall back to afford supporting fire after the fighters were committed to attacking in detail.

16.   Turning this or any other formation of bombers towards the fighters as they turn to a flank in order to swing in behind did not help appreciably to delay the attack, even when a quick turn back to the original course was made. Nor could deceleration or acceleration of the formation <u>as a whole</u> be sudden enough or great enough to upset the fighters. As mentioned above, change of depth by

dropping <u>part</u> of the formation back and closing it again when the fighters were committed would probably be much more effective.

17.   Skidding of complete box or the sliding of sections in the box round each other broke the cohesion of the bomber formation more than it worried the fighters, though slipstream effect momentarily disturbed their aim, in the latter manoeuvre.

18.   Sections Clear – When sections were flown clear of each other by 250 yards to be prepared for A.A. fire they could, if disposed roughly on a common front, protect each other well from surprise by fighters. In this formation too, they may well be able to close in time before an attack is delivered.

19.   Changing Vics – It was found that there are considerable potentialities in a big Vic. Nine is the largest number that is handy in a single Vic and when a full Squadron is present, it appears that the best position for the extra section of bombers is just in front of and below the head of the large Vic.

The vital question is the angle of this large Vic. When it is flat (say 120°), each bomber can cross-fire in support of the next effectively against single fighters attacking. When it is narrow (90° or less), the bombers in the tail can afford very strong protection to the leaders.

It is possible that peace practices exaggerate the apparently great potentialities of protective fire in a narrow Vic, because the tail bombers are not subjected to fire themselves. The leading fighters, however, present such a tempting shot that even in war the gunners would almost certainly take it. The tail bombers might be some 300 yards behind their leader so that the fighter leader might be well in their range before any fighters had opened fire at all. Scrutiny of the films shows that this was so and that the bombers aim was good.

The tails of a narrow Vic would be very vulnerable to nibbling owing to lack of supporting fire, but if the formation were under good Fighting Control, they would have time to flatten out into a wide angle Vic as soon as the fighters were committed to nibbling. On the other hand they can fall back from a wide to a narrow Vic to make fighters, committed to a mass attack, very uncomfortable,

20.   Scissors – The extension of this idea of swinging back the tails of the Vic was to cross over the right hand echelon above the left and into its position while the left reversed the process. This manoeuvre became known as the 'Scissors'.

The two flanks of Blenheims could exchange positions in 10 seconds from a Vic of about 90° and no efficacy was lost if the rear two or three bombers only on each flank moved. The manoeuvre entirely prevented a mass attack by fighters and could break it up before they reached firing position if done after they had committed themselves to conforming to the bombers' formation. Bombers' aiming results were the same as in Rotation.

21.   Fighting Control – The problem of fighting control has both more potentialities and greater difficulties in large formations than in small. The manoeuvres described above indicate clearly both the scope for initiative and the vital need for rapid decisions. The tests themselves showed the great danger of R/T jamming if, as might often happen, two air gunners attempted to transmit simultaneously. The means to overcome it are:-

    (i) Very strict wireless discipline to ensure very rapid passing of messages and avoidance of interference with a transmission just started,

    (ii) improved intercommunication to make (i) possible,

    (iii) an effective fighting control to take advantage of (i) and (ii).

Without these there appears no alternative but to accept, in spite of its slowness, the solution of Officer Commanding, No.114 Squadron of allotting special sectors to each air gunner who, on sighting an enemy, instructs his pilot to rock the aircraft until the Controller calls for the report from him or some other aircraft, which may also be rocking.

22.   Irregular formations and unco-ordinated changes of formations by individual bombers were always easy for the fighters to follow and merely decreased the volume of return fire which the bombers could deliver. This clearly showed not only that Fighting Control was necessary but also that a high standard of formation flying added enormously to the bombers' power of defence.

Fighter Attacks.

23.   General – In the interests of safety, the tests had to be carried out so that if the bombers altered formation at all, the fighters knew what to expect. This unreality permitted the fighter leader to decide and discuss on the ground with his pilots in advance, exactly what would be done, thus reducing orders in the air to the barest minimum.

Where the changes of bomber formation were such as to be likely to upset mass attacks altogether, the fighters merely viewed the manoeuvre. The programme did not allow nor did time permit for the fighters to find a means of re-organising to attack by nibbling instead of in mass, but it appeared that with the speed margin that was available they would have broken off and re-organised to change the method of attack. This problem can best be investigated with smaller numbers in the first instance and is in hand between the flights of Hurricanes and Hampdens.

24.   Delay must be expected in despatching large numbers of fighters together for interception. In present conditions, a Squadron would take some 3 minutes longer at the very least to get away than a single flight. They would also need time to form up and start on any course in the air if flights took off independently.

25.   Search – In order to retain cohesion whilst searching, individual sections flew in cruising formation, but were disposed to a fairly wide diamond to permit each section leader to concentrate mainly on searching. By allotting outward facing sectors to each section, it was possible to watch the whole forward hemisphere effectively.

26.   Head-on Approach – The first section leader to sight the enemy transmitted 'Tally Ho' and his Section Colour and at once proceeded to lead the approach by swinging to a flank. Other sections fell in behind, cutting just inside his turn to avoid losing distance on him, until the whole were in sections astern straight behind the bomber formation. In this process, each automatically took the number of its position from the front for the purpose of further manoeuvre.

27.   The turns by Sections into position showed a high standard of formation flying but no pilots felt any adverse physical effects from them.

28.   Limitations of numbers in simultaneous attacks – The fighters could only conform completely to the bomber formation when the latter flew so as to maintain the span of each clear of any other. If the bombers did this in a single layer, either the flat astern or climbing attack was possible. If they were in two layers as in two boxes alongside each other, all could be attacked simultaneously only from flat astern (with the limitations which have appeared or will be investigated in trials with single flights). In this case the boxes were separate entities from the fighter point of view. If the two boxes were to position themselves at all closely in a single vertical plane so as to present four layers, the rearmost or lower box only could be attacked.

29.   Detail of Attacks – It is considered that as soon as the fighters are in Sections Astern directly behind the bomber formation, the Squadron Commander should order "Mass Flat (or Climbing) Attack – Go" or else order

the appropriate smaller attack by its number. In the latter case Sections 1 and 2 become the leading flight and 3 and 4 the second, to act independently in waves in accordance with the order. For mass attack, No. 1 Section leader lined up on the leader of the bomber formation, No. 2 Section came up on his right, No. 3 on his left and No. 4 on the unsymmetrical bomber section when present. Once Mass Attack is ordered No. 1 Section leader should take over control.

Since 12 bombers cannot make up a symmetrical formation suitable to the development of mass attacks, and in view of the apparent predilection of foreign air forces for the flat Vic of 9 which is very convenient for such attacks, the bombers were asked at an early stage to use this Vic of 9 for the fighters' benefit. It was only with experience of it that its potentialities, when made flexible for bombers' defence, were brought to light.

30.   Film Results – The films taken in the early stages by the Spitfires showed, as a general criticism in the view of this Establishment, that the bursts were far too short. Later, however, some excellent shooting was obtained. Examinations of films by 9 aircraft attacking simultaneously shows (in confirmations of the pilots' opinions) that aim is not disturbed by numbers and consistent ranges can be obtained throughout the formation.

31.   Timing of Attacks – The amount of delay in delivering the attack that could be attributed to getting the full number of aircraft into position was exceedingly small. The squadron concerned had undoubtedly above the average ability and improved with practice, but even so, it was proved conclusively that the extra delay in large numbers is practically a negligible factor.

In order to provide some yard stick, the time was taken from the moment when the two formations passed in opposite directions to the moment of final breakaway after a 15 seconds burst. At first this varied from 2½ to 4 minutes, but later was consistently between 2¼ and 3.

In the extra tests referred to in para. 12 above, the Hurricane Squadron without any practice averaged 3½ minutes on the Blenheim at 230 m.p.h. true. The Spitfires on the Hurricanes at 270 m.p.h. took 2½ minutes, the Spitfires on Spitfires at 296 m.p.h. 5 minutes and at 325 m.p.h. 9 minutes.

The fact that the Spitfire could not close more quickly on the Blenheim than on the faster Hurricane is attributable to the fighter leader's difficulty in having to ensure, by keeping his closing speed down to 40 m.p.h. or less, that his formation is settled at the lower throttled setting before he overshoots the firing position. At the highest speed the length of time was mainly due to the great distance (about 3 miles) at which the fighters found themselves behind after the turn. It clearly shows the need for practice to get accurate judgment of the turn.

32.   <u>Limitations of the Mass Attack</u> – The only difficulty in delivering the attack was the acute sense of uncertainty in the mind of the fighter leader as to how deep the formation of bombers was and how wide it would remain. He had only a fleeting glimpse as he passed it and found much difficulty in assessing the depth from his position of deployment 800 to 1000 yards behind. Since development work to discover the best bomber defence was in progress at the same time as the attack was being developed, it is possible that more weight was given in these trials to the bombers' power of upsetting the mass attack than would be necessary in the opening stages of a war, when an enemy might not be prepared for it. If he is not prepared and flies in a formation to permit it, the attack would be entirely practicable and should be exceedingly effective.

PART IV.
CONCLUSIONS.

Bomber Defence.

33.   Against surprise, large numbers of Blenheims should be disposed on as wide a front as other considerations allow, in order to be able to keep effective look-out, particularly underneath each other.

34.   Against attack, if the object is to produce at all times the maximum volume of fire, the depth of the formation should be small and the front narrow. If the object is to hold off large numbers of fighters, the depth should be great.

35.   A flat Vic of say 120 degrees is the simplest formation that tends to supply some sort of supporting fire, because this cross-fire is reasonably effective against a nibbling attack. If, however, the bombers fly rigidly in the flat Vic, they are very vulnerable to mass attacks. But they can easily upset such attacks by a rapid closing of the Vic at the expense of some increase in range and decrease in field of cross-fire against nibbling. By further developing this movement into the 'Scissors' they can prevent a mass attack altogether. The 'Scissors' exposes the rear aircraft to nibbling, but it would be very effective if these rear aircraft were special heavily armed and armoured escorts.

36.   If it is desired to be as secure as possible against mass or nibbling attacks simultaneously, it appears that two boxes of six is still probably the best static formation for 12 bombers, at least until the above armed escorts are available. They can assist each other to avoid surprise, and in the actual attack one can fall behind the other and so delay attack on the latter without exposing itself to any more simultaneous fire, (each box being in itself the most effective formation for production of cross fire). Two boxes cannot provide supporting fire for each other without laying themselves open to simultaneous attack. The objections to boxes are that they are bad for surprise from A.A. fire, rather tiring to fly in without a great deal of practice, and possibly more open to surprise than some wider formation.

37.   Whilst bombers are still as lightly armed in relation to the fighters, boxes may be most useful to enable 12 bombers to hit back most effectively. Even now, however, if the enemy try to attack in mass or the tactical situation renders it vital for the maximum number of bombers to gain distance whilst delaying attack, then the 'Scissors' is already an exceedingly useful formation.

38.   The main lesson learnt, however, is that quite small alterations of course can produce rapid changes of dispositions for which only small increases of speed are necessary. These if properly executed may cause fighters to call off a mass attack and they should be most useful generally to the bomber leader to meet differing tactical situations. To take an extreme case, a formation might enter a long fighter zone in 2 boxes, change to independent sections through an A.A. zone and when again in boxes might throw the sections of the second box on to the top section of the first to form a Vic ready for Scissors, so as to reach a cloud area before a full fighter attack could develop.

39.   Such action calls for a very effective Fighting Control. If the leader cannot himself be carried in the rear seat of the leading Blenheim, he should have an officer in his gunner's seat to whom he can delegate Fighting Control. At least until this can be done, evasion by independent flights of Blenheims is probably a better protection than the mutual support which the two can afford each other, as long as the penetration of the raids is not so great as to render evasion hopeless. It is even an open question whether the mutual fire support of a box of Blenheims is worth the loss of the extra power of evasion which two entirely independent sections have, at least over any reasonable depth into enemy territory.

Fighter Attacks.

40.   The trials show clearly that a squadron of fighters can accurately and quite quickly deliver a concerted attack on an equivalent number of bombers, as long as the latter fly on a single shallow front and do not narrow it by increasing the depth during the final approach.

41.   The most difficult form of approach (because it is the quickest) is from head on. If first contact is made from any other direction, the fighter formation can adjust itself to the bombers with less violent manoeuvring. From head on, the leader of the 1st section to sight the bombers becomes the leader of the whole formation. He should lead the turn into a position about 800 yds. astern of the bombers in a fairly wide sweep. The remaining sections follow slightly echeloned on the first, inwards in relation to the turn. On the completion of the turn, the Squadron Commander decides whether the mass attack is possible. If so, the leader of the 1st Section lines up on the leading bomber and leads the whole attack. No. 2 Section comes up on his right, No. 3 on his left, and in the unlikely event of there being additional bombers in the enemy formation, No. 4 Section settles on the line of the remaining bombers splitting its aircraft if necessary. Alternatively, No. 4 Section hangs back to form a second wave and close on bombers that survive the first attack.

42.   If the speed superiority of the fighters is very high, great care is necessary to get the fighter formation settled to conform with the bombers before reaching firing position without overshooting; it is easiest when the speed superiority is 15% to 20%. With a speed superiority of only 10% or less, very accurate manoeuvring is necessary to avoid swinging round into position a long way behind the bombers, but with training it can be done efficiently.

43.   The above conclusions refer to Flat Astern Attacks and would apply to the Climbing Attack only if the bombers took no evasive action, otherwise the lack of horizon would cause undue collision risk. This lack of horizon might not apply to a Diving Attack, but it has not been attempted and in this case the breakaway would probably cause serious difficulties.

44.   If the enemy formation is other than a single layer Vic, the same approach would be carried out, but concerted attacks should be limited to closing only on the rear or lower echelon of bombers.

45.   The serious hindrances to these concerted attacks are the power of the bomber formation to alter its depth quickly and the difficulty which the fighter leader may have up to the last moment of finally committing himself in deciding whether the enemy formation is (and will remain) shallow enough for him to avoid undue concentration of fire on his leading aircraft. It must be remembered, too, that the positioning of a whole squadron of fighters ready for interception will almost always take longer than the despatch of a single flight.

46.   If the enemy does permit the attack, the counter-balancing considerations are that it can, with training, be carried out without undue delay, even though the fighter has only a small speed advantage, and its effect should be devastating both materially and on morale.

47.   It appears therefore that even when a squadron is in position, absolute discretion should be left to the Squadron Commander as to what form of attack he will carry out against an equivalent number of bombers. In order however that he may be able to use the mass attack efficiently when circumstances permit, the unit must be trained to carry it out.

General.

48.   Owing to the very suitable personalities of the Unit Commanders engaged, the fact that only sketchy control of progress was possible from here hardly detracted from the value of the trials. Even in this case, however, more value might have been obtained from the films and more closely related reports would have been forthcoming, if an Officer more completely au fait with recent development work here had been available.

PART V.
RECOMMENDATIONS.

49.   Bomber formations should be thoroughly trained in "Rotation", "Box" and "Scissors", and thereafter in changing both the depth of each and also from one to the other. In order to use these forms of defence, steps should be taken to enable effective Fighting Control to be exercised by the special training of selected personnel.

50.   Fighters should be trained in the delivery of mass attacks from flat astern if, as seems quite likely at least at the beginning of a war, the enemy do fly so as to allow of it. This attack can then be used to its maximum effect.

51.   When units are allotted for fighting development but not permanently allocated to this Establishment, an Officer who already has some close touch with this Establishment should normally be available to control the progress of the trials. The reports by the two sides of the combat should be co-ordinated with this Establishment before submission to the separate higher authorities of the units concerned. A long covering report repeating their findings in co-ordinated form could then be avoided and the two read together would give a clear as well as a vivid picture of the results.

AFDE/3/18/4/Air.   Group Captain, Commanding A.F.D.E.
29th June 1939.   R. A. F. Station, NORTHOLT.

CHAPTER V
David Crook's Log Book

No. 609 (West Riding) Squadron of the Royal Auxiliary Air Force was formed in 1936 at RAF Yeadon, originally as a bomber squadron, though moved to flying fighters in late 1937. The squadron received its first Spitfire Mark I in August 1939 and in 1940 was moved first to RAF Northolt providing some air cover during the Dunkirk evacuation and then on to RAF Middle Wallop in Hampshire as part of Fighter Command's 10 Group. It was based here during the Battle of Britain though also operated out of a satellite airfield at RAF Warmwell. While at Northolt Flight Lieutenant David Moore Crook had joined the squadron. This is an extract from the Flying Log he kept during the crucial days of July–September 1940. The flight time for each individual flight has been omitted.

July

1st	Spitfire P.9467	Practice Beam of 1/4 Attacks with Buchanan.[1]
	Spitfire R.6699	Dog Fighting Practice with Curchin.[2]
2nd	Spitfire R.6699	Northolt to Hawkinge.
	Spitfire R.6699	Operational Reconnaissance from Hawkinge but turned back on reaching French coast owing to bad weather
	Spitfire R.6699	Left Hawkinge about 19.30 hrs and climbed towards French coast. Our section – Blue – being "above" guard together with Green. Dived down towards Abbeville and were met by an accurate burst of AA fire. Turned and proceeded to Rouen and Dieppe without incident but had another good burst of fire from a FLAK ship off Dieppe. No enemy fighters seen. Returned to Hawkinge for the night.
3rd	Spitfire R.6699	Returned to Northolt having had to sit on the ground during a raid and see a Dornier and a Heinkel III pass over.
5th	Spitfire N.3023	To Warmwell via Middle Wallop.
6th	Spitfire N.3023	Patrol over Portland Bill.
	Spitfire N.3023	" " " "
	Spitfire P.9322	Patrol Warmwell 20,000 feet.
	Spitfire P.9322	" Portland 15,000 feet.

7th	Spitfire P.9322	Convoy patrol Portland Bill.
	Spitfire P.9322	Patrol Warmwell.
	Spitfire P.9322	" Portland Bill.
8th	Spitfire N.3023	To Warmwell and return.
	Spitfire N.3023	Patrol Portland Bill.
9th	Spitfire N.3223	To Warmwell – very bad weather.
	Spitfire N.3223	Patrol Weymouth Bay.
	Spitfire N.3223	" " "

Spitfire P.9322   After about 45 minutes patrol over Portland, we sighted two JU.87's diving into the clouds on our left. We turned towards them (I was flying No.3) when I saw above me at least 9 Me.110's diving down on us. I warned the others and then when the leading Me.110 opened fire I turned off very sharply to the left and dived through cloud. A JU.87 flew across my sights at close range and I gave him a burst – he seemed to go right through it. I then climbed up again and fired without result at an Me.110 who immediately dived into cloud and I lost him. I found myself very near to a JU.87 so stalked him through the cloud, and when he emerged into clear sky I fired all the rest of my ammunition at very close range. He turned over & dived in flames into the sea. I then returned to Warmwell and found Drummond Hay[3] missing, but Appleby[4] OK.

Spitfire P.9322   Unsuccessful search in Weymouth Bay for Drummond Hay. I think Drummond must have left his RT in the "Transmit" position and never heard my warnings about the Me.110's. He was never found.

Gordon Mitchell[5] and Pip Barran[6] were killed on the morning of July 11th. Five Spitfires, led by Pip, left Warmwell to go to the aid of a ship which was being bombed by JU.87's and Me.110's about 20 miles South of Weymouth. Though hopelessly outnumbered (about 30 to 5) Pip went straight in to attack and two JU.87's were destroyed and the enemy driven off. Gordon was never seen alive again (his body was washed ashore near Newport, Isle of Wight about 10 days later) and Pip's machine was seen flying back towards the English coast with smoke pouring from it. A moment later he baled out and descended by parachute into the sea, but was dead when picked up soon after. He was badly burnt and hit twice in the leg. I was on leave for 24 hours in London during all this.

12th	Spitfire N.3023	To Warmwell.
	Spitfire N.3023	Attempted without success to intercept He.III at 20,000 feet over aerodrome.
	Spitfire N.3023	Patrol Portland 3000'.
	Spitfire N.3023	Search for enemy a/c[7] off Ringwood.
	Spitfire N.3023	Patrol Portland
	Spitfire N.3023	Patrol Warmwell.
13th	Spitfire N.3023	Intercepted Dornier 215 over Devizes. His gunner opened fire but I gave him a long burst which must have knocked him out as there was no subsequent reply to our fire. I fired another burst but he escaped in the clouds though Blayney[8] had another three bursts at him. He was certainly damaged but got away.
14th	Spitfire N.3023	Investigation of ufid [unidentified] a/c over Wallop.
	Spitfire N.3023	To Warmwell.
	Spitfire N.3023	Patrol Warmwell Angels[9] 10.
	Spitfire N.3023	" " " 8.
15th	Spitfire N.3023	" Base " 10.
	Spitfire N.3023	To Wallop.
16th	Spitfirc R.6690	Practice Dog Fighting.
17th	Spitfire R.6690	Patrol Warmwell Angels 10.
	Spitfire R.6690	Dusk Landings.
18th	Spitfire R.6690	Patrol Warmwell Angels 18
	Spitfire R.6690	" Wallop " 6.
	Spitfire R.6690	To Warmwell.
	Spitfire R.6690	Patrol Base Angels 5.
	Spitfire R.6690	Search Party for Red.1. Frank Howell[10] in attacking a JU.87 got a bullet in his glycol[11] and had to bale out fast off Bournemouth. He was picked up almost immediately but we did not know this and went out and did a long search for him. He was quite OK.
	Spitfire R.6690	X[12]: Raid Portland Bill.
19th	Spitfire R.6690	Patrol " " Angels 5.
	Spitfire R.6690	To Middle Wallop.
21st	Spitfire R.6690	Patrol Convoy S.W. of Needles.
	Spitfire R.6690	" " Swanage.
22nd	Spitfire R.6690	To Warmwell.

	Spitfire R.6690	Patrol Base Angels 15.
	Spitfire R.6690	" " " 10
23rd	Spitfire R.6690	" Convoy.
	Spitfire R.6690	To Middle Wallop.
26th	Spitfire R.6690	To Warmwell.
	Spitfire R.6690	Patrol Portland 10,000 feet.
	Spitfire R.6690	" " " ".
27th	Spitfire R.6690	" Base " "
	Spitfire R.6690	" Weymouth X. Raid. Buchanan lost in this patrol – probably shot by Me.109's.
	Spitfire R.6690	" " Search for P/O Buchanan.
	Spitfire R.6690	To Wallop.

Summary for July 1940	1. SPITFIRE DAY – 45.15
Unit 609 SQDN Aircraft	2. " " NIGHT – 1.05
Date 1/6/40/ Type	3.

Score for July

     1 Ju. 87   Confirmed

August

3rd	Spitfire R.[13]	Practice attacks with P/O Appleby.
	Spitfire P.[14]	To Warmwell.
	Spitfire P.	Patrol Base, 15,000'.
5th	Magister[15] N.3929	[with] P/O MacKay to Wallop.
	Spitfire R.6979	Practice formation with Ovo & Novo.[16]
6th	Spitfire P.	Convoy Patrol S.E. of Swanage.
	Spitfire S.[17]	Aerobatics.
	Spitfire S.	Night flying.
7th	Spitfire S.	To Warmwell.
	Spitfire S.	Patrol Swanage 10,000'.
8th	Spitfire S.	Patrol Swanage 30 & Raid. Convoy escort off Isle of Wight.
	Spitfire S.	" Pewitt 15,000'. Big convoy raid. Got separated from others and arrived too late.
	Spitfire S.	To Wallop.
	Spitfire S.	Patrol Swanage 12,000'.

10th	Spitfire S.	To Warmwell.
	Spitfire S.	Patrol " 8,000'.
11th	Spitfire S.	Big raid on Portland. We took off at 9.45 and after patrolling round Warmwell saw some smoke trails out to sea. Investigated and found large force of Me.110's milling round in circles at 25,000 ft, Hurricanes already engaging them. We all attacked separately – I climbed well above the scrum and then saw an Me.110 some distance from others. I dived on him, fired a burst from the quarter which missed as I could not get sufficient deflection,[18] and then same into very close range astern and fired again. This hit him and he did a climbing turn to the right, stalled and started to turn over. I narrowly missed colliding with him, and did not see him again. Found myself with the Me's all round so dived away as hard as I could. Returned to Warmwell. Everybody OK and several Me.110's shot down.
	Spitfire S.	To Middle Wallop.
12th	Spitfire H.	Big attack on Portsmouth. We took off from Wallop at 12.00 and I followed about 5 minutes later owing to R.T. trouble. I did not see any of the squadron again during the action. Climbed towards the Isle of Wight and saw A.A. fire over Portsmouth and a fire raging in the Dockyard. Could not see any bombers. Then saw large enemy force off East end of Isle of Wight – Me.109 & Me.110 in three layers circling round at about 23,000 ft.

I climbed above the middle layer, selected a machine and dived onto him and opened fire and saw my bullets either hit him or narrowly miss. Almost collided with him and lost sight of him as I continued my dive. I pulled out about 3000 feet below and at that moment an Me.110 enveloped in a sheet of flame dived past me within 200 yards. This machine was certainly destroyed but don't know if it was mine. I think it quite probably was as did not see any other British fighters in action when I attacked.

When I pulled out of my dive, found myself in very vulnerable position with many enemy round and above, and so dived away hard. Saw over 500 mph indicated air speed – actual speed probably nearly 600 mph.

Almost blacked out as I pulled out. I later found wings damaged and landing lamp torn out of wing. Everybody got back safely and several more Huns shot down. My Spitfire went back to factory for new pair of wings!!

13th	Spitfire L.	To Warmwell.
	Spitfire L.	Patrol Warmwell.
	Spitfire L.	"Best effort yet" for 609. Took off at 3.30pm & climbed

through cloud. After patrolling for some time (during which I could hear a lot of German talk on the RT) we sighted a large number – 60 or 70 – Me.109 and JU.87 approaching. We climbed above them with Blue Section (McArthur,[19] Nowierski and self) as top guard. Suddenly I saw a few Me.109's pass beneath us. I immediately broke away and attacked one which was some distance behind the rest. I came up behind & fired a good burst from dead astern. He rocked violently and then turned over and dived away & burst into flames and crashed near Hardy's Monument behind Weymouth. Everybody got back OK, and we shot down 9 JU.87 and 4 Me.109 confirmed and damaged & possibly destroyed a good many more. Altogether a good five minutes work!

Note:- Just before we attacked I heard a German voice (presumably the Wing Commander) saying repeatedly – "Achtung, achtung, Spit and Hurri". He sounded a bit fed up about something!

Actual score was: 13 destroyed confirmed, 3 destroyed probably, 4 damaged. N.B. 13 is our lucky number! August 13th – 13 of us in the fight and 13 Huns down.

[Written later] This was the record "bag" for one squadron in one fight during the whole Battle of Britain.

	Spitfire L.	Patrol Ringwood 10,000'.
14th	Spitfire L.	To shoot down Balloon (cancelled).
	Spitfire L.	Patrol base 10,000'.
	Spitfire L.	To Wallop.
	Spitfire L.	Wallop bombed by single JU.88 which hit hanger &

killed several men. Shot down about 10 miles away. We took off as bombs fell and patrolled aerodrome for some time and I fired without apparent result at 2 Heinkel III which I saw for a moment in the clouds.

609 shot down 2 Heinkels during the course of the afternoon – one of them containing 1 German Group Captain & 2 Wing Commanders. Unfortunately Goodwin[20] was missing and we never knew really what happened to him – his body was washed up on the Isle of Wight 10 days later. He must have chased a Hun out to sea and been shot down.

15th	Spitfire K.	Middle Wallop again bombed, this time by fairly large force of JU.88 & Me.110. We shot down 4 Me.110 confirmed. A Blenheim attacked the German formation and I shot it down by mistake. Crew OK (save for a cut in rear gunner's bottom) & machine landed at Wallop looking fairly well peppered. Not a very good show!
16th	Spitfire D.	Patrol Needles Angels 24.
18th	Spitfire Q.	Investigation of smoke trail.
	Spitfire Q	Patrol Ringwood Angels 10.
	Spitfire Q.	" Base " 10.
19th	Spitfire S.	Local flying practice.
24th	Spitfire P.	Patrol St Catherine's Point Angels 10.
25th	Spitfire P.	" Base 15,000'.

Big fight over Warmwell. Dived much to fast on an Me.110 and blazed away but missed and overshot badly. His gunner got 3 bullets through my wing root within 2 feet of me! But quite a good day for the squadron – 6 Huns confirmed without any losses to us. I learnt not to be over enthusiastic after this show, and always took my time! Much better! – and safer.

26th	Spitfire T.	" Portsmouth 15,000'.
27th	Spitfire T.	Dog Fighting with P/O Gaunt.[21]
29th	Spitfire P.	" " " P/O Nowierski.
30th	Spitfire P.	Local flying practice [L.F.P.].

Summary for August 1940	1. SPITFIRE	DAY	32.00
Unit 609 SQDN Aircraft	2. " "	NIGHT	1.15
Date 1/9/40/ Type	3.MAGGY	DAY	.30

Score for August

1 Me 109	destroyed
1 Me 110	"
1 Me 110	probable
1 Blenheim	shot down

September

1st	Spitfire R.6961	Patrol Guildford 10,000.
	Spitfire R.6961	" " 20,000'.
	Spitfire R.6961	Circuits & Landings.
2nd	Spitfire R.6961	L.F.P. & Beam attacks.
3rd	Spitfire R.6961	Patrol Base, 15,000'.
4th	Spitfire R.6961	" Northolt, 12,000'.
	Spitfire R.6961	Beam attacks.
5th	Spitfire R.6961	Patrol Brooklands & Kenley 8,000'.
	Spitfire R.6961	" " 20,000'.
6th	Spitfire R.6961	" " 10,000'.
7th–8th		
	Magister 3929	[with] F/O Dundas.[22] To Yeadon. Yeadon to M. Wallop. L.F.P. & Dog Fight with Gaunt.
9th	Spitfire X.4165	Brooklands & Guildford. Cloud base.[23]
10th	Spitfire X.4165	L.F.P. & Beam attacks.
11th	Spitfire X.4165	Patrol Base, 10,000'.
12th	Spitfire X.4165	L.F.P.
	Spitfire X.4165	Patrol Felton, 15,000'.
18th	Spitfire R.6961	Brooklands & Croydon 15,000' (cancelled).
	Spitfire R.6961	" & Northolt, 10,000'.
20th	Spitfire R.6961	L.F.P.
21st	Spitfire R.6961	Patrol Guildford 10,000'.
22nd	Spitfire R.6961	Weather Test.
23rd	Spitfire R.6961	L.F.P.
24th	Spitfire N.3288	L.F.P.
	Spitfire R.6961	Patrol Base, 20,000'.
	Spitfire R.6961	" Black West Rock (West End I. of Wight).

25th	Magister N.3929	[with] Sgt. Fitzgerald.
		To Yeadon. (Geoff's Funeral).[24]
26th	Magister N.3929	[with] Sgt Fitzgerald. From Yeadon.
	Magister N.3929	To Hamble.
	Magister N.3929	[with] P/O Hancock. From Hamble.
	Spitfire R.6961	Patrol Base 20,000'.
27th	Spitfire R.6961	Me.110 Destroyed. Shared with P/O Bisdee. In this

27th Spitfire R.6961 — Me.110 Destroyed. Shared with P/O Bisdee. In this fight at 25,000 feet above Swanage, Miller[25] was killed when he collided head on with an Me.110. I chased one out to sea, put out the rear gunner and started his port engine smoking furiously, but ran out of ammunition. Bisdee[26] arrived on the scene and finished him off.

28th	Spitfire R.6961	Patrol Needles, 25,000'.
30th	Spitfire X.4165	Kenley & Biggin Hill, 20,000'.
		2 Me109's Destroyed; Me109 Probable

Morning. We intercepted some Me.109's at 23,000 feet over Swanage. The fools tried to escape by diving and we all went down after them. I got up to about 600 mph and easily caught mine, gave him a burst and he crashed into the sea. I then chased another one and put him into the sea about 25 miles from Cherbourg. It took me a long time to get back to the English coast. I was pleased to see the white cliffs!

Afternoon. I was leading Green Section and we attacked 6 Me.110's about 10 miles North of Poole. I had a very enjoyable few minutes dog fighting with one and though I was behind him all the time, could not get my sights properly on him. Finally he dived for cloud, but I chased him to Weymouth and gave him a good burst. He turned over on his back and spun into cloud streaming glycol smoke. I couldn't claim him as definite as did not see him actually crash but he certainly never got back to France. This was my best day yet – 2 Me.109 destroyed, 1 Me.109 probably destroyed.

Summary for September 1940	1. SPITFIRE	DAY	20.30
Unit 609 SQDN Aircraft	2. " NIGHT	1.15	
Date 1/10/40/ Type	3.MAGISTER		8.50

Score for September

½ Me 110	Destroyed
2 Me 109	Destroyed
1 Me 109	Probably destroyed

Eventually scoring 6 confirmed kills during the Battle of Britain, David Crook would be awarded the Distinguished Flying Cross. In 1942 he published his personal account of the Battle of Britain entitled *Spitfire Pilot*. In 1944, while flying a Photo Reconnaissance mission in a Spitfire Mark IX, David Crook crashed into the sea and was killed.

Spitfire Mark I X4590, which joined 609 Squadron in October 1940, can be seen on display at RAF Hendon.

[1] Pilot Officer J. R. Buchanan.

[2] Flight Lieutenant 'Johnny' Curchin.

[3] Flying Officer Peter Drummond-Hay.

[4] Pilot Officer Michael Appleby.

[5] Pilot Officer Gordon Thomas Manners Mitchell.

[6] Flight Lieutenant Philip Henry Barran.

[7] a/c – aircraft.

[8] Pilot Officer Adolf Jarvis Blayney.

[9] Angels – RAF term used in airborne communications, an Angel was 1,000ft altitude, hence 'Angels 10' is flying at 10,000ft.

[10] Flying Officer Frank J. Howell.

[11] The glycol tank, located near the nose, contained the Merlin's coolant ethylene glycol.

[12] 'X' was used to signify enemy aircraft.

[13] Presumably Crook is referring to R.6690.

[14] Presumably Crook is referring to P.9322.

[15] The Miles M.14 Magister or 'Maggie' was a two-seat monoplane basic trainer aircraft which served as an introduction to the Spitfire for new pilots.

[16] Pilot Officer Charles Neville 'Teeny' Overton; Pilot Officer Tadeusz 'Novo' Nowierski.

[17] For the remainder of August Crook's Log only provides letter references to the Spitfires he was flying, I can find no reference as to what airframe S. pertains to.

[18] Deflection shooting – the art of firing a burst ahead of a moving target.

[19] Flight Lieutenant James Henry Gordon 'Butch' MacArthur.

[20] Flying Officer Mac D Goodwin.

[21] Pilot Officer Geoff Gaunt.

[22] Flying Officer John Dundas.

[23] Lowest altitude of visible portion of cloud.

[24] Geoff Gaunt, one of Crook's oldest friends.

[25] Pilot Officer Roger Freeman Garland Miller.

[26] Pilot Officer John Derek Bisdee.

CHAPTER VI
Spitfire Mark V Pilot's Notes

May 1941
(Reprinted January 1943)
AIR PUBLICATION 156E
Pilot's Notes

SECTION I
PILOT'S CONTROLS AND EQUIPMENT

Introduction

1 The Spitfire, VA, VB and VC are single seat, low-wing monoplane fighters, each fitted with a Merlin 45 or 46 engine and a de Havilland 20° (P.C.P.), Rotol 35° or de Havilland hydromatic constant speed propeller. Mark VB aeroplanes are fully tropicalised and particulars of additional equipment are given in the Addendum at the end of this section.

Main Services

2. **Fuel system.** – Fuel is carried in two tanks mounted one above the other (the lower one is self-sealing) forward of the cockpit. The top tank feeds into the lower tank and fuel is delivered to the carburettor by an engine-driven pump. The tank capacities are as follows:

Top tank: 48 gallons.
Bottom tank: 37 gallons.

On early aeroplanes the top tank is fitted with a separate cock and an immersed pump is fitted in the lower tank. On tropicalised aeroplanes the main fuel tanks are pressurised (see Addendum) and these and later aeroplanes are fitted to carry a long-range jettisonable tank of 30 or 90 gallons capacity under the fuselage.

3. **Oil system.** – Oil is supplied by a tank of 5.98 gallons capacity under the engine mounting and two oil coolers in tandem are fitted in the underside of the port plane. The above tank is placed by one of 8.5 gallons capacity when the aeroplane is fitted with a 90 gallons jettisonable fuel tank.

4. **Hydraulic system.** – An engine-driven hydraulic pump supplies the power for operating the undercarriage.

5. **Pneumatic system.** – An engine-driven air compressor feeds two storage cylinders for operation of the flaps, brakes, guns and landing lamps. The cylinders are connected in series, each holding air at 300 lb/sq.in. pressure.

6. **Electrical system.** – A 12 volt generator, controlled by a switch above the instrument panel supplies an accumulator which in turn supplies the whole of the electrical installations. There is a voltmeter in the left of the switch.

Aeroplane Controls

7. (a). **Primary flying controls and locking devices.** – The control column is of the spade-grip pattern and incorporates the brake lever (13) and gun cannon firing control (11). The rudder pedals (28) have two positions for the feet and are adjustable for leg reach by rotation of star wheels (82) on the sliding tubes. Control locking struts are stowed on the right hand side of the cockpit, behind the seat.

(b). To lock the control column, the longer strut should be clamped to the control column handle at one end and the other end inserted in a key-hole slot in the right hand side of the seat. The fixed pin on the free end of the arm attached to this strut at the control column end should then be inserted in a lug (64) on the starboard datum longeron, thus forming a rigid triangle between the column, the seat and the longeron.

(c) To lock the rudder pedals, a short bar with a pin at each end is attached to the other struts by a cable. The longer of the two pins should be inserted in a hole in the starboard star wheel bearing (82) and the shorter in an eyebolt (891) on the fuselage frame directly below the front of the seat. The controls should be locked with the seat in its highest position.

8. **Flying instruments.** – A standard blind flying instrument panel is incorporated in the main panel. The instruments comprise: airspeed indicator, altimeter, directional gyro, artificial horizon, rate of climb and descent indicator, and turn and bank indicator.

9. **Trimming tabs.** – The elevator trimming tabs are controlled by a hand wheel (52) on the left hand side of the cockpit, the indicator (3) being on the instrument panel. The rudder trimming tab is controlled by a small hand wheel (57) and is not provided with an indicator. The aeroplane tends to turn to starboard when the hand wheel is rotated clockwise.

10 (a) **Undercarriage control and Indicators.** – The undercarriage selector lever (80) moves in a gated quadrant, on the right hand side of the cockpit. An automatic cut-out in the control moves the selector lever into the gate when it has been pushed or pulled to the full extent of the quadrant. A hydraulic valve indicator in the quadrant shows DOWN or IDLE, or UP depending upon the position of the hydraulic valve. UP or DOWN should normally show only when the selector lever is operated to raise or lower the undercarriage, and IDLE when the lever has automatically sprung back into the gate after raising or lowering the undercarriage. If, with the engine not running, the indicator shows DOWN, it should return to IDLE when the engine is started.

(b) *To raise the undercarriage* the lever is pushed forward, but it must first be pulled back and then across to disengage it from the gate. When the undercarriage is raised and locked, the lever will spring into the forward gate.

(c) *To lower the undercarriage* the lever is pulled back, but it must first be pushed forward and then across to disengage it from the gate. When the undercarriage is lowered and locked, the lever will spring into the rear gate.

(d) *Electrical visual indicator.* – The electrically operated visual indicator (5) has two semi-transparent windows on which the words UP on a red background and DOWN on a green background are lettered; the words are illuminated according to the position of the undercarriage. The switch (44) for the DOWN circuit of the indicator is mounted on the inboard side of the throttle quadrant and is moved to the ON position by means of a striker on the throttle lever; this switch should be returned to the OFF position by hand when the aeroplane is left standing for any length of time. The UP circuit is not controlled by this switch.

(e) *Mechanical position indicator.* – A rod that extends through the top surface of the main plane is fitted to each undercarriage unit. When the wheels are down the rods protrude through the top of the main planes and when they are up, the top of the rods – which are painted red – are flush with the main plane surfaces.

(f) *Warning Horn.* – The push switch (43) controlling the horn is mounted on the throttle quadrant and is operated by a striker on the throttle lever. The horn may be silenced, even though the wheels are retracted and the engine throttled back, by depressing the button (48) on the side of the throttle quadrant. As soon as the throttle is again advanced beyond about one quarter of its travel the push-button is automatically released and the horn will sound again on its return.

11. **Flap Control.** – The split flaps have two positions only, up and fully down. They cannot therefore, be used to assist take-off. They are operated pneumatically and are controlled by a finger lever (7).

12. (a) **Undercarriage emergency operation.** – A sealed high-pressure cylinder containing carbon-dioxide and connected to the undercarriage operating the jacks is provided for use in the event of failure of the hydraulic system. The cylinder (70) is mounted on the right hand side of the cockpit and the seal can be punctured by means of a red painted lever (77) beside it. The handle is marked EMERGENCY ONLY and provision is made for fitting a thin copper wire seal as a check against inadvertent use.

(b) If the hydraulic system fails, the pilot should ensure that the undercarriage selector lever is in the DOWN position (this is essential) and push the emergency lowering lever forward and downward. The angular travel of the emergency lever is about $100°$ for puncturing the seal of the cylinder and then releasing the piercing plunger; it must be pushed through this movement and allowed to swing downwards. NO attempt should be made to return it to its original position until the cylinder is being replaced.

13. **Wheel brakes.** – The control lever (13) for the pneumatic brakes is fitted on the control column spade grip: differential control of the brakes is provided by a relay valve connected to the rudder bar. A catch for retaining the brake lever in the on position for parking is fitted below the lever point. A triple pressure gauge (2), showing the air pressure in the pneumatic system cylinders and at each brake, is mounted on the left hand side of the instrument panel.

Engine Controls

14. **Throttle and mixture controls.** – The throttle and the mixture levers (33 and 42) are fitted in a quadrant on the port side of the cockpit. A gate is provided for the throttle lever in the take off position and an interlocking device between the levers prevents the engine from being run on an unsuitable mixture. Friction adjusters (47) for the controls are fitted on the side of the quadrant. On later aircraft there is no mixture control or, if fitted, it is rendered inoperative.

15. **Automatic boost cut-out.** – The automatic boost control may be cut out by pushing forward the small red painted lever (1) at the forward end of the throttle quadrant.

16. **Airscrew controls.** – The control levers (50) for the de Havilland 20° or Rotol 35° constant speed airscrew is on the throttle quadrant. The de Havilland 20° airscrew has a Positive Coarse Pitch position which is obtained in the extreme aft position of the control lever, when the airscrew blades are held at their maximum coarse pitch angles and the airscrew functions are a fixed airscrew. Some aircraft are fitted with a de Havilland hydraulic propeller.

17. **Radiator flap control.** – The flap at the outlet end of the radiator duct is operated by a lever (31) and the ratchet on the left hand side of the cockpit. To open the flap, the lever should be pushed forward after releasing the ratchet by depressing the knob at the top of the lever. The normal minimum drag position of the flap lever for the level flight is shown by a red triangle on the top of the map case fitted beside the lever. A notch beyond the normal position in the aft direction provides a position of the lever when warm air is diverted through ducts into the main planes for heating the guns at high altitude.

18. **Slow-running cut-out.** – The control on the carburettor is operated by pulling the ring (22) on the right-hand side of the instrument panel.

19. **Fuel cock controls and the content gauges.** – The fuel cock controls (25), one for each tank, are fitted at the bottom of the instrument panel. With the levers in the up position the cocks are open. Either tank can be isolated, if necessary. The fuel contents gauge (20) on the instrument panel indicates the contents of the lower tank, but only when the adjacent push button is pressed. On later aircraft there is only one fuel cock control. For jettisonable tank cock control and jettison lever see Addendum.

20. **Immersed fuel pump.** – An immersed fuel pump is fitted in the lower fuel tank for use at the heights over 25,000 ft., when the fuel pressure falls. The pump is electrically operated and the switch controlling it is mounted on the left hand side of the cockpit, adjacent to the seat.

21. **Fuel priming pump.** – A hand-operated pump (23) for priming the engine is mounted below the right hand side of the instrument panel.

22. **Ignition switches.** – The ignition switches (83) are on the left hand side bottom corner of the instrument panel.

23. **Electric starting.** – On early aeroplanes the starting magneto switch (60) is at the right hand bottom corner of the instrument panel and the engine starting push-button (24) is under a shield above the fuel cock controls. On later aeroplanes the starting magneto switch is not provided but a booster coil push switch is fitted adjacent to the starter push-button. Current for the starter motor is normally supplied by an external battery, which is connected to the socket on the engine mounting U-frame, accessible through a door in the engine cooling panel on the starboard side. The general service accumulator carried in the aeroplanes is also connected to the starter, but as its capacity is small for such heavy duty it should be used only as a stand-by.

24. **Hand starting.** – A starting handle is stowed behind the seat. A hole in the engine cowling panel in the starboard side gives access for connecting the handle to the hand starting gear.

25. **Oil dilution.** – A push-button for operating the solenoid valve is on the left hand side in the cockpit.

26. **Engine instruments.** – The engine instruments are grouped on the right hand side of the instrument panel and consist of an engine speed indicator (14), fuel pressure gauge (15), boost gauge (16), oil pressure gauge (17), oil inlet temperature gauge (18) radiator outlet temperature gauge (19), and fuel contents gauge (20). On later aircraft the fuel pressure gauge (15) is replaced by a fuel pressure warning lamp which lights when the pressure drops to 6 lb./sq.in.

Cockpit Accommodation and Equipment

27. **Pilot's seat control.** – The seat (34) is adjustable for height by means of a lever on the right hand side of the seat.

28. **Safety harness release.** – In order that the pilot may lean forward without unfastening his harness, a release catch (68) is fitted to the right of the seat.

29. **Cockpit door.** – To facilitate entry to the cockpit a portion of the coaming (37) on the port side is hinged. The door catches are released by means of a handle at the forward end. Two position catches (39) are incorporated to allow the door to be partly opened before taking off or landing in order to prevent the hood from sliding shut in the event of a mishap.

30. **Hood locking control.** – The sliding hood is provided with spring catches for holding it either open or shut: the catches are released by two finger levers at the forward end of the hood. From outside, with the hood closed, the catches can be released by depressing a small knob at the top of the windscreen. Provision is made on the door to prevent the hood from sliding shut if the aeroplane overturns on landing.

31. **Direct vision panel.** – A small knock-out panel is provided on the right hand side of the hood for use in the event of the windscreen becoming obscured.

32. **Cockpit lighting.** – A floodlight (40) is fitted on each side of the cockpit. Each is controlled by a switch immediately below the instrument panel.

33. **Cockpit heating and ventilation.** – A small adjustable flap on the starboard coaming above the instrument panel is provided for ventilation of the cockpit. The flap is opened by turning a knurled nut underneath the flap.

34. **Oxygen.** – A standard regulator unit (6) is fitted on the left hand side of the instrument panel and a bayonet socket (63) is on the right hand side of the cockpit. A separate cock (72) is provided in addition to the regulator.

35. **Mirror.** – A mirror providing a rearward view is fitted at the top of the windscreen.

36. **Map cases.** – A metal case (49) for a writing pad and another (54) for maps, books, etc. are fitted on the left hand side of the cockpit. Stowage (65) for a height-and-airspeed computor is provided below the wireless remote contractor.

Operational Equipment and Controls

37. (a) **Guns and cannon.** – The machine guns and cannon are fired pneumatically by means of push-buttons on the control column spade grip. The compressed air supply is taken from the same source as the brake supply, the available pressure being shown by the gauge (2).

(b) The single push-button for firing the eight machine guns on the Spitfire VA is surrounded by a milled sleeve which can be rotated by a quarter of a turn to a safe position in which it prevents operation of the button. The SAFE and FIRE positions are engraved on the sleeve and can also be identified by touch, as the sleeve has an indentation which is at the bottom when the sleeve is in the SAFE position and is at the side when the sleeve is turned to the FIRE position.

(c) The triple push button (11) for firing the machine guns and the cannon on the Spitfire VB is fitted with a milled finger which extends out of the bottom and is a means of locking the button in the SAFE position, SAFE and FIRE being engraved on the adjacent casing. When the catch is in the FIRE position, a pip also extends out of the top of the casing so that the pilot can ascertain by feel the setting of the push button.

(d)   The cannon cocking valve (67) is mounted on the starboard side of the cockpit.

38. (a) **Reflector gun sight.** – For sighting the guns and cannon a reflector gun sight (12) is mounted on a bracket above the instrument panel. A main switch and the dimmer switch are fitted below the mounting bracket. The dimmer switch has three positions marked OFF. NIGHT and DAY. Three spare lamps for the sight are stowed in the holders (61) on the right hand side of the cockpit.

(b)   When the sight is used during the day the dimmer switch should be in the DAY position in order to give full illumination, and if the background of the target is very bright, a sun-screen (10) can be slid behind the windscreen by pulling on the ring (9) at the top of the instrument panel. For night use the dimmer switch should be in the NIGHT position; in this position a low-wattage lamp is brought into circuit and the light can be varied by rotating the switch knob.

39. (a) **Camera.** – A G. 42B cine-camera is fitted in the leading edge of the port place, near the root end, and is operated by the gun firing button on the control column spade grip, a succession of exposures being made during the whole time the button is depressed. When cannon are fitted the cine-camera is operated off the cannon-firing pipe line.

(b)   A footage indicator and an aperture switch are mounted on the wedge plate (38) above the throttle lever. The switch enables either of the two camera apertures to be selected, the smaller aperture being used for sunny weather. A main-switch (53) for the cine-camera is mounted on the left hand side of the cockpit. The camera can also be controlled independently by means of an electrical push switch on the control column spade grip, below the gun firing control button.

Navigational, Signalling and Lighting Equipment

40. (a) **Wireless.** – The aeroplane is equipped with a combined transmitter-receiver, either type T.R. 9D or T.R. 1133, and an R.3002 set.

(b)   With the T.R. 9D installation a type C mechanical controller (45) is
fitted on the port side of the cockpit above the throttle lever and a
remote contractor (21) and contractor master switch are fitted on the
right hand side of the cockpit. The master contractor is mounted
behind the pilot's headrest and a switch controlling the heating element
is fitted on the forward bracket of the mounting. The heating element
should always be switched OFF when the pilot leaves the aeroplane.
The microphone/telephone socket (74) is fitted on the right hand side
of the pilot's seat. The R.3002 push buttons (66) are on the right hand
side of the cockpit, and the master switch (69) immediately aft of these.

(c)   With the T.R.1133 installation the contractor gear and the
microphone/telephone socket are as for the T.R.9D installation, but
the type C mechanical controller is replaced by a push-button
electrical control unit.

41. (a)   **Navigation and Identification lamps.** – The switch (46) controlling
the navigation lamps is on the instrument panel.

(b)   The upward and downward identification lamps are controlled from
the signalling switch box (62) on the right hand side of the cockpit. This
switch box has a switch for each lamp and a morsing key, and provides
for steady illumination or morse signalling from each lamp or both. The
switch lever has three positions: MORSE, OFF and STEADY.

(c)   The spring pressure on the morsing key can be adjusted by turning
the small ring at the top left hand corner of the switch box, adjustment
being maintained by a latch engaging one of a number of notches in
the ring. The range of movement of the key can be adjusted by
opening the cover and adjusting the screw and locknut at the centre
of the cover.

42. **Landing Lamps.** – The landing lamps, one on each side of the aeroplanes,
are housed in the under surface of the main plane. They are lowered and
raised by a finger lever (30) below the instrument panel. Each lamp has an
independent electrical circuit and is controlled by a switch (29) above the
pneumatic control lever (30). With the switch in the central position both

lamps are off; when the switch is moved to the left or to the right, the port or starboard lamp respectively, is illuminated. A lever (32) is provided to control the dipping of both landing lamps. On pulling up the lever the beam is dipped. On later aircraft no landing lamps are fitted.

43. **Signal discharger.** – A straight pull of the toggle control (58) fires the cartridge out of the top of the fuselage, aft of the cockpit.

De-Icing Equipment

44. (a) **Windscreen de-icing.** – A tank (78) containing the de-icing equipment solution is mounted on the right hand side of the cockpit directly above the bottom longeron. A cock (79) is mounted above the tank, and a pump (75) and a needle valve (76) to control the flow of the liquid are mounted below the undercarriage emergency lowering control. Liquid is pumped from the tank to a spray at the base of the windscreen, from which it is sprayed upwards over the front panel of the screen.

    (b) The flow of the liquid is governed by the needles valve, after turning ON the cock and pushing down the plunger to its full extent. The plunger will return to the extended position on its own, and if required, it can be pushed down again. When de-icing is no longer required the cock should be turned to the OFF position.

45. **Pressure head heater switch.** – The heating element in the pressure head is controlled by a switch (55) below the trimming tab handwheels. It should be switched off on landing in order to conserve the battery.

Emergency Equipment

46. **Hood jettisoning.** – The hood may be jettisoned in an emergency by pulling the lever mounted inside the top of the hood in a forward and downward movement, and pushing the lower edge of the hood outboard with the elbows.

47. **Forced landing flare.** – A forced landing flare is carried in the tube inside the fuselage. The flare is released by means of a ring grip (56) on the left of the pilot's seat.

48. **First aid.** – The first aid outfit is stowed aft of the wireless equipment and is accessible through the hinged panel on the port side of the fuselage.

Addendum

1. **Jettisonable tank controls.** – On aeroplanes fitted for carrying a long range jettisonable fuel tank, the cock control and jettison lever are mounted together on the right hand side of the cockpit, below the undercarriage control unit. The jettison lever is pulled up to jettison the fuel tank, but cannot be operated until the cock control is moved forward to the OFF position.

2. **Fuel tank pressurising.** – To meet the possibility of engine cutting due to fuel boiling in the warm weather at high altitudes, the main tanks can be pressurised (operative above 20,000 feet). Pressurising however impairs the self sealing of the tanks and should, therefore, be turned ON only when fuel pressure drops to 6 lb./sq. in. or the fuel pressure warning lamp (if fitted) comes on. In very warm weather at very high altitudes a rich cut may occur with the tanks pressurised and pressure must be turned OFF.

3. **Air cleaner.** – On tropicalised aeroplanes cleaner is fitted and a control is provided for cutting it out should it become choked. This consists of a lever below the throttle quadrant which is pushed forward from COLD to HOT to cut out the cleaner and admit warm air from the engine bay.

4. **Desert equipment.** – The following desert equipment is stowed in the fuselage of tropicalised aeroplanes, aft of the pilot's seat:

> Flying and emergency rations.
> Drinking water tank and water bottle.
> Screwdriver, adjustable spanner and pair of pliers.
> Five signalling strips and mirror
> Very signal pistol and container for six cartridges.

> A second cockpit ventilator is fitted on these aeroplanes, on the port coaming above the instrument panel.

SECTION II – ILLUSTRATIONS

INSTRUMENT PANEL SPITFIRE VA, VB & VC, ALSO SEAFIRE I & II

FIG. 1

FS/9

Key to Fig. I

2. Brake triple pressure gauge.

3. Elevator tabs position indicator.

5. Undercarriage position indicator.

6. Oxygen regulator.

7. Flaps control.

8. Blind flying instrument panel.

9. Lifting ring for sun screen.

9a. Reflector sight switch.

10. Sun screen.

12. Reflector sight base.

12a. Voltmeter.

12b. Ventilator control.

14. Engine speed indicator.

15. Fuel pressure warning lamp.

16. Boost pressure gauge.

17. Oil pressure gauge.

18. Oil temperature gauge.

19. Radiator temperature gauge.

20. Fuel contents gauge and push button.

24. Engine starting push button.

24a. Booster coil push button.

24b. Cockpit light switches.

46. Navigation lights switch.

83. Ignition switches.

84. Arrestor hook warning lamp (Seafire only).

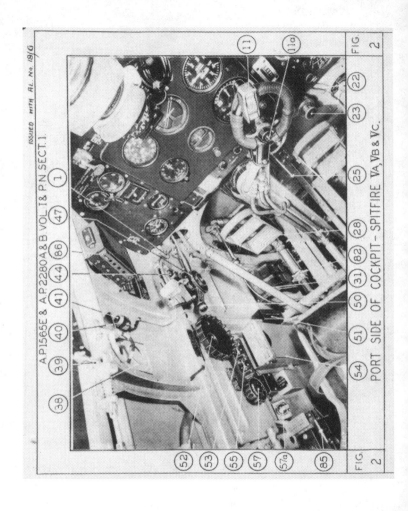

PORT SIDE OF COCKPIT – SPITFIRE VA, VB & VC.

FIG. 2

ISSUED WITH A.L. No. 19/G

A.P.1565E & A.P.2280A & B VOL. I & P.N. SECT. 1.

Key to Fig. 2

1. Boost control cut-out.
11. Gun and cannon three-position push-button.
11a. Cine-camera pushbutton.
22. Slow-running cut-out.
23. Fuel cock control.
28. Rudder pedal.
31. Radiator flap control lever.
38. Wedge plate for camera footage indicator.
39. Two position door catch.
40. Cockpit floodlight.
41. Camera indicator supply plug.
44. Undercarriage indicator master.
47. Control friction adjusters.
50. Propeller speed control lever.
51. Radio controller plug stowage.
52. Elevator trimming tab handwheel.
53. Camera-gun switch.
54. Map case.
55. Pressure head heater switch.
57. Rudder trimming tab handwheel.
57a. Oil dilution pushbutton.
82. Rudder pedal adjusting starwheel.
85. Signal discharger control (Spitfire V only).
86. T.R.1196 or T.R.1304 controller.

STARBOARD SIDE OF COCKPIT – SPITFIRE VA, VB & VC.

A.P. 1565E & A.P. 2280A & B. VOL. I & P.N. SECT. 1

ISSUED WITH A.L. N°. 196/

FIG. 4

FIG. 4

Key to Fig. 4

21. Remote contractor and contractor switch (Spitfire V only).

61. Stowage for reflector sight lamps.

62. Signalling switch box.

64. Lug for flying control locking gear.

66. R.3002 push buttons.

68. Harness release control.

69. R.3002 master switch.

70. CO_2 cylinder for undercarriage emergency system.

71. Oxygen mask hose.

72. Oxygen supply cock.

75. Windscreen de-icing pump.

76. Windscreen de-icing needle valve.

77. Undercarriage emergency lowering control.

79. Windscreen de-icing cock.

79a. Jettisonable tank jettison lever.

80. Undercarriage control unit lever.

80a. Jettisonable tank cock control.

89. Fuel tank pressurising cock control.

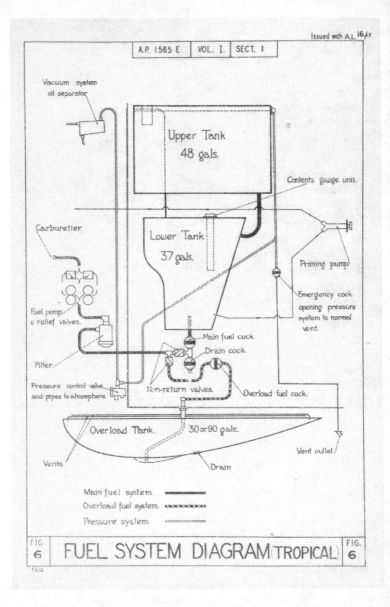

A.P. 1565 E | VOL. I | SECT. 1

Vacuum system oil separator

Upper Tank
48 gals.

Contents gauge unit.

Carburetter

Lower Tank
37 gals.

Priming pump

Emergency cock opening pressure system to normal vent.

Fuel pump & relief valves.

Main fuel cock.

Drain cock.

Filter.

Pressure control valve and pipes to atmosphere.

Non-return valves.

Overload fuel cock.

Overload Tank. 30 or 90 gals.

Vent outlet.

Vents.

Drain

Main fuel system.
Overload fuel system.
Pressure system.

FIG. 6 — FUEL SYSTEM DIAGRAM (TROPICAL) — FIG. 6

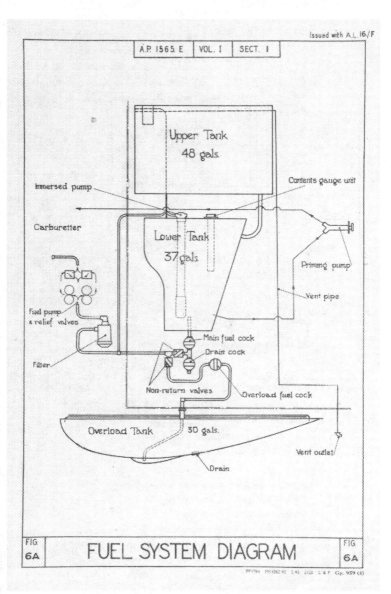

Issued with A.L. 16/F

A.P. 1565. E | VOL. I | SECT. I

Upper Tank
48 gals.

Immersed pump

Contents gauge unit

Carburetter

Lower Tank
37 gals.

Priming pump

Vent pipe

Fuel pump
& relief valves

Main fuel cock

Drain cock

Filter

Non-return valves

Overload fuel cock

Overload Tank   30 gals.

Vent outlet

Drain

FIG
6A

FUEL SYSTEM DIAGRAM

FIG
6A

SECTION III
HANDLING AND FLYING NOTES FOR PILOT

NOTE: The flying technique outlined in these Notes is based on AP.129, Flying Training Manual Part 1, Chapter III and AP.2095, Pilot's Notes General, to which reference should always be made if further information is required.

1. **Engine data:** Merlins 45, 45M, 46, 50, 50A, 50M, 55 and 55M.
(i) *Fuel:* 100 octane only.
(ii) *Oil:* See AP.1464/C.37.
(iii) *Engine limitations:*

	R.p.m.	Boost lb/sq.in.	Clnt. Temp °C	Oil. Temp °C
Max take-off to 1,000 feet	3,000	+12	-	-
Max climbing 1 hr, limit	2,850	+9	125	90
Max rich continuous	2,650	+7	105 (115)	90
Max weak continuous	2,650	+4	105 (115)	90
Combat 5 ins limit	3,000	+16	135	105
		+18		

NOTE:
(a)   +18 lb/sq.in. boost is obtained, only on "M" type engines, by moving the throttle lever through the gate. On other engines +16 lb/sq.in. boost is obtained by operating the boost control cut-out.

(b)   Combat boost is permitted only at 2,850 to 3,000 rpm.

(c)   The figure in brackets is permitted for short periods if necessary.

Oil pressure	Normal:	60/80 lb/sq.in
	Minm:	45 lb/sq.in
Minm. temp for take-off	Oil:	15°C
	Clnt:	16°C
Fuel pressure	8-10lb/sq.in	

2. **Flying limitations**
(i) Maximum speeds:

Diving:	450 m.p.h. I.A.S.
Undercarriage down:	160 m.p.h. I.A.S.
Flaps down:	160 m.p.h. I.A.S.
Landing lamos lowered:	140 m.p.h. I.A.S.

(ii) Restrictions:

(a) When fitted with a 90-gallon drop tank the aircraft is restricted to "straight flying" (see A.P. 2095, IA.3) until the tank is jettisoned. This restriction does not apply when fitted with a 30-gallon drop tank.

(b) For restrictions when carrying 170 and 29-gallon tanks see Para. 22.

(c) Drop tanks should be jettisoned only in straight and level flight, and then only if absolutely necessary.

(d When carrying a bomb, spinning is not permitted and violent manoeuvres must be avoided. The angle of dive must at no time exceed 400.

3. **Management of fuel system**
When fitted with a drop tank:

(i) Start and warm up in the normal way on the main tanks.

(ii) Take off on the main tanks and change over to the drop tank at a safe height (say 2,000 feet). Turn OFF the main tanks.

(iii) Normally the aeroplane should be flown on the jettisonable tank until the fuel is exhausted. When the engine cuts turn ON the main tanks and turn OFF the jettisonable tank at once.

(iv) If the tank is to be jettisoned before the fuel in it is exhausted, first turn ON the main tanks and then move the jettisonable tank cock control to OFF before operating the jettison lever.

NOTE: The jettisonable tank cock must be kept OFF when the tank is jettisoned or when the fuel in it is exhausted, other-wise air may be sucked into the main fuel system.

(v) For maximum range and endurance the tank should be jettisoned as soon as the fuel in it has been exhausted.

4. **Preliminaries**

On entering the cockpit check the following:

Undercarriage lever – DOWN (check that indicator shows DOWN; switch on light indicator and check that green lights appear)

Flaps – UP

Landing lamps – UP

Contents of lower fuel tank.

5. **Starting the engine and warming up**

(i) *Set:*

Fuel cock lever(s) – ON

Throttle – ½ inch open.

Mixture control (if fitted) – RICH

Propeller speed control – Fully back (D.H. 20°) or fully forward (Rotol 35° or DH Hydromatic)

Radiator shutter – OPEN

(ii) High Volatility fuel (Stores ref. 36A/111) should be used if possible for priming pump until the suction and delivery pipes are full; this may be judged by a sudden increase in resistance.

(iii) Switch on the ignition and starting magneto (if fitted) and press the starter and booster coil buttons (if fitted). Turning periods must not exceed 20 seconds, with a 30 second wait between each. Work the priming pump as rapidly and as vigorously as possible while the engine is being turned, and it should start after following number of strokes:

Air Temperature °C	+30	+20	+10	0	-10	-20
Normal Fuel	3	3½	7	12½		
High Volatility Fuel				4	7½	15

(iv) At temperatures below freezing it will probably be necessary to continue priming after the engine has fired and until it picks up on the carburettor.

(v) When the engine is running satisfactorily, release the booster coil button, or switch off the starting magneto (if fitted) and screw down the priming pump.

(vi) Run the engine as slowly as possible for half a minute, then warm up at a fast tick-over.

(vii) If fitted with a D.H. 20° C.S. propeller, move the speed control slowly fully forward when the engine has been running for a minute or more.

6. **Testing engine and installations**
   While warming up:

(i) Make the usual checks of temperatures, pressures and controls. Brake pressure should be at least 120 lb/sq.in.

(ii) See that the cockpit is locked open and the emergency exit door is set at the "half-cock" position.
   After warming up:

(iii) See that there are TWO men on the tail, and with the propeller speed control fully forward, test as follows:

   (a) Open up to a maximum boost for WEAK mixture cruising; exercise and check operation of constant speed propeller.
   (b) Open the throttle fully and check take-off boost and r.p.m.
   (c) At maximum boost for RICH mixture cruising test each magneto in turn. The drop should not exceed 150 r.p.m.

(iv) Running of the engine must not be unduly prolonged because, if the coolant temperature before taxying out exceeds 100°C, it may become excessive before take-off is completed.

(v) When engines are being kept warm in readiness for immediate take-off, de Havilland 20°C.S. propeller should be left in fine pitch – control lever fully forward.

7. **Final preparations for take-off**
   The drill of Vital Actions is "T.M.P., Fuel, Flaps and Radiator."
   T – Trimming tabs – Elevator: about one division nose down from neutral.
   Rudder – Fully to st'bd.
   M – Mixture control (if fitted) – RICH
   P – Pitch – Propeller speed control fully forward.
   Fuel – Cock levers ON and check contents of lower tank.
   Flaps – UP
   Radiator – Fully open.

8. **Take-off**

(i) Open the throttle slowly to the gate (RATED BOOST position). Any tendency to swing can be counteracted by coarse use of the rudder. If taking off from a small airfield with a full load, maximum boost may be obtained by opening the throttle through the gate to the TAKE-OFF BOOST position.

(ii) After raising the undercarriage, see that the red indicator light – UP – comes on (it may be necessary to hold the lever hard forward against the quadrant until the indicator light comes on).

(iii) Do not start to climb before a speed of 140 m.p.h. I.A.S. is attained.

9. **Climbing**

The speeds for maximum rate of climb are as follows:

From S.L. to 10,000 feet	170 m.p.h. I.A.S.
From 10,000 to 16,000 feet	160 m.p.h. I.A.S.
From 16,000 to 21,000 feet	150 m.p.h. I.A.S.
From 21,000 to 26,000 feet	140 m.p.h. I.A.S.
From 26,000 to 31,000 feet	130 m.p.h. I.A.S.
From 31,000 to 37,000 feet	120 m.p.h. I.A.S.
Above 37,000 feet	115 m.p.h. I.A.S.

10. **General flying**

(i) *Stability:* The aircraft is stable about all axes.

(ii) For normal cruising flight the radiator shutter should be in the minimum drag position.

(iii) Change of trim:

Undercarriage down	Nose down
Flaps	Nose down

(iv) For combat manoeuvres climbing r.p.m. should be used.

(v) For stretching a glide in the event of a forced landing, the propeller speed control should be pulled right back and the radiator flap set at the minimum drag position.

11. **Maximum range**

(i) *Climbing:*
Climb at +p lb/sq.in. boost and 2,850 r.p.m. at the speed recommended for maximum rate of climb. Mixture control (if fitted) at RICH.

(ii) *Cruising:*
Maximum range will be obtained at intermediate heights. The recommended speeds are as follows:

(a) Without auxiliary tanks, or if fitted with 30 gallon drop tank:

Below 8,000 feet	180 m.p.h. I.A.S.
Between 8,000 and 15,000 feet	160 m.p.h. I.A.S.
Above 15,000 feet	150 m.p.h. I.A.S.

(b) At very low altitude the speed may be increased to 200 m.p.h. I.A.S. without seriously affecting range.

If fitted with 90 gallon drop tank:

Below 8,000 feet	180 m.p.h. I.A.S.
Above 8,000 feet	170 m.p.h. I.A.S.

Fly in WEAK mixture (if control fitted) at maximum obtainable boost not exceeding +4 lb/sq.in. (the mixture richens automatically at higher boosts) and reduce speed by reducing r.p.m. which may be as low as 1,800 if this will give the recommended speed, but check that the generator is charging. If at 1,800 r.p.m. the speed is higher than that recommended, reduce boost.

NOTE: For maximum range when fitted with 170 gallon and 29 gallon auxiliary fuel tanks see para. 22.

12. Stalling

(i) At the stall one wing will usually drop with flaps either up or down and the aircraft may spin if the control column is held back.

(ii) This aircraft has sensitive elevators, and if the control column is brought back too rapidly in a manoeuvre such as a loop or a steep turn, stalling incidence may be reached and a high speed stall induced. When this occurs there is a violent shudder and clattering noise throughout the aircraft which tends to flick over laterally, and unless the control column is put forward instantly, a rapid roll and spin will result.

(iii) Stalling speeds when loaded to about 6,400 lbs are:

Flaps and undercarriage up:	73 m.p.h. I.A.S.
Flaps and undercarriage down:	64 m.p.h. I.A.S.

13. Spinning

(i) Spinning is permitted by pilots who have written permission from the C.O. of their squadron (C.F.I. of and O.Y.U.). The loss of height involved in recovery may be great, and following height limits are observed:

(a)   Spins are not to be started below 10,000 feet.

(b)   Recovery must be started not lower than 5,000 feet.

(ii)   A speed of over 150 m.p.h. I.A.S. should be attained before starting to ease out of the resultant dive.

14. Aerobatics

The following speeds are recommended:

Looping: Speed should be about 300 m.p.h. I.A.S. but may be reduced to 220-250 m.p.h. I.A.S. when the pilot is fully proficient.

Rolling: Speed should be anywhere between 180 and 300 m.p.h. I.A.S. The nose should be brought up to about 30° above the horizon at the start, the roll being just enough to keep the engine running throughout.

Half-roll off loop: Speed should be 320-350 m.p.h. I.A.S.

Upward roll: Speed should be about 350-400 m.p.h. I.A.S.

Flick manoeuvres: Flick manoeuvres are not permitted.

15. Diving

(i)   The aircraft becomes very tail heavy at high speed and must be trimmed into the dive in order to avoid the dangers of excessive acceleration in recovery. The forward trim should be wound back as speed is lost after pulling out.

(ii)   A tendency to yaw to the right should be corrected by use of the rudder trimming tab.

16. Approach and landing

(i)   During the preliminary approach see that the cockpit hood is locked open, and the emergency exit door is set at the half-cock position. Take care not to get the arm out into the airflow.

(ii)   Reduce speed at 140 m.p.h. I.A.S. and carry out the Drill of Vital Actions "U.M.P. and Flaps."

U – Undercarriage – SOWN (Watch indicators and check green lights).

M – Mixture control (if fitted) – RICH

P – Propeller control – Fully forward

Flaps – DOWN

(iii) Approach speeds (m.p.h. I.A.S.):

		(flaps up)
Engine assisted:	85	(95)
Glide:	95	(100)

(iv) When lowering the undercarriage hold the lever fully forward for about two seconds. This will take the weight off the locking pins and allow them to turn freely when the lever is pulled back. The lever should then be pulled back smartly to the down position and left there. It should NOT be pushed into the gate by hand. As soon as the undercarriage is locked down the lever should automatically spring into the gate and hydraulic valve indicator return to IDLE. If it cannot be pulled fully back, hold it forward again for at least two seconds. If it becomes jammed it may generally be released by a smart blow of the hand. If this fails it is necessary to take the weight of the wheels off the locking pins, either by pushing the nose down sharply or by inverting the aircraft. The lever can then be pulled straight back.

(v) If the green indicator light does not come on, hold the lever fully back for a few seconds. If this fails, raise the undercarriage and repeat the lowering. If this fails also, use the emergency system (see section 1, Para. 12).

NOTE: Before the emergency system can be used, the control lever must be in the down position. It may be necessary to push the nose down or invert the aircraft in order to get the lever down.

(vi) If the undercarriage is lowered too late on the approach, with insufficient engine speed to develop full hydraulic pressure, the selector lever may not automatically spring from the fully back position into the gate, so indicating that the operation is not complete. This may cause the undercarriage to collapse on landing. (As previously mentioned, the lever must NOT be pushed into the gate by hand.) It is advisable therefore, to lower the undercarriage early on the circuit prior to landing and not in the later stages of the approach.

(vii) *Mislanding*: Climb at about 120 m.p.h. I.A.S.

17. After landing

(i) Raise the flaps before taxying.

(ii) If fitted with a D.H. 20°C.S. propeller, after taxying in set the speed control fully back and open up the engine sufficiently to change pitch to coarse.

(iii) Run the engine at 800-900 r.p.m. for two minutes, then pull the slow-running cut-out and hold it out until the engine stops.

(iv) Turn OFF the fuel cocks and switch OFF the ignition.

18. Oil dilution

See A.P. 2095/4. The dilution period should be:

Atmospheric temperatures above – 10°C: 1 minute

Atmospheric temperatures below – 10°C: 2 minutes

19. Flying at reduced airspeeds

In conditions of bad visibility near the ground, reduce speed to about 120 m.p.h. I.A.S. and lower the flaps. The radiator shutter must be opened to keep the temperature at about 100°C and the propeller speed control should be set to give cruising r.p.m.

20. Position error

From	100	140	160	180	200	240	270 &	m.p.h. I.A.S.
To	140	160	180	200	240	270	over	m.p.h. I.A.S.
Add	4	2	0	-	-	-	-	m.p.h.
Subtract	-	-	-	2	4	6	8	m.p.h.

21. Fuel capacities and consumption

(i) Fuel

Normal capacity:

Top Tank:	48 gallons
Bottom Tank:	37 gallons
Total:	85 gallons

Long-range capacity:

With 30 gallons drop tank:	115 gallons
With 60 gallons drop tank:	175 gallons
With 170 gallons drop tank and 29 gallons rear fuselage tank:	284 gallons

(ii) Oil:

Normal capacity:

5.8 gallons

Long-range capacity:

With 90 gallon tank:	115 gallons
With 170 +29 gallon tank:	14.5 gallons

(iii) Fuel consumption (approximate gals/hr)

(a) WEAK mixture (or as obtained at +4 lb/sq.in. boost and below if control not fitted) at 6,000-20,000 feet:

Boost (lb/sq.in.)	2,650 R.p.m.	2,400 R.p.m.	2,200 R.p.m.	2,000 R.p.m.	1,800 R.p.m.
+4	56	53	51	47	43
+2	51	48	46	43	39
0	47	44	42	39	35
-2	43	40	38	35	31
4	39	36	34	31	26

(b) RICH mixture (or as obtained above +4 lb/sq.in. boost if control not fitted):

R.p.m.	lb/sq.in.	Gals/hr
3,000	+9	88
2,850	+9	84
2,600	+7	67

22. Management of 170 and 29 gallon auxiliary fuel tanks

(i) The aircraft is restricted to straight flying until the drop tank and the rear fuselage tank are empty.

(ii) It is most important that at no time should the drop tank cock and the rear fuselage tank cock be ON together, or fuel in the rear fuselage tank will be lost. This applies whether or not the tank has been jettisoned.

(iii) The drop tank should be jettisoned only in straight and level flight.

(iv) Start, warm up and take-off on the main tanks, and change over to the drop tank at a safe height (say 2,000 feet). Turn OFF the main tanks.

(v) When the engine cuts, turn OFF the drop tank, turn ON the rear fuselage tank, and if maximum range is required, or in other special circumstances, jettison the tank at once. If the tank is carried throughout the flight, the still air range is reduced by approximately 120 miles.

(vi) If the tank has to be jettisoned before it is empty, first turn ON the main tanks and then turn OFF the drop tank. Then change over to the rear fuselage tank when convenient.

NOTE: The drop tank cock must be off when the tank is jettisoned, otherwise air may be sucked into the main fuel system, and fuel from the rear fuselage tank will be lost.

(vii) When the engine cuts again, turn OFF the rear fuselage tank and turn ON the main tanks.

(viii) Climb in RICH mixture (if control fitted) at +9 lb/sq.in. boost and 2,850 r.p.m. at 170 m.p.h. I.A.S.
For level cruising flight the following are the recommended speeds:

(a) With 170 gallon tank on:
185 m.p.h. I.A.S. when the drop tank is empty.
(b) After jettisoning tank while using fuel in rear fuselage tank (for medium or high altitudes):
170 m.p.h. I.A.S. when the rear fuselage tank is full, reducing as fuel is consumed, to 160 m.p.h. I.A.S. when the rear fuselage tank is empty.

(x) Fly in WEAK mixture (if control fitted) at +4 lb/sq.in. boost (if obtainable) (do not exceed +4 lb/sq.in. because the mixture is automatically richened at boosts in excess of this) and reduce speed by reducing r.p.m. which may be as low as 1,800 (but check that the generator is charging). By reducing r.p.m. by 50 at the end of each half-hour the I.A.S. will be reduced by approximately the correct amount. If at 1,800 r.p.m. the speed is higher than that recommended, reduce boost.

CHAPTER VII
Spitfire Aircraft for Malta, 1942

Reinforcement of Middle East Command

1. It has been decided to reinforce the Middle East Command by means of a carrier operation. The ship to be used will be a special carrier and aircraft are to be embarked in the Clyde on approximately 10th April.

2. <u>Aircraft.</u> 52 Spitfire VC aircraft, with Merlin 46 engines, tropicalised and fitted with long range jettisonable tanks and VHF wireless, are to be prepared for this operation and are to be flown to Abbotsinch under arrangements to be made by No.41 Group. The maximum possible number of these aircraft are to be fitted with 4 cannons. The first 12 aircraft are to arrive at Abbotsinch on Wednesday, the 8th of April, followed by 10 per day on the 9th, 10th, 11th and 12th April. The exact capacity of the carrier being employed is not known but 50 aircraft are to be available at Abbotsinch for embarkation. The aircraft will be embarked in the fully erected state.

3. The aircraft after flying off the carrier are to proceed without escort. Special care is therefore to be taken that:-

    (i) Compasses are correctly swung and deviation cards fitted.

    (ii) Fuel consumptions are checked and proved to be normal.

    (iii) Wireless is correctly tuned and serviceable.

    (iv) Aircraft are complete with Appendix 4 equipment [not included here].

    (v) Guns are tested and sights harmonised.

4. <u>Pilots.</u> 55 pilots are to be provided by Fighter Command of whom 52 are to be embarked. These pilots are to be detailed as follows:-

    (i)   40 including the 2 Commanding Officers are to be taken as squadron teams from 2 of the 6 Spitfire Squadrons detailed for operation "Corry". Loose Minutes DDOII/358 dated 24th March and 366 dated 29th March refer.

    (ii)   The remaining 15 pilots are to be detailed from Fighter Command resources. They are to be experienced and carefully selected.

All pilots must be fully conversant with the correct methods of operating long range tanks and of the correct methods of manipulating engine controls to obtain most economical cruising.

5. Care is to be taken that all pilots are fully equipped with full flying clothing, parachutes, dinghies, radio equipment, etc.

6. Arising out of the above arrangements a new C.O. is to be appointed of the 2 "Corry" Squadrons from which the 40 pilots mentioned in para 4(i) above have been taken. These 2 officers are to accompany the Squadrons overseas in convoy W.S.18. The remaining 38 pilots required to bring these 2 "Corry" Squadrons to establishment will be supplied from the normal flow of fighter pilots through Takoradi.

7. It is intended that Wing Command McLean, who is returning from Operation "Quarter", should sail in this operation, but to allow for eventualities, another Wing Commander, who has had previous experience of this type of operation, is to be detailed to stand by. This officer is to report to D.C. Ops as early as possible.

8. Maintenance arrangements. An experienced maintenance party, provided with all necessary equipment, is to be detailed by D.S.M. to sail in the carrier. Where possible personnel should be chosen to include those who have had previous experience of this type of operation and those with specialist Spitfire knowledge. Three or four experienced specialist personnel have been recalled from "Quarter". It must not, however, be assumed that they will return in time, and therefore stand-bys are to be detailed.

9. D.S.M. must also arrange for an Engineer Officer to be responsible for the general technical control of aircraft at Abbotsinch after they have been handed over by 41 Group. It is understood that S/Ldr. Wall has been detailed for this duty.

10. Spares. A small parcel of spares is to be carried in each aircraft. The weight of each parcel is to be decided by D.S.M. in conjunction with D.O.Ops.

11. Batmen. R.A.F. batmen are to be detailed at the normal scale. If these should not be required, they will be released at the port of embarkation.

12. Fuel. A supply of 100 octane fuel, a quantity of the appropriate oil and any coolant required is to be available in the carrier.

13. <u>Armament</u>. As stated in para.2, as many aircraft as possible are to be equipped with 4 cannon, whether the aircraft are fitted with 4 cannon or 2 cannon and Browning guns, the ammunition carried when the aircraft take off from the carrier will be the same; that is, 2 cannons to be loaded with 60 rounds each.

14. Will:-

(i)   <u>0.7.</u> in conjunction with 41 Group arrange for the allotment of aircraft and for their delivery at Abbotsinch on the date and at the rate stated in para. 2.

(ii)   <u>41 Group</u> arrange for the preparation of the aircraft as detailed in para. 3. As no experts are being provided on this occasion it is specially important that aircraft should be complete and serviceable in all respects before embarkation.

(iii) <u>Fighter Command</u>:-

(a) Detail 55 pilots as required in para.4 and ensure that they are fully kitted and equipped. Fighter Command is also to ensure that all pilots are fully conversant with the methods of using long range tanks and the methods of obtaining most economical petrol consumption.

(b) Detail new Commanding Officers for the 2 "Corry' squadrons. These officers are to sail in convey W.S.18 with the remainder of their squadrons.

(c) Detail an officer experienced in carrier operations to accompany the party and instruct him to report to D.O.Ops as soon as possible. This officer will only sail if W/Cdr. McLean does not return in time from operation "Quarter".

(iv)   <u>P.P.6 and M.6:</u> please note arrangements set out in this loose minute in so far as they affect postings and take the necessary action. Will M.6. also send the requisite number of batmen to Abbotsinch.

(v)   <u>D.S.M.</u> arrange for an officer for technical supervision at Abbotsinch and also for an experienced maintenance party to sail in the carrier.

(vi)   <u>C.D.S.8.</u> in conjunction with D.S.M. arrange:-

      (a) for the supply of spares for use at Abbotsinch and also for use in the carrier.

      (b) fuel and oil and coolant for the carrier.

      (c) ammunition as required by the conditions set out in para.13 above.

(vii)   <u>D.D.Movements</u> Please issue the necessary Movement orders for personnel and aircraft, informing Fighter Command on what date pilots should report at Abbotsinch. It is understood that they will not be called upon to report there before the 8th April and the Command has been so informed.

15. <u>Code names.</u> A code name for this operation is being issued separately. Care should be taken by all concerned to maintain the utmost secrecy and that only information is divulged to those concerned preparing aircraft, etc., sufficient to enable them to carry out their particular task.

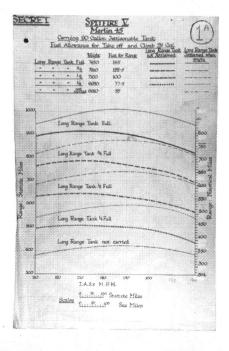

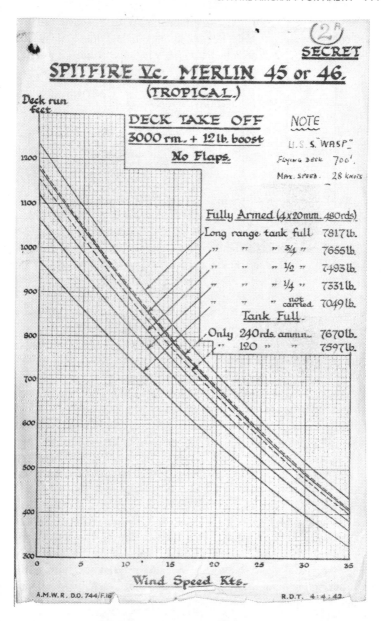

SECRET

SPITFIRE Vc. MERLIN 45 or 46.
(TROPICAL.)

Deck run feet

DECK TAKE OFF
3000 rm. + 12 lb. boost
No Flaps.

NOTE

U.S.S. "WASP"

FLYING DECK 700'.

MAX. SPEED. 28 knots

Fully Armed (4×20mm. 480rds)

Long range tank full			7817 lb.
" " " 3/4 "			7655 lb.
" " " 1/2 "			7493 lb.
" " " 1/4 "			7331 lb.
" " " not carried			7049 lb.

Tank Full.

Only 240 rds. ammn. 7670 lb.
" 120 " " 7597 lb.

Wind Speed Kts.

A.M.W.R. D.O. 744/F.16

R.D.T. 4:4:42

SECRET CYPHER MESSAGE

To: Fighter Command, Maintenance Command, 41 Group, Abbotsinch, Rafshipper Glasgow. Repeat Admiralty – F.O.I.C.Glasgow and
F.O.I.C.Greenock.

From: Air Ministry, Kingsway.

Received	A.M.C.S.	1406	hours	6.4.42.	
Despatched	"	1515	"	"	

OX 5622 6/4. Immediate – Secret

Movement Order 436. Following in six parts.

Part One. Following procedure to be followed in shipment of 52 Spitfires VC in ship commencing loading Clyde Friday tenth April. Aircraft tropicalised fitted long range jettisonable tanks and V.H.F. provided by and flown under 41 Group arrangements to Abbotsinch. Twelve by Wednesday eighth April followed by ten on Thursday Friday Saturday and Sunday. After delivery ferry pilots at disposal of 41 Group.

Part Two. At Abbotsinch all petrol tanks including long range tanks to be drained and aircraft prepared for manhandling completely erected to Blackburns Wharf on own undercarriages. Aircraft completely erected to be loaded on barges and conveyed to ship under arrangements to be made by Rafshipper Glasgow. Three sets slings for Spitfires VC will be manufactured and despatched 47 MU Sealand to Abbotsinch to arrive p.m. Tuesday seventh April. Abbotsinch will arrange provision of ropes and tackle to secure aircraft to barges guide ropes for use during loading and handling party of thirty-three airmen. Rafshipper Glasgow will arrange for barges and use of Blackburns Crane. Hoisting aircraft aboard ship will be carried out under arrangements of Ships Captain. Four Cannon of which two are to be loaded with sixty rounds each are fitted in aircraft to accompany each aircraft throughout if available. Otherwise two Cannon and four Browning guns same loading.

Part Three. Fighter Command to provide fifty-five pilots of whom fifty-two will travel in ship and three reserves will remain at Abbotsinch. Pilots to assemble at Abbotsinch by 1200 hours on Tuesday fourteenth April. They are to be fully equipped to Middle East scale with full flying clothing flying topees anti-glare goggles parachutes and harness radio equipment life saving jacket K type dinghies blue uniform revolvers and ammunition. Total personal Kit to accompany each pilot in addition limited to ten pounds weight. Balance of pilots personal kit to be packed handed into unit store and Unit Commanders instructed to apply to Air Ministry (Movements 3) for shipping instructions.

Part Four. Fifty-two sets of Maps arranged by Air Ministry (A.D.O.P) will be despatched to Rafshipper Abbotsinch by Friday 10th April. 40 Group are providing twelve Skates six Trollies two hundred and twenty-four Chocks three Slings one Compressor one Jack and four Steering Arms under arrangements made by Air Ministry (S.M.2. and E.16). Maintenance Command will provide fifty-two sandfly nets and fifty-two jars of Bamber oil or equivalent amount of substitute anti mosquito cream of Sketofax. One net and one jar are to be fixed to each aircraft. Any equipment required to be loaded in ship only repeat only to be marked NEWMAN/SKATES NEWMAN/CHOCKS et cetera.

Part Five. Air Ministry (D.G.M.S.) will arrange lecture on health precautions on board ship about Tuesday fourteenth April. In order to deny details of complete movement to all individuals only such portions of this order appropriate to each individual or unit to be communicated. Rafshipper Glasgow to consult Ships Captain regarding quantities and method of delivery of 100 Octane petrol and oil Reference 34a/115 and Glycol Reference 33c/559.

Part Six. Squadron Leader WALL is responsible for general technical control of aircraft at Abbotsinch after they have been handed over by ferry pilots. Wing Commander Parsons is responsible for all matters relating to movement of aircraft pilots maintenance party and equipment from Abbotsinch to ship. Acknowledge.

Time of origin: 1230 hours 6.4.42.

CHAPTER VIII
Spitfire Mark IX Tactical Trials

Report No.46
Air Fighting Development Unit,
R.A.F. Station, Duxford, 1942

INTRODUCTION

1. In accordance with instructions from Headquarters, Fighter Command, one Spitfire IX aircraft, AB.505, was delivered from Messrs. Rolls-Royce, Ltd., to this Unit on 26th April 1942, for a period of one week, for tactical trials.

2. In order to bring the weight of the aircraft up to its full war load it was necessary to fit 2 x 20 mm. cannons, full ammunition for all guns, V.H.F., and I.F.F. The aircraft has fittings for a jettisonable fuel tank but this was not available. Without this tank the all-up weight is about 7,400 lbs.

3. During the trials minor adjustments had to be made to the undercarriage and sliding hood, and after 5 days flying engine failure occurred. It was found that the butterflies in the carburettor were pitted, one spray nozzle on the enrichment side was missing, and several pieces of metal had reached the oil filters. A new engine is being sent from Messrs. Rolls-Royce, Hucknall.

BRIEF DESCRIPTION OF THE AIRCRAFT
General

4. The Spitfire IX is a Spitfire VC modified to incorporate a Merlin 61 engine fitted with the latest negative 'G' carburettor. The main differences between the two aircraft are the slightly longer nose due to the larger engine, a 4-bladed Rotol constant speed propeller, two thermostatically controlled radiators and two-speed superchargers which are automatically controlled. The fuel capacity is increased by approximately 10 gallons and the tanks are pressurised.

Pilot's Cockpit

5. The cockpit is similar to that of the Spitfire VC but has additional controls for ground testing the full supercharger gear and radiators, and for pressurising the fuel tanks. There is only one fuel cock.

6. The supercharger gear is fully automatic, so that M.S. gear only is in operation below about 22,000 feet and F.S. gear above that height. For ground

testing there is a push button to bring the F.S. gear into operation. A red light illuminates when the button is pressed and also in the event of the aneroid failing to change down to M.S. on descent so as to warn the pilot that there will be a loss of power should he have his landing baulked and have to go round again. If the aneroid is functioning correctly F.S. is not available below 22,000 feet, nor is M.S. available above this height.

7. The radiator is thermostatically controlled so that the pilot does not have to operate it manually. For ground testing there is a push button which will open the radiator while the button is held down, otherwise the shutters open when the coolant temperature reaches 115°C. This press button and the button for testing F.S. gear are situated on a plate aft of the throttle box and are in the way of the pilot's arm.

9. A cock is provided for pressurising the fuel tanks and must always be kept on above 20,000 feet to avoid engine failure due to vapour locks. In the event of a tank being holed by enemy action it is essential to turn off the pressure to avoid excessive loss of fuel. The cock is on the starboard side of the cockpit and is liable to be fouled by the pilot's elbow. A rod fuel pressure warning light is fitted instead of a pressure gauge on the dash-board and lights when the pressure falls to 3 lbs.

10. There is a gauge mounted on the port side of the dash-board showing the temperature of the mixture charges, which should read about 40°C. in M.S. gear and 60-80°C. in F.S.

11. There is an efficient system of heating the cockpit which can be regulated by the pilot.

12. The constant speed control for the airscrew is in the usual position and controls between 1700 and 3000 r.p.m. The travel of the lever is, however, very short indeed and the selection of desired r.p.m. far too critical.

Sighting View

13. The Spitfire IX is fitted with the G.M.2 pilots reflector sight and although the aircraft is no longer in the nose than the Spitfire VC, the 100 m.p.h. ring of the sight is still just clear of the nose.

Oxygen Equipment

14. The oxygen supply is obtained from two bottles provided with an economiser and is the same as that used in the standard Spitfire.

TACTICAL TRIALS

15. The Spitfire IX was compared with a Spitfire VC with similar armament, and a Typhoon I for performance and manoeuvrability; all aircraft were carrying full war load.

Flying Characteristics

16. The Spitfire IX is similar to the Spitfire VC for take-off and landing, although the landing speed is slightly higher. The extra weight and length of the aircraft has made the elevators a little heavier and as a result controls are better harmonised. It was noticed that during dives there was loss tendency for the aircraft to yaw and this was thought to be due to the extra radiator fitted on the port wing. Tight turns were made up to 5G and there was no sign of 'tightening up', the aircraft recovering normally when the control column was released.

Performance

17. The speed of the Spitfire IX was compared with a Spitfire VC and a Typhoon I at various heights. Its maximum true speed in M.S. gear is developed at a height of 16,300 feet and is approximately 386 m.p.h., and in F.S. gear at 28,000 feet and is approximately 409 m.p.h. These figures are slightly less than those obtained by Messrs. Rolls-Royce, but it is understood that the aircraft they used was not fitted with cannons and did not carry full war load. The speed of the Spitfire IX at all heights was vastly superior to that of the Spitfire VC.

18. Two speed runs were made against a Typhoon I from an operational squadron. At 15,000 feet the Spitfire IX was approximately 10 m.p.h. faster, and at 18,000 feet approximately 2 m.p.h. faster. (See Appendix 'B').

Climb

19. Comparative climbs were carried out and it was found that the Spitfire IX was superior to the Spitfire VC and Typhoon I at all heights. This superiority becomes even more marked as height increases. The Spitfire IX was climbed under maximum continuous climbing conditions, to an indicated height of 39,500 feet where the rate of climb was about 700 feet per minute. It was particularly noticed that the oil and glycol temperatures were normal throughout. The operational ceiling is considered to be about 38,000 feet where the rate of climb is 1,000 feet per minute. This height can be reached by a single aircraft in 18½ minutes. The results obtained from the various climbs are shown in Appendix 'C'.

Manoeuvrability

20. The Spitfire IX was compared with a Spitfire VC for turning circles and dog-fighting at heights between 15,000 and 30,000 feet. At 15,000 feet there was little to choose between the two aircraft although the superior speed and climb of the Spitfire IX enabled it to break off its attack by climbing away and then attacking again in a dive. This manoeuvre was assisted by the negative 'G' carburettor, as it was possible to change rapidly from climb to dive without the engine cutting. At 30,000 feet there is still little to choose between the two aircraft in manoeuvrability, but the superiority in speed and climb of the Spitfire IX becomes outstanding. The pilot of the Spitfire VC found it difficult to maintain a steep turn without losing height, whereas the pilot of the Spitfire IX found that he had a large reserve of power which enabled him to maintain height without trouble. The all-round performance of the Spitfire IX at 30,000 feet is most impressive.

21. Short trials were carried out against a Typhoon I and the Spitfire IX was found to be more manoeuvrable and superior in climb but inferior in dive. During a dog-fight at 18,000 feet the Spitfire out-turned the Typhoon and got on its tail after 1½ turns.

High Flying

22. Several climbs were made to heights between 39,000 and 40,000 feet and the pilot felt that the aircraft was capable of going even higher. Although the operational coiling is considered to be 38,000 feet, it is thought that Sections of two could operate up to 39,000 feet and probably higher. The aircraft is easy to fly at high altitudes, but freezing up of the trimming tabs occurred. It was therefore difficult to keep the aircraft level as it was still trimmed for climb. During manoeuvres there is otherwise little tendency to lose height even at 38,000 feet. At this height the aircraft was dived for 1,500 feet and zoomed up to 39,000 feet. Stoop turns were carried out at 38,000 feet where it was necessary to maintain an indicated airspeed of at least 110 m.p.h. to prevent stalling. The cockpit heating kept the pilot warm at all heights and flying clothing was unnecessary.

23. Slight icing up of the cockpit was experienced during turns but this dispersed as soon as the aircraft was flown straight. The cold air spray to the windscreen was turned on during descents and no misting up was experienced.

24. During the high flying trials vapour trials were formed between 30,000 and 36,000 feet, but above this height trails were not visible. All flights took

place under conditions of no cloud and extremely low temperatures, -64°C. being reported on one occasion.

Endurance

25. The fuel capacity of the Spitfire IX is 92 gallons, 57 in the top tank and 35 in the bottom tank. This is 10 gallons more than the Spitfire VC. There are fittings under the fuselage for a jettisonable tank holding 39 gallons. Petrol consumption during the trials was high and during a comparative flight of 75 minutes the Spitfire IX used 76 gallons and the Spitfire VC 54 gallons. In a flight of one hour, three speed runs of 4 minutes each and a maximum continuous climb to 39,000 feet were carried out and the Spitfire IX used 76 gallons. On investigation of engine trouble experienced at the latter stage of the trials it was found that the aircraft had been delivered with the mixture control locked in the "RICH" position instead of "WEAK".

Armament Characteristics

26. The Spitfire IX, like the Spitfire VC, is fitted with the universal wing and for the trials 2 x 20 mm. cannons and 4 x .303" Brownings were carried. When fitting the 20 mm. cannons it was found that the inboard rib on the gun panel housing fouled the feed mechanism and the gun panel had to be cased by filing. Time did not permit firing trials to be carried out but this installation has already been reported on by this Unit. (See A.F.D.U. Report No. 42).

Cine Camera Gun

27. It was impossible to fit a G.45 cine camera gun as ducts for the radiator system obstructed the camera mounting.

CONCLUSIONS

28. The performance of the Spitfire IX is outstandingly better than the Spitfire V, especially at heights above 20,000 feet. On the level the Spitfire IX is considerably faster and its climb is exceptionally good. It will climb easily to 38,000 feet and when levelled off there, can be made to climb in stages to above 40,000 feet by building up speed on the level and a slight zoom. Its manoeuvrability is as good as a Spitfire V up to 30,000 feet, and above that is very much better. At 38,000 feet it is capable of a true speed of 368 m.p.h., and is still able to manoeuvre well for fighting.

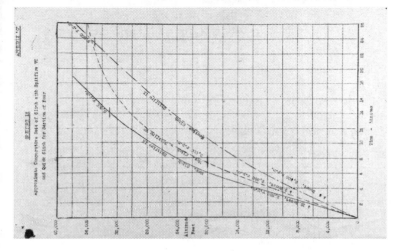

APPENDIX 'D'

SPITFIRE IX

Approximate Comparative Rate of Climb with Spitfire VC and Quick Climb for Series of Four

Altitude Feet

Time - Minutes

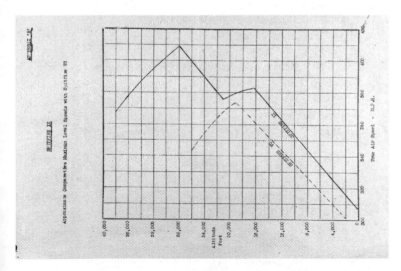

APPENDIX 'E'

SPITFIRE IX

Approximate Comparative Maximum Level Speeds with Spitfire VC

Altitude Feet

True Air Speed - M.P.H.

CHAPTER IX
No. 11 Group Report on Circus No. 252, 1943

1. Information.

It was decided to carry out Circus 252 against Tricqueville and Caen Aerodromes: Tricqueville with a force consisting of 12 Bostons in two boxes of six, and Caen with a force consisting of 18 Venturas in three boxes of six, with escort. The operation took place during the afternoon of the 21st January, 1943, in accordance with No. 11 Group Operation Order No. 362 dated 17th January, 1943, the following forces taking part:-

Part I. Target: Caen Aerodrome.

Bombers: 18 Venturas of No. 2 Group.

Fighters:

Escort: Nos. 335 and 336 Squadrons (Debden).

No. 350 Squadron (Hornchurch).

Target Support. Nos. 331 and 332 Squadrons (Spit.IX's) (North Weald).

1st Bouncing Wing. Nos. 306 and 315 Squadrons (Spit.IX's) (Northolt).

Part II. Target; Triqueville Aerodrome.

Bombers: 12 Bostons of No. 2 Group.

Fighters:

Escort. Nos. 401 and 402 Squadrons (Spit.IX's), and Nos. 412 and 416 Squadrons (Spit.V's) (Kenley).

1st Bouncing Wing. Nos. 340 and 611 Squadrons (Spit.IX's) (Biggin Hill).

Mopping-up Wing. Nos 340 and 611 Squadrons (Spit.IX's) (Hornchurch).

Appledore Wing. Nos. 165 and 485 Squadrons (Tangmere).

2. Weather.

Part I.

6/10ths cloud at 16,000 ft. over France: visibility 15 miles. Over Channel to 30 miles north of Le Havre, clear.

Part II.

10/10ths cloud over target at 10/12,000 ft: visibility above and below cloud 30 miles.

3. Narrative of Operations.

Part I.

Bombers.

12 Venturas attacked the target with 12 x 500 lb. M.C., 2 x 500 lb. G.P. and 26 x 250 lb. G.P. bombs. A number of D.A. and Incendiary Bombs were also dropped. Runway and dispersal areas received direct hits.

Fighters.
Escort.

The Debden squadrons made rendezvous with the Venturas and the operation was carried out according to plan. The French coast was crossed west of Ouistreham with the bombers at 11,000 ft. and our aircraft to starboard at 12,000 ft. Moderate accurate heavy flak over the target area where six bomb bursts were seen on the S.W. corner of the aerodrome. On the return journey, when our aircraft were at 500 ft. about 15 miles out from the French coast, two FW.190's were seen approaching at sea level. The enemy aircraft steered off on sighting out aircraft. Four pilots fired from extreme range but could not close and saw no results. The Hornchurch squadron joined up with the two Debden squadrons and completed the operation according to plan. They too experienced much light and heavy flak in the target area, whilst they saw bombs drop on small buildings outside the aerodrome and hits between the hangars and runway.

Target Support.

The North Weald Wing operated according to plan, arriving over Caen Aerodrome ready to bounce any enemy aircraft. Only two FW.190's were seen and one section chased them S.E. but they dived inland as though to encourage our fighters to follow. The first section broke away and as they did so, a second section dived from astern and fired at long range without result.

1st Bouncing Wing.

The Northolt Wing reached Shoreham below 500 ft. according to plan and from there flew for 22 minutes at sea level. Climbing, they made French landfall at Trouville between 10,000 and 13,000 ft. After sweeping over Tricqueville aerodrome in an effort to bounce any aircraft there, the French coast was recrossed west of Fecamp. No signs of activity were seen on Tricqueville aerodrome. When about 25 miles N.W. of Fecamp, the Wing was ordered to return towards Le Havre, where they orbited west of the port without seeing any enemy aircraft. They were then instructed to set course for home, and the English coast was recrossed at Shoreham at 1302 hours. No enemy aircraft or flak was observed at any time.

Part II.

Bombers.

3 Bostons attacked the target, dropping 48 x 30 incendiaries and 48 x 40 G.B. bombs from 10,000 ft. 10/10ths cloud over the target made it invisible after bombs had been released but some bursts were seen although their positions could not be plotted. 5 aircraft abandoned the attack, after circling the aerodrome a second time, owing to 10/10ths cloud at 5,000 ft.

Fighters.
Escort.

The Kenley Wing completed the operation according to plan, proceeding for 13 minutes at sea level and then climbing rapidly to bombing height. Smoke trails were seen on the way out approaching from the N.E. at approximately 20,000 ft., but no enemy aircraft were identified.

1st Bouncing Wing.

The Biggin Hill Wing flew to Shoreham and set course for Granville at zero feet: began to climb after 22 minutes and French coast was crossed just south of the Seine at 12,000 ft. The Wing turned south and made a very wide orbit over the target area. The Bombers and some Spitfires were soon disappearing through cloud over the target but were not seen again. Crossed the French coast between Fecamp and St. Valery at 12,000 ft., whilst the English coast was crossed over Beachy Head. No enemy aircraft seen.

Mopping-up Wing.

Rendezvous was made at Hornchurch and the Wing climbed steadily to Beachy Head where, at 20,000 ft., thin hazy cloud was encountered. Climb continued but still in cloud so the Wing came down to 20,000 ft. until 55 miles off French coast when the formation came out of cloud at 13,000 ft. They then climbed back again and crossed the French coast E. of St. Valery at 18,000 ft. The Wing swept right, climbing over Bolbec at 24,000 ft. They were ordered to proceed to the Abbeville area as Huns reported at 10,000 and 25,000 ft.

They orbited Abbeville/Le Crotey area at 28,000 ft. Huns being then reported off Berck. The formation did a right orbit, diving to get under cloud layer which was 10,000 ft. 15 FW.190's were sighted coming from sun about 2 miles distant. The formation was ordered to climb and dive on Huns but as climb commenced, Huns went down vertically through cloud. It was impossible to follow the formation and our Wing then did a left orbit and went out over Le Crotey, recrossing the English coast at Dungeness.

Appledore Wing.

The Tangmere Wing made a rendezvous over Beachy Head, crossing the French coast at Cayeux at 16,000 ft. The formation then climbed to Abbeville to cloud base at 18,000 ft. Here, 485 Squadron report accurate heavy flak from the aerodrome. No aircraft were seen on the aerodrome and the formation continued to climb through 8-10/10ths cloud to a point about 8 miles S.E of Abbeville, reaching a maximum of 21,500 ft. The formation then flew towards Hesdin and Montreuil. Enemy aircraft were reported at 25,000 ft. to the E. of the Wing but nothing was seen but smoke trails at 25/28,000 ft. in the St. Pol area. The Wing Leader then ordered the Wing below cloud and the formation crossed the French coast just north of Berck at 16,000 ft. Passing through a thin layer of misty cloud, No. 165 Squadron then lost touch with No. 485 Squadron, who said they were five miles E. of Berck. 165 Squadron orbitted over Berck and suddenly saw two batches of unidentified aircraft totalling about 12. They were three miles away, heading due West and at same height. The Wing Leader then called up and said he was just passing over top of No. 165 Squadron and No. 165 Squadron reported the unidentified formation to the Wing Leader, who at the same moment saw 16 FW.190's travelling across from left to right about two miles ahead. No. 485 Squadron pursued these enemy aircraft and the Wing Leader got within 400 yds. range of a straggler and fired a short burst. The FW.190 belched out brown smoke and dived down steeply but pulled out at sea level. The other 13 enemy aircraft dived steeply away and were not seen again. Several pilots had brief squirts at very extreme range with unobserved results. No. 165 Squadron were unable to get within range. Our Wing then set course for home. Two FW.190's were seen at about 13,000 ft. near Berck and these followed the Squadron a short way out but some distance behind. One of our sections was detached to try and get round behind these two enemy aircraft but lost them in cloud. The FW.190's were camouflaged dark green-brown.

4. Summary of Casualties.

Enemy Casualties: Nil.
Our Casualties: Bombers. Nil.
Fighters. Nil.

5. Notes.

1. Debden report that the 2 FW.190's seen at sea level attempted to position themselves for a head-on attack on the Venturas prior to being chased off.

2. Enemy Reaction.
(a) See by our Squadrons:- 35.
(b) Plotted: Le Havre area 15+
Pas de Calais area 25
Belgium 10
Total 50+

CHAPTER X
Tactical Paper No. I

Air Ministry D.D.A.T.
February 1947

AIR FIGHTING TACTICS USED BY SPITFIRE FIGHTER SQUADRONS OF 2ND T.A.F. DURING THE CAMPAIGN IN WESTERN EUROPE

Introduction

1. In June, 1944, when the Allied forces invaded Normandy, the Royal Air Force had experienced almost five years of aerial warfare and had accumulated a wealth of knowledge upon which to base its plans and tactics. The types of formation flown over Normandy, the tactics the day-fighters used, and the different methods of "tree top" and high altitude fighting had been slowly and carefully evolved throughout the preceding five years, and a brief outline of this period illustrates the development of the various fighter tactics until there were attained a style, method, and degree of combat flying which inflicted the maximum number of casualties upon the enemy whilst keeping our own losses at a minimum.

Formations

Dunkirk

2. When carrying out standing patrols over Dunkirk beaches in May/June, 1940, most of the squadrons flew in tight compact formations consisting of four sections of three aircraft in line astern as illustrated at Appendix "A", Fig. 1. This was a poor formation as individual aircraft were so close to each other that only the leaders had any opportunity of keeping a sharp lookout: the aircraft in the rearmost section, therefore, were very easy to "bounce". The Luftwaffe had already learned the lesson of the "open" formation in the Spanish Civil \War and in Poland. Later, such experienced G.A.F. leaders as Moelders, Galland and Weike declared that our fighter formations over Dunkirk were far too compact and often presented easy targets. Furthermore, the basic section of three aircraft proved to be cumbersome and unwieldy, and later squadron formations were built upon the pair, similar to the "rotte" in the Luftwaffe, which proved effective and lasted throughout the war.

Battle of Britain

3. During the Battle of Britain, although many fighter squadrons still flew in four sections of three, others adopted the three sections of four aircraft flying in line astern as shown in Fig. 2 of Appendix "A". This, undoubtedly, was a better fighting formation but it was still far from ideal, as Nos. 2, 3 and 4 in each section had to pay most of their attention to their leader in order to keep in position, and, therefore, were not able to keep a good lookout. This formation, however, remained very popular for a long time and some squadrons were still using it at the end of the war in Europe. Usually the first man to be hit out of this formation was, of course, No. 4, or "Tail-end-Charlie", as he was most vulnerable, and for this reason this position was unpopular, particularly with new pilots, who generally carried out their first few operations in this unenviable position. In order to keep a better lookout and to prevent the No. 4 from being picked off, some squadrons adopted the "weaving" principle, in which each section of four weaved when over enemy territory. Although this did allow the leader to keep a better lookout "weaving" seriously affected the radius of action of a Wing or Squadron.

Sweeps

4. The early sweeps over France in 1941 developed yet another type of formation known as "finger-fours", as illustrated at Appendix "A", Fig. 3. This formation was a step in the right direction as every one was "well up" and had an equal chance of spotting the enemy, and, if properly flown, it was difficult to "bounce". Each section of four was, if necessary, quite independent, as Nos. 1 and 2 guarded Nos. 3 and 4, and vice-versa. Similarly in squadron formation, yellow section guarded red and blue sections whilst blue section, out on the port flank, guarded red and yellow sections. The main disadvantage of this formation was that it was unwieldy and covered a large area, especially when a wing operated with three squadrons, and, after any fighting, the wing was seldom reformed as a whole and because of this a large percentage of its striking power was lost. Nevertheless, it was a popular formation with the pilots, both leaders and No. 2's, and it is one of the few formations which survived throughout the remaining four years of air fighting. It was especially popular with ground attack aircraft during the campaign in Western Europe.

1942–43 Period

5. During operations over Europe and North Africa in 1942–43 there emerged what is probably the most nearly perfect fighter formation of the war,

the "fluid-six", which is shown at Appendix "A", Figs. 4.(*a*) and 4.(*b*). It is a loose manoeuvrable formation suitable for freelance fighter sweeps, bomber escort, fighter-bombing, armed reconnaissance, patrols and straffing. It was extremely popular with pilots, particularly newcomers, as there was no "Tail-end-Charlie" feeling, and, if the formation is flown properly, all pilots are "well-up" and in position should a fight be imminent. It is both an offensive and defensive formation, as twelve pairs of eyes are continually searching the sky. It has the great advantage over other formations, that the Flight Commander is always leading his own Flight of six aircraft and thus he can watch carefully the flying discipline, skill and development of his pilots. Since the squadron flies in two sixes ("A" and "B" Flights) it eliminates the "bastard" section of four aircraft found in most other formations when a four is made up of two aircraft from each flight, which is most unsatisfactory. From the illustrations in the Appendix it can be seen that the whole formation is based upon the pair and relies for its success upon team-spirit and co-operation. Red 5 and 6 look after the tails of 3 and 4, and vice versa, thus Red 1 and 2 are doubly covered. Similarly it is Blue Section's duty to guard Red Section from a surprise attack, and vice versa. A wing of up to and including three squadrons is easy to operate and lead when this formation is flown (see Appendix "A" Figs. 5 and 6).

Formation Technique – Fluid Sixes

Take-off

6. Throughout the campaign in Western Europe squadrons using the "fluid-six" formation invariably took off in pairs, the leader waiting until all his squadron was in position behind him on the runway in order to ensure a quick form-up after take-off. The pairs of aircraft behind the leader positioned themselves at a slight angle to the runway to facilitate judgment of the exact moment to turn into wind and open up. The leader executed a long wide climb to port so that Blue Section, particularly Nos. 5 and 6, could "cut-the-corner" and achieve a quick squadron form-up. With this method it was possible to form up a squadron within one-half to three-quarters of the circuit. This form of mass take-off would not, of course, have been possible without complete local air-superiority as the squadron forming up on the ground makes an ideal target for a ground straffing attack.

Climbing

7. When climbing, a squadron flying in "fluid sixes" in conditions where it was unlikely that 10/10 cloud would be met with, "B" Flight formed up immediately astern of "A" Flight as shown in Fig. 9 (*a*) of the Appendix. A fairly compact formation was then flown during the climb and when the leader deemed it necessary the formation opened out to its battle positions (Fig. 4 (*a*)). When it was necessary to climb the squadron through 10/10 cloud the formation shown at Fig. 9 (*b*) was adopted. It is a very small departure from the previous formation but it ensures that an experienced pilot is leading each "vic" of three aircraft. The four sections of three aircraft then climbed steadily through cloud at one minute intervals and reformed above the overcast. When the leader decided to open up into battle formation (Fig. 4 (*a*)), Red 2 and 3 and Blue 2 and 3 simply changed positions, Blue Section taking up its position and the battle formation being quickly arrived at.

Landing

8. After a sortie a squadron would return to its base in two sixes, "B" Flight line astern of "A" Flight and as the circuit was approached "B" Flight dropped back. The formation leader then, for a left hand circuit, ordered the sections into echelon starboard, and the squadron landed in the order, Red 1, 2, 3, 4, 5 and 6 followed by Blue 1, 2, 3, 4, 5 and 6 as shown in Fig. 10 (*b*).

Battle Tactics

General

9. Fighter tactics vary from month to month and from year to year, but at the end of the campaign in Western Europe there were certain general rules that did apply to all Spitfire squadrons. These were:-

    (*a*) The pair had been proved to be the basis of the present day fighter formations, and all later formations were designed and built up on this principle.

    (*b*) Strict flying discipline, good drill and immediate obedience to the formation leader's orders were essential to the success of a fighter squadron.

    (*c*) Strict R/T discipline was most important and with a well trained squadron no air to air R/T chatter was necessary until enemy aircraft were sighted. Vectors from Controllers and other ground to air messages were acknowledged with a minimum of speech.

"Ultimate Pursuit"

10. During the air fighting over the occupied countries previous to "D" Day, the German fighters generally took evasive action by half rolling and diving to ground level. They could dive at a steeper angle and at a higher speed than the Spitfire, and as a result, during the 1941–43 period, they were seldom pursued to ground level as it was considered highly dangerous to do so. Over Normandy, however, this decision was reversed as it was the aim to destroy the enemy's fighter arm completely and furthermore, as a result of their experience in straffing sorties and low-level "Rangers", the Royal Air Force fighter pilots were well trained in low-level work. The enemy was surprised to find that he was now followed and engaged at tree-top height, and he showed little skill at this hedge-hopping type of air fighting. As a result he suffered a considerable number of casualties.

Rangers

11. A very popular type of operation was known as the "Ranger", and it paid handsome dividends. No more than six aircraft, fitted with long-range tanks, would take-off. They would first climb in order to cross the bomb-line and flak belts at a safe height, then having flown well inside enemy territory and flown several widely differing courses to confuse enemy radar, they would go down to ground level. Here they settled down, No. 2's slightly echeloned from their leaders, to follow the prescribed route. With Spitfire IX's using a 90-gallon jettison tank, the radius of action was about 270-280 miles which made it possible to visit a great many enemy airfields on this type of operation. Enemy aircraft were easy to spot, especially if there was any low cloud, and when one was sighted a pair would be detailed to deal with it and they climbed steadily and attacked from below into the belly of the enemy aircraft. The success of this operation depended entirely on the leader, who was always a first-class low-level navigator, and who naturally spent most of his time map-reading and checking his navigation. The other members of the formation were thus able to devote all their energies to keeping a sharp look-out for enemy aircraft or other targets of opportunity. The height at which this operation was carried out made detection by radar extremely difficult.

Bomber Escort

12. The size of fighter escorts for bombers varied greatly during the different stages of the war, and whereas in 1941 as many as nine fighter squadrons

escorted three Stirlings on daylight bombing operations, in 1944–45 the escort for the medium bombers was cut to a bare minimum. This was due to the fact that the American Air Forces were operating deep into enemy territory whilst our medium bombers, in their role of close support air arm, were bombing targets on, and a few miles inside, the bomb line. It was a generally accepted principle that one-third of the escorting fighters could break away and engage any enemy fighters they could see in the vicinity of the bombers, even though they were some miles away. This was an important factor, as during the Battle of Britain, we are now told, Goering strictly ordered his fighters to stay with the bombers at all costs even when they could see R.A.F. fighters manoeuvring for position some distance away. If this is true the German fighters were at a great disadvantage as they could not break away and fight until our attack had actually commenced. Close co-operation with the bomber squadrons was essential and visits were paid to their bases to discuss formations and tactics.

Fighter v. Fighter

13. The better known German fighters, the Me. 109 and F.W. 190, presented little difficulty to the versatile Spitfire IXB, and the Spitfire XIV was vastly superior to either of them as it was faster and could out-turn and out-climb with ease. Whenever there was a warning of German fighters in the vicinity, as much advantage as possible was taken of the prevailing weather conditions, sun and cloud, and if enemy forces were engaged, one third of the Spitfires were detailed as high cover in order to keep a look-out for further enemy formations. Occasionally the high cover was brought down into the fight if the leader thought it advisable.

14. The Me.262 presented quite a different problem as it was very fast and quite impossible to catch even when the Spitfires possessed a good height advantage. Fortunately all of this type of enemy aircraft encountered appeared to be of the bomber, not fighter, variety, and they did not appear to be interested in attacking the Spitfire formations. The only method of cornering the Me.262 with Spitfires was to discover the airfield from which they were operating, pay frequent visits to it during the day and endeavour to destroy them as they took off or landed. This scheme worked on several occasions, and the operation was extremely interesting, largely because of the efforts of the flak defences of the G.A.F. airfields.

Fighter v. Bomber

15. The Battle of Britain offered the only opportunity for the R.A.F. fighters to develop their tactics in attacking large formations of enemy bombers. Since that time, the day fighters operating from the United Kingdom, and later from the Continent, rarely encountered enemy bombers, and even when they did, the enemy was never present in strength. The Luftwaffe, however, had ample opportunity of developing fighter attacks against the large formations of American day bombers, and a study of the lessons they learned are well worth while.

Re-forming

16. It is very necessary that a fighter wing be able to fight, re-form and proceed with its planned flight after an engagement with the enemy. On many occasions Fighter Wings crossed the bomb line, engaged the enemy and returned in ones and twos to their base within a few minutes of taking-off, very often with nearly full petrol tanks and ammunition drums which, as can be seen, is a great waste of effort. To avoid this the leaders of certain Wings always gave, after an engagement, clear and concise instructions as to the rendezvous and height at which he wished the Wing to re-form. For example he might say, "Wing will re-form over Caen, No. 1 Squadron at *angels* 20, No. 2 Squadron at *angels* 22, and No. 3 at *angels* 24, Course 180." All aircraft were then able to make their way to the rendezvous which the leader would orbit for two or three minutes before setting course.

Camera Guns

17. When the cine films were developed and returned to the Wing, it was customary for the Wing Commander Flying to show the films to all pilots, compare them with the actual combat report, and criticise range, length of bursts and accuracy of shooting. Unfortunately the films produced by the type of camera in use were generally of such poor quality that it made this task practically impossible, and on most films all that could be seen was a dark blur on a greyish scratched background. Even at the end of the war the Spitfires were carrying a camera which took only 14 frames per second as compared to the camera fitted to the American fighters which took 72 frames per second. Furthermore, on the British camera, there was no "override" fitted, consequently the best cannon strikes at the end of the combat were never seen.

Gun Sights

18. During 1944–45 all Spitfires were fitted with the gyro-sight and it was discovered that it had several disadvantages when pilots were engaging in "close fighting". It consisted of a large piece of mechanism which obstructed the forward view of the pilot, and it required quite a lot of ranging and tracking and rudder and stick juggling in order to get an enemy aircraft correctly lined up in the sight; as a result the pilot was apt to spend too much time over his sight in a combat where every second counted. When used for long steady shots at enemy bombers, however, it was found to be ideal.

Briefing

19. During the Western European campaign the briefing of a Spitfire Wing fell into two categories.

(a) When the Wing operated together and purely in a fighter roll, such as freelance fighter sweeps in Wing strength and escorts to bombers, it was customary for the Wing Commander Flying to brief pilots in detail. On these occasions the procedure followed was:–

(i) To give a general description of the operation with special emphasis on other friendly forces likely to be encountered. This was most important as there were numerous cases of American and British aircraft attacking one another through faulty recognition and bad training.

(ii) To discuss the role of the Wing, i.e. close escort, escort cover or sweeping ahead of the bombers.

(iii) To make clear the route, rendezvous, heights and targets, which were always displayed on a map of suitable scale, and the Wing Commander Flying traced the whole operation from start to finish. The squadrons were then given the order to go and exactly what time individual squadrons would press starter buttons and take-off. The time for the whole Wing to set course from base was then given and watches synchronised. (It was found that from most bases with a reasonable runway and taxi tracks a Wing of three squadrons could take-off, form up and set course in ten to twelve minutes.)

(iv) To give the positions of the heavy and light flak – an important point, especially if the bombers were attacking heavily defended targets. Special flak maps were always on view in the briefing tents.

(v) To ensure that all pilots were aware of the correct R/T call signs, emergency homing and air/sea rescue procedure.

(vi) To give the weather forecast with special reference to high altitude wind speed and direction.

(vii) To give general hints such as any new types of enemy aircraft that may be encountered, decoys and any other items of importance.

(viii) For the senior A.L.O., who generally wound up the briefing, to point out on his maps the positions of the forward troops, the bomb line, and enemy dispositions. This served to keep all pilots up to date with the land battle and was invaluable when squadrons were switched from a purely fighter role to ground attack or close support duties.

(b) When the day's operations consisted of aircraft operating in section or flight strength only, such as standing patrols, armed reconnaissance, dive bombing ground attacks. On these occasions the same flight sometimes flew on three and even four operations of an exactly similar nature in one day. It was the custom for the formation leader to bring his pilots to the briefing tent in order to study the bomb line, dispositions of friendly and enemy troops, enemy flak batteries, enemy vehicle recognition, weather forecast etc. It was the duty of the Wing Commander Flying to be present at all these small briefings and also at the interrogation of the pilots concerned after the operation was completed. The A.L.O's were found to be extremely valuable and they stimulated the pilots' interest in the land battle a great deal.

Conclusion

20. It must be appreciated that Battle Tactics are entirely dependent upon the existing circumstances and it is impossible to lay down any hard and fast rules. A close study of tactics which have been used successfully, along with the conditions existing at the time of their use can, however, be invaluable as very often it is possible to adapt well tried ideas to a new set of circumstances. The chief requirement for successful tactics is, however, for the Wing Leaders to "keep abreast of the times" and constantly review their tactics in the face of new developments.

PLAN VIEW OF FORMATIONS.   APPENDIX "A".

FIG. I.

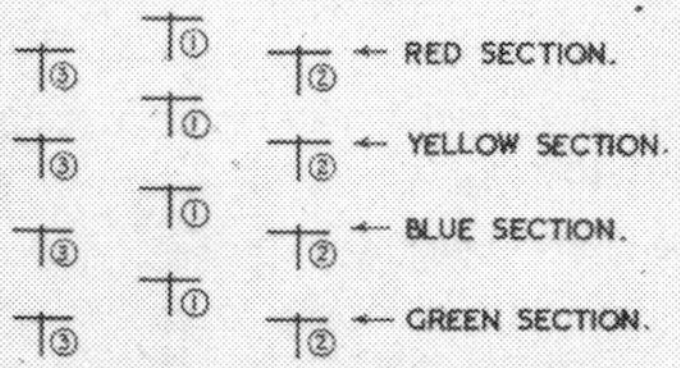

← RED SECTION.

← YELLOW SECTION.

← BLUE SECTION.

← GREEN SECTION.

FOUR SECTIONS OF THREE AIRCRAFT
SECTIONS LINE ASTERN, AIRCRAFT IN VIC.

FIG. 2.

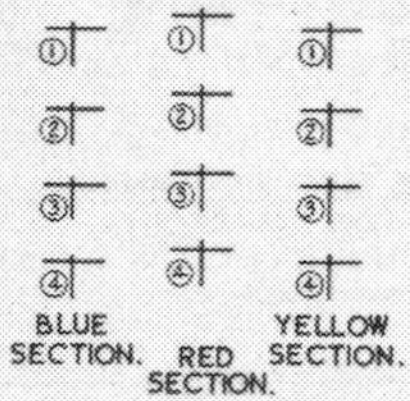

BLUE
SECTION.   RED
SECTION.   YELLOW
SECTION.

THREE SECTIONS OF FOUR AIRCRAFT SECTIONS ABREAST,
AIRCRAFT LINE ASTERN

FIG. 3.

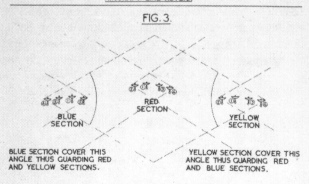

BLUE
SECTION

RED
SECTION

YELLOW
SECTION

BLUE SECTION COVER THIS
ANGLE THUS GUARDING RED
AND YELLOW SECTIONS.

YELLOW SECTION COVER THIS
ANGLE THUS GUARDING RED
AND BLUE SECTIONS.

THREE SECTIONS OF FOUR AIRCRAFT SECTIONS ABREAST,
AIRCRAFT ABREAST.

APPENDIX "A". PLAN VIEW OF FORMATIONS.
FIG. 4 (a).

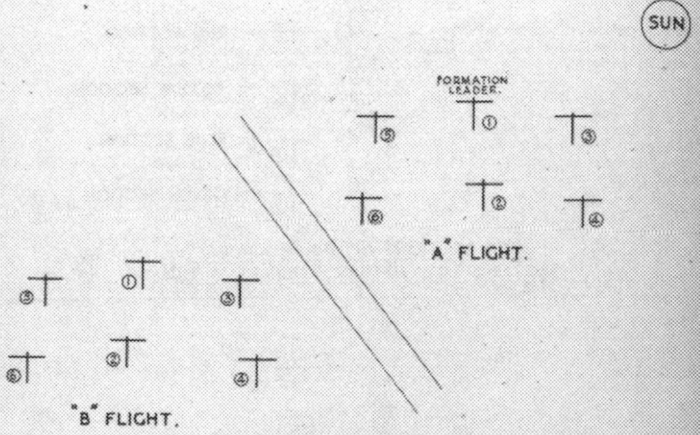

SUN

FORMATION
LEADER.

"A" FLIGHT.

"B" FLIGHT.

THE FLUID SIX FORMATION.
(ONE SQUADRON)

HEAD ON VIEW OF FORMATIONS.
FIG. 4 (b).

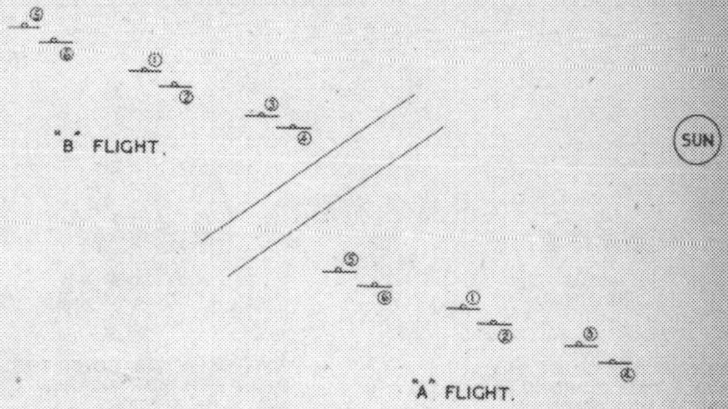

"B" FLIGHT.

SUN

"A" FLIGHT.

THE FLUID SIX FORMATION
(ONE SQUADRON)

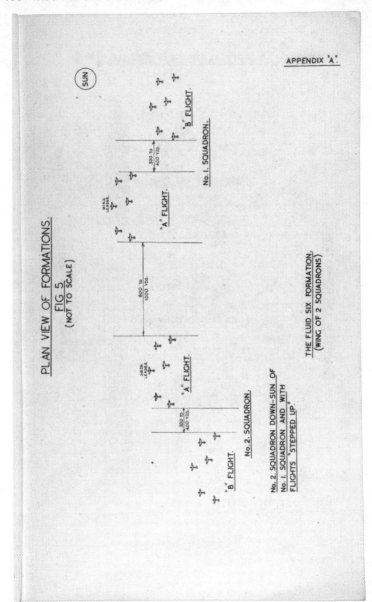

PLAN VIEW OF FORMATIONS.
FIG 5
(NOT TO SCALE)

No. 1. SQUADRON.

"B." FLIGHT.

"A." FLIGHT.

No. 2. SQUADRON.

"A." FLIGHT.

"B." FLIGHT.

No. 2. SQUADRON DOWN-SUN OF
No. 1. SQUADRON AND WITH
FLIGHTS "STEPPED UP."

THE FLUID SIX FORMATION.
(WING OF 2 SQUADRONS)

APPENDIX 'A'.

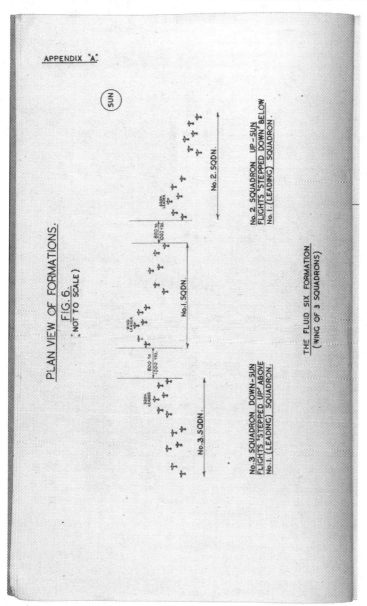

APPENDIX 'A'.

PLAN VIEW OF FORMATIONS.

FIG. 6.
(NOT TO SCALE)

SUN

No.3. SQDN.

SQDN. LEADER

800 TO 1200 YDS.

WING LEADER

No.1. SQDN.

800 TO 1200 YDS.

SQDN LEADER

No.2. SQDN.

No.3 SQUADRON DOWN-SUN
FLIGHTS 'STEPPED UP' ABOVE
No.1. (LEADING) SQUADRON.

No.2 SQUADRON UP-SUN
FLIGHTS 'STEPPED DOWN' BELOW
No.1. (LEADING) SQUADRON.

THE FLUID SIX FORMATION
(WING OF 3 SQUADRONS)

PLAN VIEW OF FORMATIONS. FIG. 7.

APPENDIX 'A'.

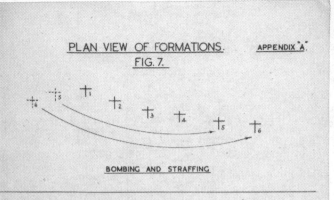

BOMBING AND STRAFFING

PLAN VIEW OF FORMATIONS. FIG. 8.

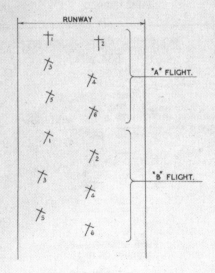

LINE-UP FOR TAKE OFF.

APPENDIX "A".   PLAN VIEW OF FORMATIONS.
FIG. 9 (a)

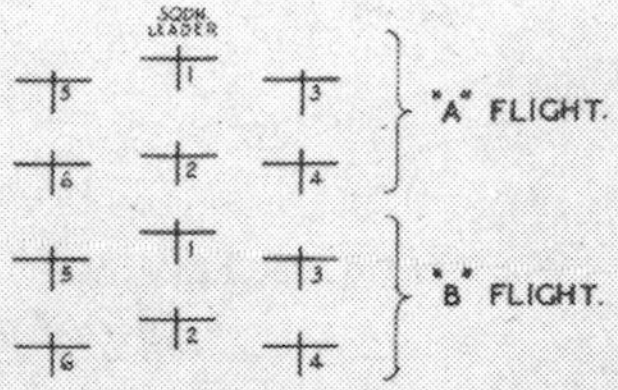

CLIMB IN CONDITIONS OF
CLEAR VISIBILITY.

PLAN VIEW OF FORMATIONS.
FIG. 9 (b).

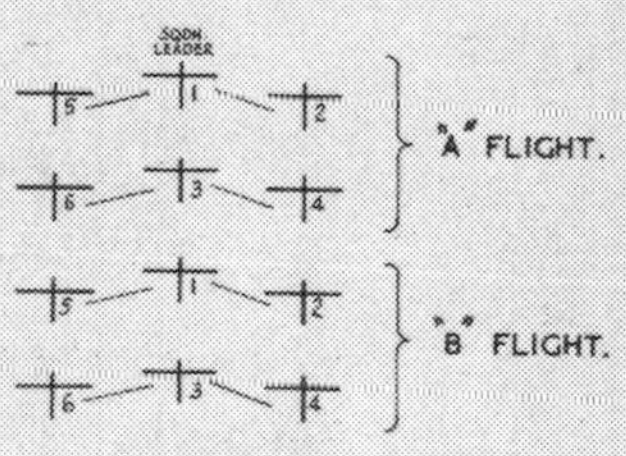

CLIMB THROUGH CLOUD.
SECTIONS OF THREE.

PLAN VIEW OF FORMATIONS.
FIG. 10 (a).

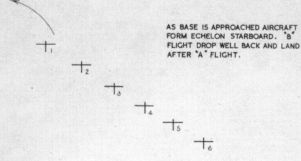

"A" FLIGHT.

"B" FLIGHT.

RETURN TO BASE.

PLAN VIEW OF FORMATIONS.
FIG. 10 (b).

AS BASE IS APPROACHED AIRCRAFT
FORM ECHELON STARBOARD. "B"
FLIGHT DROP WELL BACK AND LAND
AFTER "A" FLIGHT.

RETURN TO BASE.

CHAPTER XI
Tactical Paper No. 4

Air Ministry, D.D.A.T.
September, 1947.

TACTICS USED BY SPITFIRE DAY FIGHTER/BOMBER SQUADRONS OF 2ND T.A.F. DURING THE CAMPAIGN IN WESTERN EUROPE

Introduction

1. The Tactical Air Force, which was created for the invasion of the Continent, was based mainly on the fighter force which was then existing in Great Britain.

2. The aircraft deployed by the new force were the same fighter aircraft modified so as to carry bombs and rocket-projectiles. In their role in 2nd T.A.F. the aircraft of the Spitfire XVI Squadrons normally carried the following armament:–

   (a) Two 20-mm. cannons with 260 rounds of ammunition.

   (b) Two 0.5-in, machine-guns with 500 rounds of ammunition.

   (c) One 500-lb. bomb plus two 250-lb. (fully loaded).

   (d) Two 250-lb. plus drop tank (45 gallons).

The bombs were of two types, high explosive and incendiary. The high explosive bombs were either instantaneous or had delayed action fuses from 0.025 second to 72 hours, depending on the kind of target. The bombing was carried out from low level or from a dive. In the case of low level bombing the normal fuse was of at least 11 seconds delay in order that it should not endanger the bombing aircraft.

3. The first trials of using fighter aircraft for new purposes were the operations "Rhubarb". From the experience gained in these operations and in mass exercises of the fighter squadrons in Great Britain in the years 1943–1944, the basis of the formation of a Tactical Air Force was formed. The employment of fighter aircraft in the Tactical Air Force necessitated new tactics being evolved because of:–

   (a) Flying at lower altitude in the reach of enemy flak defences.

   (b) The employment of fighter aircraft in attacks on ground targets.

   (c) The arming of fighter aircraft so that they could carry bombs and rocket projectiles.

4. The creation of a Tactical Air Force did not change the main tasks of the Fighter Force. It only added new tasks and the personnel and material had to carry out a more varied programme.

5. The general tactics of the Fighter Force were only changed inasmuch as the technical improvements of the material allowed it. We will limit ourselves in the review of the Tactical Air Force to the experience of certain Units who had Spitfires Mk. XVI at their disposal. These Squadrons had the following tasks to carry out:-

(*a*) Direct co-operation with our own first-line troops.

(*b*) Attacks on the enemy's front line and rear.

(*c*) Normal fighter force tasks.

Outline of Operations
Direct Co-operation with First-Line Troops

6. This co-operation had three main aims:-

(*a*) The attacking of targets which were supplied in advance by the Army to the Air Force through regular channels. It used to take some time before the attack on the supplied target could be carried out. Thus, this method of co-operation could only be effective when the front was more or less stabilised or in the case of immobilised points of resistance such as dug-in artillery or tanks.

(*b*) Attacks on targets passed to the pilot from the Contact Car. The pilot who was linked by R/T to the Contact Car could attack any target upon receipt of instructions. The target could be a small one and even mobile.

(*c*) Patrols of defined regions with attacks on enemy artillery and personnel whose location was normally observed by the pilot patrolling or was betrayed through their own fire. Such patrols and eventual attacks forced the enemy personnel to seek cover and enabled our own troops to have more freedom of movement. These patrols were being carried out as a supplement or instead of the normal co-operation with Contact Car, and only in very special circumstances as, for example, during the crossing of Siegfried Line when the Sappers of the Polish 1st Armoured Division were completing a bridge on the river Mark, during the liquidation of the enemy bridgehead at Breskens opposite Walcheren Island etc.

Attacks on the Enemy's First Line and Rear up to a certain Depth

7. This activity was not a result of direct requests by the Ground Forces, but was carried out by the Air Force on general lines supplied by higher authority, and had two main tasks:–

(a) Attacks on targets supplied and strictly defined as for example, Enemy H.Q.'s, launching points of V.1 and V.2 factories, groups of enemy units, motorised enemy formations, enemy airfields, etc. This kind of task required very minute preparations and especially exact data about the target. Preparation for this type of operation was, therefore, somewhat lengthy.

(b) In reconnaissance and attacks on targets in defined regions, the fighter force had to reconnoitre a defined region and find its own targets for attack. This kind of operation was called "Armed Recce" and was mainly directed against enemy's lines of communication (road and rail transport). It was also directed against the enemy units and had as a general aim the disorganisation of the enemy in the line and in the rear of the front-line. Once the Air Force gained a definite superiority, and the enemy units were disorganised, this kind of attack was also carried out to an extended depth.

Normal Fighter Force Tasks

8. The activity of the Tactical Air Force on the Continent was exercised in rather specific conditions, seeing that the enemy air force hardly ever appeared in order to resist any ventures by the Tactical Air Force. But the "New Year's" attack of the German Air Force on the 1st January, 1945, was a proof that the general task of the fighter air force should not be left out of the programme of the Tactical Air Force. It was a proof that the Tactical Air Force should be ready at any time to carry out tasks normally carried out by a Fighter Force.

9. The three main tasks are:–

(a) To gain and maintain air superiority. For that purpose, sections or whole squadrons of the Tactical Air Force were prepared for combating the enemy Air Force, for maintaining readiness and for offensive patrols.

(b) To act as escort for other aircraft; this task being carried out on the lines of the strict fighter force system.

(c) Reconnaissance, which was the duty of every aircraft of Tactical Air Force. As the front line was very mobile, ordinary tactical reconnaissance could not be effective. The time for carrying out an attack on a reconnoitred target was limited owing to the very mobile nature of most targets. As a result of the above all Tactical Air Force aircraft were carrying out a continuous reconnaissance during their operations. Any target which was suitable for attack and destruction but could not be effectively tackled by the pilot who located it, for any reason at all, was passed by the pilot immediately by R/T to any other section or formation who were operating in the same region and could be directed to the target. If the target was a large one, for example, concentrations of enemy motorised units or steamed-up trains at railway junctions, the pilot passed his information to G.C.C. All other information as for instance enemy movements etc. the pilot used to pass to the Intelligence Officer upon landing.

Factors Influencing the Carrying-out of a Task

Nature of Target

10. The nature of the target was the deciding factor of the number of aircraft which were to take part in the operation. On large targets or on targets whose destruction was essential two or even three squadrons were sent out. On small or mobile targets one or two sections (of two aircraft) were employed. The nature of the target was also the deciding factor with regard to the type and number of bombs. In the attacks on the enemy transport the aircraft were not bombed-up as a rule, and normally carried drop tanks to enable the pilot to remain as long as possible over enemy territory. The only exceptions to this rule were attacks on trains and water-ways transport, bombs being very effective in attacks on the latter. For the purpose of attacking fortifications, enemy Headquarters, factories and "Interdiction" (cutting of railway lines) the full load of bombs was considered best, and very often both high explosive and incendiary bombs were used. If the distance to the target or the time over target warranted it two 250-lb. bombs were carried in addition to a drop tank.

Flak

11. The enemy's flak defences influenced the tactics during flight and the carrying out of the attack. In the front line zone the enemy had a terrific concentration of small calibre flak, the fire of which was not visible to the attacking pilots. This kind of defence was very effective up to 3,000 ft. and so,

as a rule, the aircraft flew higher, and only came below 3,000 ft. when carrying out the attack.

12. The light flak fire was effective up to 6,000 ft. and could be easily seen by the pilot (smoke and explosions). In the orbit of the enemy flak fire the following tactics were employed:–

(*a*) Widening of formation.

(*b*) Constant changes in the height and direction of flight.

In most cases the enemy's light flak defences would not open fire at aircraft which were flying past. This was because they did not wish to betray their position and during the final stages of the war, to economise ammunition. They normally opened fire only on attacking aircraft.

13. Heavy flak was also easy to see and in the orbit of this kind of artillery the tactics employed were the constant change of the flying height and, if necessary, the direction. For instance, a formation of aircraft which got into the orbit of heavy flak at 12,000 ft, used to dive to 10,000 ft. and after 30 seconds at that height used to climb to 11,000 ft.

Weather

14. The weather conditions had a greater influence in the T.A.F. than in any other Air Force. The carrying out of a task and the tactics to be employed were dependent upon the time of day, visibility, cloud-base, direction and strength of wind.

The minimum requirements, as regards weather, for carrying out a tactical flight were:–

(*a*) Visibility not less than 2,000 yards.

(*b*) The base, at an amount of 7/10 cloud, could not be lower than 3,000 ft. for strafing or 5,000 ft. for bombing. There were some operations which were carried out with a cloud base lower than 3,000 ft. but the losses were quite extensive and only very important targets could justify such a venture. When carrying out such missions special care was taken to avoid concentrations of enemy flak. In some cases this amount of cloud, especially when the clouds were thin ones, used to be exploited for the purpose of surprise attacks. Then the flight to the target was made above clouds (6,000 ft.) and only when over enemy territory did the aircraft go below cloud in the look-out for a target. After having carried out the attack they climbed above cloud again. These tactics were carried out until all ammunition was exhausted.

(c) When the amount of cloud was less than 7/10, the base cloud, even if lower than 3,000 ft. did not interfere with the operations. In many instances such atmospheric conditions were used for making surprise attacks, as it was often possible to catch larger numbers of enemy transport on the move.

(d) Strong wind always made operations difficult. Most of the airfields had only one run-way and the strong cross wind made take-offs more hazardous, especially with a full load, and the time required for take-offs or landings of formations was much longer. During bombing, a strong wind had the following influence:–

It dictated to the pilots their direction of approach, thus preventing them from making use of the position of the sun, the form of the target and the position of our own lines.

It also affected the accuracy of the bombing. If the target in question could only be attacked from one certain direction, the strong wind made such bombings very problematical (railway lines which could only be bombed along the line).

(e) The time of day. The activity of our aircraft forced the enemy to limit his movements by road and rail to a minimum during daylight. Because of this factor, special tactics were used. A section of two aircraft would take-off 45 minutes before first light and carry out a reconnaissance of the enemy territory. When this section saw a train they would attack the locomotive and with the aid of R/T would transmit the position of the target. Upon receipt of the section's communication, the appropriate number of aircraft loaded with bombs would be despatched for the purpose of destroying the train.

The position of the sun was exploited in order to make the attack a full surprise; the technique of attack being to come out of the sun, bomb the train and leave the target by climbing towards the sun.

Execution of the Task

15. A brief outline of the whole procedure from the briefing of the pilots to their reporting on landing gives a clear picture of how a typical task was executed.

Briefing

16. The accuracy of the briefing depended on the nature of the task, the

amount of information available about the target and on the amount of time available for briefing. The main principle was that there should be no sortie without an appropriate briefing and that all pilots who were taking part in the operation should be present. The briefing had as its aim the acquainting of the pilots with the following information:–

(*a*) Particulars about the force taking part. The number of aircraft, the formation to be used, the armament (number and type of bombs), the sequence of take-off etc.

(*b*) Information about the target. Whenever possible, photographs and an exact plan and description of the target were provided. All the possible interferences such as enemy defences, observation posts, and flak were pointed out. Special attention was given to the terrain around the target.

(*c*) Navigation and maps. The maps generally used were 1 : 250,000 on which the bomb line was always kept up to date. In the case of targets which were difficult to locate or extremely important for destruction more accurate maps were used such as 1 : 50,000 and sometimes 1 : 25,000. For the purpose of co-operation with Contact Cars the 1 : 50,000 were used with a special grid, duplicate maps being held by the Contact Car.

(*d*) R/T. The button, the call signs and all homing procedure were repeated for the pilots' information.

(*e*) The leader informed the pilots as to his intended tactics of approach, flight, rendezvous, etc.

If only experienced pilots had to be briefed, the briefing could be limited to the essential points; but, taking into consideration that many pilots were young and inexperienced, the general rule was to repeat instructions and remind the pilots of the usual things, such as what they were to do in case of being hit, emergency landing, how to attack, how to dive, at what height to release bombs, etc.

Take-off

17. The take-off depended on the kind and state of the run-way. It also depended on the load of bombs and on weather conditions. If the aircraft were bombed-up they normally took off singly with such a distance between them that one aircraft did not start taking off until the aircraft in front of it was just leaving the ground. With the exception of bombed-up aircraft, and when weather conditions permitted, the take-off was done in sections of two. In the

case of a fully loaded aircraft, or even an aircraft with two 250-lb. and a drop tank, special care was taken that take-offs were three-point ones and that there was no excessive bouncing of the aircraft as it endangered the machine and the pilot. In the case of bigger formations the aircraft used to form up whilst circling over their own base (3,000 ft.).

Navigation

18. It was taken as a rule that the whole operation should be carried out without the navigational aid of the Ground Control with the exception of special cases, very bad weather etc. In the case of difficult and small targets which were difficult to locate, a certain point of orientation was chosen somewhere near the target which was easy to find in the terrain and on the map.

Each pilot had to know:-
   (*a*) The course back.
   (*b*) The position of the bomb line and forward troops so that he could be certain at every moment on which side of, and how far from, the forward troops he was.
   (*c*) The position of the nearest airfield in case of emergency landing.

Flight to Target

19. The flight to the target was divided into three parts:-
   (*a*) Over own territory. If there were no special restrictions from our own A.A. or troops, the flight to the targets was left to the discretion of the leader of the formation. The general rule was that the formation should fly as close as possible but not as close a formation as would tire the pilots. The height of the flight was decided by the visibility, base of clouds and ease of navigation.
   (*b*) Crossing of the front line. Before reaching the front line the aircraft would take up battle formation and would climb so as to cross the front line at a minimum height of 5,000 ft. It was usual to climb to a greater height (10,000 ft.) and cross the front line at high speed in a slight dive. At this stage the pilots would switch on their cameras and their sights and get the bombs ready for release so that in the event of meeting enemy aircraft they could release the bombs and be ready for dog-fighting.
   (*c*) Over enemy territory. As a rule the height of 5,000 ft. was kept and the aircraft flew at high speed (+ 2 boost). They never flew on a

straight line so as not to reveal to the enemy to which target they were flying, and as a safe-guard against enemy flak.

Bombing

20. Bombing by T.A.F. was divided into two main categories: dive-bombing and low-level bombing. Most of the bombing missions were dive-bombing as the accuracy of the bombing did not suffer and the aircraft were less vulnerable to flak. Sometimes it was essential to bomb from low-level, although in most cases the use of aircraft with rocket projectiles was more effective in this type of attack. Bombing could be carried out with a whole formation bombing at once or with one aircraft following the other. In the first case the aircraft were less endangered by flak, and in the second case, greater accuracy was achieved. Polish Squadrons normally bombed one aircraft after another. This ensured both liberty of action for each pilot and more accurate bombing, as the pilot who followed could correct his own bombing by the result achieved by the pilot who preceded him. In addition, the leader could give advice on aiming to the pilots by R/T, the main point being the effect of wind on bombs.

Approach

21. The approach to the attack was made in level flight at speed 220 to 230 m.p.h At the moment when the target hid itself under the wing on a line of about 1/3 from the end of the wing-tip, the pilot made a gentle turn under the horizon in the direction of the target. (Appendix "A"). He regulated the speed of the turn so that the target should be visible all the time. This turn had to be a very steady one and made without the excessive use of the rudder, so that the pilot could very quickly catch the target in his sight. There was another method of flying straight at the target and attacking it from a half roll, but in this case the aircraft gathered high speed and the pilot had great difficulty steadying it and bringing it on the target.

Attack

22. The attack was usually carried out from a dive and at angle of 60 to 45 degrees. The leader dived at a steep angle, while the aircraft who were behind him and at his side were forced to dive at a shallower angle. When diving the pilots had to remember:–

(a) The danger of a traverse as in this case the bombing was inaccurate.

(b) Not to get the aircraft into high speed as the aiming time would pass too quickly and the pulling out from the dive would be much more difficult and unpleasant.

The bombs were released at 3,000 ft. The angle of release for the bombs depended on the direction and strength of the wind. (Appendix "B".)

Departure

23. The departure from the target after bombing was carried out in level flight at full boost in order to get out as quickly as possible from the orbit of enemy flak. Only after having travelled some distance did the pilot start to climb. Climbing immediately after the release of bombs was one of the most common mistakes and resulted in:–

(a) Unnecessary danger to the pilot from the enemy flak. (Appendix "C".)

(b) "Black-out".

(c) Wing wrinkling.

Low Level

24. Bombing at low level. This was carried out on the same lines as strafing.

Co-operation

25. Co-operation between aircraft during bombing tasks. The squadron was divided into three sections of four aircraft. The sections usually had different colours (Red, Blue, Yellow, White) while the aircraft in the sections were Red 1, Red 2, etc. Red 1 was the leader of the formation. Once the formation reached the region of their target, the leader would issue last minute instructions before attack, such as the location of the target, the direction of attack, direction of departure, etc. Upon receipt of these instructions, the pilots would get into the correct order ready for bombing and keep a distance of about four hundred yards between themselves. (Appendix "D".) They kept this distance so that the formation should not be too long and in order that every aircraft should start diving at more or less the same point end of the same angle as the leader. (Appendix "E".) Every pilot, upon the release of his bombs, informed the others that he had done so by R/T, for example "Red 4, dropped". Each pilot observed the hits of the bombs of the pilot who preceded him. Thus, after the attack, it was possible to decide how accurate the bombing was. If a pilot for any reason did not drop his bombs in his turn, he reported this by R/T and dropped his bombs as the last of the formation.

Strafing

26. Strafing with cannon and machine-guns was limited to special targets and was not usually carried out together with bombing. A typical case for strafing during Armed Recce on mobile targets. The attack followed these general lines:–

(*a*) General remarks. After locating the target the leader of the formation decided on the time, place and way of approach, passing the information by R/T to the rest of the pilots. The enemy had look-outs on all his transport vehicles. On the M.T. they normally had two, one on the mudguard and one on the roof or at the back of the vehicle in question. As soon as our aircraft were sighted the vehicle usually hid under trees or in the vicinity of buildings. Thus the pilots were forced to leave the moving vehicles and not attack until they were on a part of the road where it could not easily find cover. The attack had to be carried out rapidly so as to deny the vehicle time to find cover.

(*b*) The approach to attack was usually carried out from a wide turn with a loss of height so that when levelling out for the attack, the aircraft should not be higher than 1,500 ft. and as far as possible at normal speed. (Appendix "F".)

(*c*) After steadying the aircraft and getting the target in the sights, the pilot would open fire at a height of about 700 ft. from a distance of about 500 yards and at an angle of 25 to 30 degrees. The angle of attack in relation to the direction of the moving target used to vary from 0 to 90 degrees and dependent mainly on the nature of the target, its position and the outlines of the terrain. The attacks on motor transport and locomotives were normally carried out as far as possible at an angle of 30 degrees from the front. (Appendix "G".)

(*d*) The departure from the target after attack was carried out at full throttle low level flying for about 30 seconds with a turn in order to get out of the line of fire of the next aircraft. Thus, in the case of a convoy, the leader would attack the first car on the side to which he intended to turn after carrying out his attack.

(*e*) Co-operation between aircraft. The usual practice was to send out two aircraft on such missions. In the case of more aircraft, the aircraft would take up a formation to be on the straight line for attack when the first aircraft started its attack. The following aircraft only started firing at the moment when the one who preceded him passed the target with a slight turn. On small targets or single targets, if there were not more targets than the number of aircraft, one attack should be sufficient. Only in the case of a greater number of vehicles, and after making sure that the flak was not dangerous, did the leader decide to repeat the attack. Normally, when the front line was more or less stabilised, the enemy had a great amount of flak concentrated and the repetition of an attack after the flak positions were manned was very risky. The enemy sometimes used dummy motor transport and locomotives, concentrating round those dummies a great amount of light flak, and pilots had to be very careful to avoid being caught.

(*f*) Effectiveness of the cannon and machine-guns in the Spitfire Mk. XVI was very great, especially in attacks on road and rail transport or moving columns of enemy troops. Attacks on trains usually exploded the locomotive. The shooting up and destruction of the rail trucks, however, depended on the freight they were carrying. The attacks on road transport usually set fire to vehicles and completely destroyed them.

Special Tasks

27. The special tasks that were normally carried out consisted of patrols over the front line, which attacked targets of opportunity, and co-operation with the Contact Car which directed fighters to particular targets.

Patrols

28. Patrols over our own first line troops were normally carried out by two aircraft at a time. They patrolled a certain region at a certain time and attacked any targets, such as artillery and enemy troops, that were proving obstacles to the advance of our own troops.

Contact Car

29. The co-operation with a Contact Car was carried out by 2 or 4 aircraft at a time, sometimes carrying bombs. The aircraft would proceed to a rendezvous at about 5,000 ft. and then report by R/T to the Contact Car. The Contact Car would then pass to them the tasks and give them the information about the target with the aid of special grids which were previously drawn on

the maps or with the aid of landmarks. (Hills or valleys could not be taken as landmarks for the pilot.) After carrying out the attack the pilot would return to the rendezvous point. The co-operation between the aircraft and Contact Car would go on until all ammunition was spent or the defined time elapsed. Other sections, if required, would then take the place of the one which had just finished its task.

Return

30. The return to base was normally carried out on the same lines as the flight to the target, our own front line being crossed at a minimum height of 5,000 ft. in order to give our own A.A. a chance to recognise the aircraft.

Emergencies

31. Airfield conditions and flying in the orbit of enemy flak often resulted in technical defects as well as damage caused by the enemy. Thus it was essential that each pilot should be mentally and technically prepared for all eventualities. Over enemy territory the closest co-operation between aircraft was essential. Pilots were instructed to watch whether their fellow pilots managed to get rid of their drop-tanks or drop their bombs. Pilots were told to escort their fellow-pilots who were hit by flak at least to the moment when they crossed our own lines, but usually until the aircraft in distress managed to land. The purpose of such an escort was to defend the damaged aircraft, to help the pilot find the nearest airfield or landing ground and then inform the base of the exact spot and how the landing was carried out. If the pilot did not manage to release his bombs or his drop tank, he used to land as the last in the formation. This was so that if he did damage the runway it would not stop the other aircraft landing.

Landing

32. Landings were made by single aircraft on the same lines as those practised by fighter squadrons in Great Britain.

Interrogation

33. The interrogation after the completed task had as its aim:–
    (a) to decide on the effectiveness of the attack.
    (b) to discuss any errors that may have been committed.
    (c) to draw conclusions for future attacks.
    (d) to pass information achieved from reconnaissance.

Conclusions

34. Apart from the change of armament (i.e. the carrying of bombs) and the novel circumstances of activity, the main characteristics of the T.A.F. as compared with Fighter Command was the fact that there was not a single sortie which did not result in some kind of action. On the whole the pilot could not return from a flight without having found a target for his bombs or cannons and machine-guns unless there were special instructions to the contrary. Most of the sorties were carried out by sections of two aircraft and each pilot was personally responsible for carrying out his task.

35. Thus we can assert that pilots who took part in sorties in T.A.F. had to possess all the characteristics required of a fighter pilot and had to display great courage, speed of decision and speed of action. Taking into consideration that it is very difficult to repeat an attack on the same target and that most of the targets are mobile, the main characteristic which should be sought in the future T.A.F. pilot should be accuracy of bombing and firing. This, apart from the technical side of it, depends mostly on the speedy orientation and quick action on the part of the pilot. Pilots should be good navigators, as the targets will be small ones, mobile and difficult to observe in the terrain, and the whole flight will have to be carried out at comparatively low altitude.

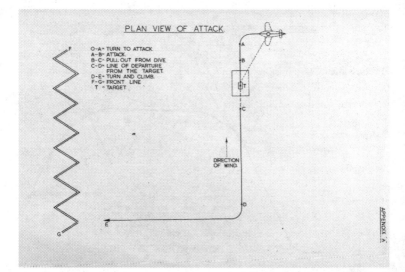

PLAN VIEW OF ATTACK

O-A = TURN TO ATTACK.
A-B = ATTACK.
B-C = PULL OUT FROM DIVE.
C-D = LINE OF DEPARTURE
     FROM THE TARGET.
D-E = TURN AND CLIMB.
F-G = FRONT LINE.
T = TARGET

DIRECTION
OF WIND.

APPENDIX A

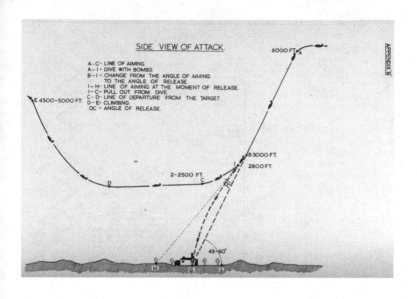

SIDE VIEW OF ATTACK.

A–C = LINE OF AIMING.
A–I = DIVE WITH BOMBS.
B–I = CHANGE FROM THE ANGLE OF AIMING
       TO THE ANGLE OF RELEASE.
I–H = LINE OF AIMING AT THE MOMENT OF RELEASE.
I–C = PULL OUT FROM DIVE.
C–D = LINE OF DEPARTURE FROM THE TARGET.
D–E = CLIMBING.
OC = ANGLE OF RELEASE.

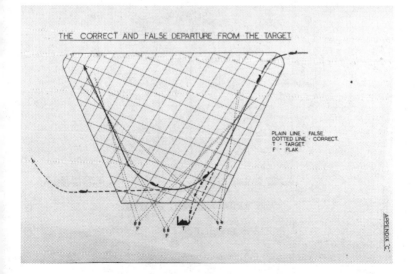

THE CORRECT AND FALSE DEPARTURE FROM THE TARGET.

PLAIN LINE = FALSE
DOTTED LINE = CORRECT.
T = TARGET
F = FLAK

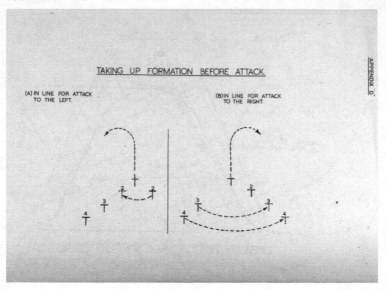

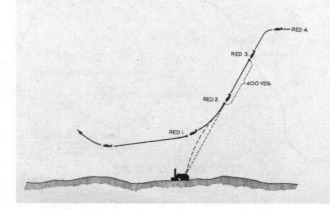

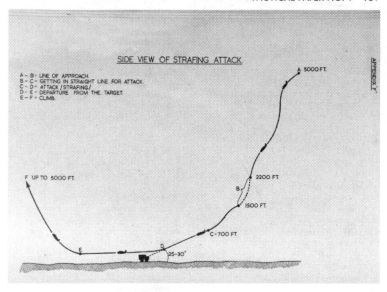

SIDE VIEW OF STRAFING ATTACK.

A – B = LINE OF APPROACH.
B – C = GETTING IN STRAIGHT LINE FOR ATTACK.
C – D = ATTACK /STRAFING/
D – E = DEPARTURE FROM THE TARGET.
E – F = CLIMB.

A 5000 FT.

F UP TO 5000 FT.

2200 FT.

B

1500 FT.

C – 700 FT.

E

D

25–30°

APPENDIX F

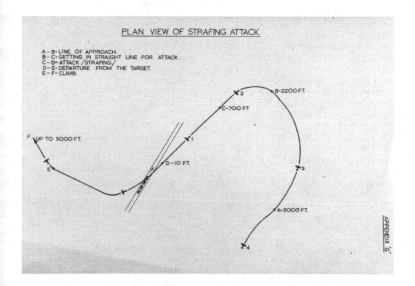

PLAN VIEW OF STRAFING ATTACK.

A – B = LINE OF APPROACH.
B – C = GETTING IN STRAIGHT LINE FOR ATTACK.
C – D = ATTACK /STRAFING/
D – E = DEPARTURE FROM THE TARGET.
E – F = CLIMB.

2

B – 2200 FT.

C – 700 FT.

F UP TO 5000 FT.

E

1

D – 10 FT.

3

A – 5000 FT.

4

APPENDIX G

INDEX

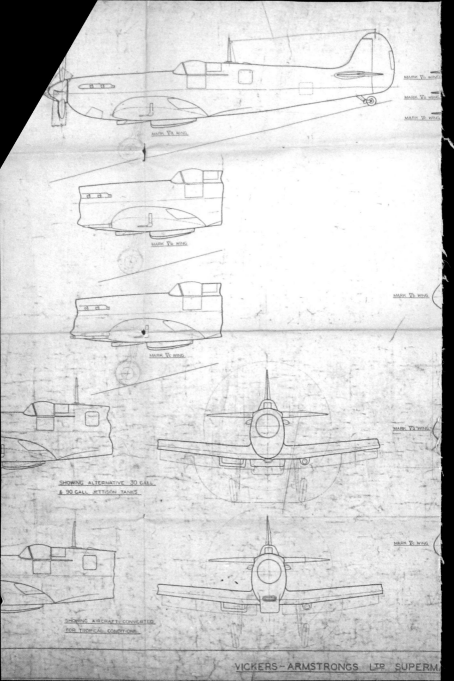

MARK Vb WING

MARK Vc WING

MARK Vc WING

MARK Va WING

MARK Vb WING

MARK Vb WING

MARK Vc WING

MARK Vb WING

SHOWING ALTERNATIVE 30 GALL.
& 90 GALL JETTISON TANKS

MARK Vc WING

SHOWING AIRCRAFT CONVERTED
FOR TROPICAL CONDITIONS

VICKERS-ARMSTRONGS LTD SUPERMA

Lancashire Waterways

by
Gordon Biddle

Drawings and maps
by Peter Fells

Dalesman Books
1980

The Dalesman Publishing Company Ltd.,
Clapham (via Lancaster), North Yorkshire

First published 1980

©Gordon Biddle 1980

ISBN: 0 85206 572 8

46055264

0114239+

By the same author:
  PENNINE WATERWAY: A Pictorial History of the
  Leeds & Liverpool Canal

Of related interest:
  CHESHIRE WATERWAYS
  YORKSHIRE WATERWAYS

Printed by Galava Printing Co. Ltd., Nelson, Lancashire

Contents

Front cover photograph of the Lancaster Canal at Barton, near Preston, by S. C. Sedgwick. Back cover photograph shows M. V. **Manchester Faith** at No. 6 Dock, Manchester.
Photographs in the text are on pages 41 - 48.

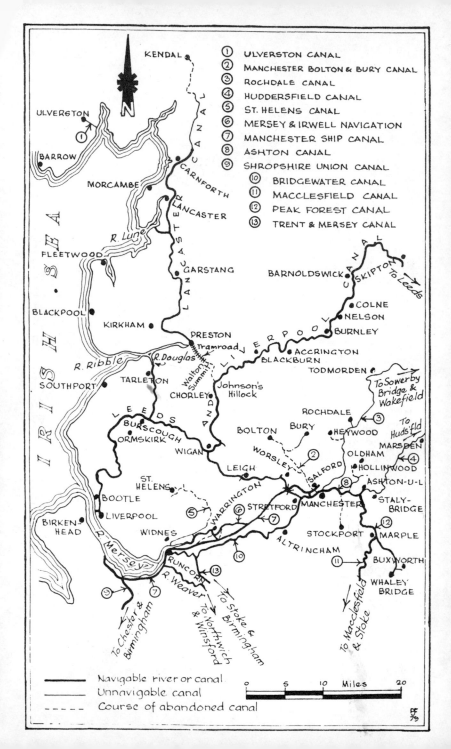

①	ULVERSTON CANAL
②	MANCHESTER BOLTON & BURY CANAL
③	ROCHDALE CANAL
④	HUDDERSFIELD CANAL
⑤	ST. HELENS CANAL
⑥	MERSEY & IRWELL NAVIGATION
⑦	MANCHESTER SHIP CANAL
⑧	ASHTON CANAL
⑨	SHROPSHIRE UNION CANAL
⑩	BRIDGEWATER CANAL
⑪	MACCLESFIELD CANAL
⑫	PEAK FOREST CANAL
⑬	TRENT & MERSEY CANAL

N

KENDAL

ULVERSTON

BARROW

MORCAMBE

CARNFORTH

LANCASTER

R. Lune

FLEETWOOD

GARSTANG

BARNOLDSWICK

SKIPTON

To Leeds

COLNE

BLACKPOOL

KIRKHAM

PRESTON

Tramroad

R. Douglas

NELSON

BURNLEY

ACCRINGTON

BLACKBURN

TODMORDEN

To Sowerby Bridge & Wakefield

IRISH SEA

R. Ribble

SOUTHPORT

TARLETON

Walton's Summit

CHORLEY

Johnson's Hillock

ROCHDALE

BOLTON

BURY

HEYWOOD

To Huds'fld

MARSDEN

LEEDS

BURSCOUGH

ORMSKIRK

WIGAN

WORSLEY

OLDHAM

HOLLINWOOD

ASHTON-U-L

LEIGH

SALFORD

ST. HELENS

BOOTLE

LIVERPOOL

WIDNES

WARRINGTON

STRETFORD

MANCHESTER

STALY-BRIDGE

BIRKEN-HEAD

RUNCORN

R. Weaver

STOCKPORT

ALTRINCHAM

MARPLE

BUXWORTH

WHALEY BRIDGE

R. Mersey

To Chester & Birmingham

To Stoke & Birmingham

To Northwich & Winsford

To Macclesfield & Stoke

▬▬▬	Navigable river or canal
───	Unnavigable canal
-----	Course of abandoned canal

0   5   10   Miles   20

EF 79

Introduction

AS in so many other fields of human invention, Lancashire has been first in new forms of inland transport: the first British motorway, the Preston bypass, was opened in 1958; the first main line railway, the Liverpool and Manchester in 1830; the first canal of the industrial era, the St. Helens, in 1757. For centuries rivers had been used for transporting goods as far inland as possible before trans-shipping to carts or packhorses and many, like the Mersey and Irwell, were improved over the years by making short cuts and locks to avoid bends and weirs. The Roman Fossdyke in Lincolnshire is the first known wholly artificial navigable waterway in this country, although it was cut primarily for drainage. This was followed by the short Exeter Canal opened in 1566 to allow coastal craft to avoid the River Exe. But it is to the Continent, where canals crossing watersheds had been in use from the seventeenth century—and to the curiously overlooked Newry Canal in Ireland, of 1745—that we have to turn for the inspiration behind the network of British Canals that gave such impetus to the Industrial Revolution.

The St. Helens Canal was built in 1757 to take coal from south Lancashire pits to the Mersey and thence up the River Weaver to the salt works of north Cheshire. Meanwhile the Duke of Bridgewater was anxious to improve the market for his coal mined at Worsley, which had to be carted to rapidly expanding Manchester and Salford, with the result that he opened his canal to Castlefield, Manchester in 1765, and extended it to the Mersey at Runcorn in 1776. The advantages of an artificial waterway over a river, however much improved, were immediately obvious. A canal boom hit the country so that by 1790 it was possible to travel by water between Mersey, Humber, Thames and the Bristol Channel, and by 1835 Manchester was the centre of a network of waterways serving the North West with three trans-Pennine connections to Yorkshire and two links with the Midlands and the South.

These seventy years between 1765 and 1835 formed the great age of the canals although, promoted as they were by a multitude of independent competing companies, through passage was not

5

always possible. Before constructing a canal an Act of Parliament was necessary to authorise a company to issue shares, compulsorily purchase land, levy tolls for carriage of goods once the canal was built, fix bye-laws, take water from streams and exercise many other powers. Restrictions also were imposed. In the North West most canals were built wide enough to take a fourteen feet barge, although lengths varied, while Midlands canals generally were built to 'narrow' standards for seventy-two feet long boats only six feet ten inches wide. They were cheaper and used less water. This inadequate vision by the early builders eventually led to their undoing. Lack of uniformity was a major impediment when competition with the new railways began in the 1840s. The railways were also faster and more reliable—no droughts, floods and frosts —so many canal companies either sold out to railways or, in a few cases, converted themselves into railway companies. Others competed for local traffic with varying success but in general from that time the story over the next century was one of slow, gradual decline.

In 1947 most of the inland waterways system was nationalised, Lancashire exceptions being the Rochdale, Bridgewater and Manchester Ship Canals, and today those canals that remain open have no regular commercial traffic but fulfil a growing amenity role for pleasure boating, angling and walking, and provide habitats for wildlife of all kinds. Organisations like the Inland Waterways Association and local canal amenity societies are anxious that further deterioration should be halted and, where possible, restoration should take place. The importance of inland waterways for varied recreation is now recognised by the British Waterways Board but it operates on a public subsidy and is hamstrung by lack of funds. Until the government is prepared to release enough money for clearing arrears of maintenance there is unlikely to be cash for actual improvements, which means that reliance will have to continue on the numerous volunteer bodies who have done such sterling work, particularly in the Manchester area. Most canals also perform important land drainage functions.

This book covers Lancashire as it was before 1974, that is including Greater Manchester, Merseyside and Cheshire north of the Mersey, and Furness, thus being complementary to the recently published Dalesman books, **Yorkshire Waterways** by Peter L. Smith and **Cheshire Waterways** by David Owen. The county is rich in waterway history and industrial archaeology. Many of the canals have high scenic value, from the flat, fen-like country of west Lancashire to the wide views gained from the cross-Pennine and north Lancashire canals. Conversely there are no better ways of appreciating the effect of the Industrial Revolution than to walk along the towing path through, for instance, Ashton, Burnley or Rochdale. Much has been forgotten too. How many people realise that it is possible to take a boat through the heart of Manchester beneath Piccadilly. Only a few will remember the days when boats were hauled up the Irwell valley to discharge cargoes at Bolton and Bury, although there are still plenty of visual reminders; more may perhaps remember canal boats at Rochdale and Mossley.

This book is not a detailed guide—there are others far better, as listed on p. 80 but an introduction for those wishing to know something of the waterways heritage that gave life to Lancashire industry, and an encouragement to walk their banks or cruise their waters and appreciate the county from a different angle. I hope it will give some indication of what can still be seen on and off the towing path, and from places where boats can no longer go.

A short glossary of some canal terms

Barge—a broad-beamed craft, as opposed to 'narrow boat' (see below).

Clough—see 'lock'.

Cut—nickname for a canal.

Flat—a barge used on the Rivers Mersey and Weaver, originally sailing craft and capable of coastal work.

Legging—a method of propelling a boat through a tunnel by two men lying head-to-head on boards placed across the bow, and 'walking' along the walls. Many tunnels had professional legging gangs.

Lock—a chamber with gates at both ends and sluices for admitting or emptying water so that a boat can be raised or lowered from one level to another. The sluice gates are called 'paddles' or, on some northern canals, 'cloughs' (pronounced 'clows'). Gate paddles are sluices fitted in the gates; ground paddles are fitted in culverts behind the lock walls. Most locks had both types for rapid emptying and filling. Locks may be single, in flights or in staircases, in the latter the bottom gate of one forming the top of the next, each called a 'rise'.

Narrow boat—a boat six feet ten inches wide and seventy feet long for the narrow canals of the Midlands and, in the North West, the Ashton, Peak Forest, Macclesfield and Huddersfield Canals.

Pound—a stretch of water between two locks.

Roving bridge—a bridge carrying the towing path over a canal or a branch.

Staith—a wharf, usually for coal or minerals, with loading chutes.

Summit level—the highest level on a canal crossing a watershed, from which locks descend on either side.

Tramroad—a primitive forerunner of the railway, comprising wooden or, later, cast iron rails laid on stone sleeper blocks, along which horses could draw short trains of wagons. Many were built to connect quarries, pits and factories to canals.

being cheaper to build than a branch canal. Some had 'edge' rails to take flanged wheels, as on a railway. Others had flanged rails on which ordinary road wagons with flat-tyred wheels could run, provided they were to the appropriate gauge.

The Ashton-under-Lyne Canal

MANCHESTER had two great canal ports close to the city centre, Castlefield on the Bridgewater and, just over a mile away, Piccadilly, where the Ashton Canal meets the Rochdale which connects the two centres by a series of nine locks. The Ashton was a narrow canal only 6¾ miles long; in fact its branches totalled almost twice the distance. It was authorised in 1792, to bring coal to Manchester from the Ashton and Oldham districts at a time when the Rochdale, Huddersfield and Peak Forest Canals were also being promoted and which would thus form connections at both ends. As a short but vital link its fortunes became closely associated with the other three, particularly the Peak Forest running from Dukinfield to Marple and Whaley Bridge which, when the Macclesfield Canal was completed in 1831, made the Ashton into a second canal route from Manchester to the Midlands as well as to Yorkshire.

The branches were completed before the main line: Hollinwood, 4 5/8 miles, in 1796; Fairbottom, 1 1/8 miles, and Stockport, 4 7/8 miles, in 1797. Because of financial problems, not to mention a quarrel with the Rochdale which considered that the Hollinwood Branch took away traffic from its territory (the two canals were within half a mile of each other), opening of the final short stretch from Ancoats to Piccadilly was delayed until 1800, the same year that the Peak Forest was opened. The Huddersfield followed in 1811.

The Ashton Canal rose from Manchester by eighteen locks; the Hollinwood Branch had seven locks and the Stockport Branch was level. There were numerous short branches to collieries and mills in Manchester—many of them privately owned—the longest being the Clayton Branch, 3/8 mile, and the 1 1/8 mile Fairbottom Branch running off the Hollinwood Branch. The principal traffic was coal and limestone with general goods in addition, but the company was only mildly profitable. Between 1797 and 1802 there were short-lived passenger boat services to Ashton and Stockport from Piccadilly. Then in 1846 the company sold out to the Manchester, Sheffield & Lincolnshire Railway, along with the Peak Forest and the Macclesfield, which the railway (later to become the Great

Central and then part of the London & North Eastern) operated as one concern, running boats from Manchester to a timetable, connecting with their goods trains at Guide Bridge station. Road transport began to erode canal traffic in the present century; the Hollinwood and Fairbottom Branches closed in 1932 and the Stockport Branch about the same time, although statutory abandonment did not take place until 1955 and 1961-2 by which time the main line had also become unnavigable.

Then a remarkable event took place that was to mark a turning point in the plight of derelict canals throughout the country. In 1961 the Inland Waterways Association organised a cruise by eight boats from Marple to Manchester, although owing to last minute vandalism only one boat got right through. However, the point had been made, publicly, and in 1964 the Peak Forest Canal Society was formed with the aim of restoring that canal and the Ashton, which with the Manchester section of the Rochdale, the Bridgewater, Trent & Mersey and Macclesfield Canals made up the Cheshire Ring of waterways. The two organisations persuaded the Waterways Board and local authorities to put money into restoration, voluntary labour was provided and, despite major setbacks, enthusiasm and resources grew. In 1968 'Operation Ashton', a weekend memorable if only for the weather, was organised on a nation-wide scale to clear rubbish from the top seven locks and pounds at Clayton, resulting in equally wide publicity. Six hundred people turned up to cheerfully work in mud and rain, and again in 1972 'Ashtac' was staged on a similar scale to assist the Board in clearing the top length. As a result of this uniquely co-operative effort between a nationalised body, local authorities and voluntary organisations the Minister of Transport reopened the canal in 1974.

Looking at the canal itself, until recent years there was a group of large Ashton Canal warehouses around Ducie Street, where the towing path is gained just beyond the junction with the Rochdale, but now the area has been flattened and landscaped. Store Street aqueduct follows, a strongly buttressed, single skew-arched stone structure, from where it is a short distance to the three Ancoats Locks, the first one almost beneath Great Ancoats Street bridge. Between Nos. 1 and 2 locks the Islington Branch led off to the left, now filled in and marked only by two bridges, and after the third lock mills and factories line both sides for half a mile to Cambrian Street. Then there is a confusion of bridges. A road and railway bridge cross side by side on the skew above the canal which itself is on an aqueduct over the murky River Medlock, seen deep below emerging from a tunnel under Bradford gasworks. The four Beswick Locks are close to Bradford colliery which had its own branch between Nos. 6 and 7, and are quickly followed by the deep Clayton nine. The site of the Stockport Branch can be seen beneath the roving bridge between Nos. 10 and 11., from which there is a good view across Manchester. The branch can be traced by gaps between houses and some remaining bridges to its terminus in Lancashire Hill, Stockport, beside Albion Mills where Wharf Street and some fragments of parapet are the only remains.

Aqueduct, Hollinwood Branch — Ashton Canal

To open the three swing bridges in this vicinity a key has to be obtained from the lock-keeper. They are at Crabtree Lane (over a lock), Buxton Lane and Copperas Lane. Although the entire route is drab, the landscaped locks and neat waterside make an enormous difference. Local firms have also co-operated, the works of Ciba-Geigy and Anchor Chemicals alongside Clayton Locks showing most creditable canalside development that has incorporated the waterway instead of ignoring it.

At Fairfield there is a gracefully arched stone footbridge just below the top lock and a boathouse dated 1833, from the days of the packet boats. Above is a broad junction where the Hollinwood Branch led off, now a short spur, while the main canal turns right for 2¾ level miles to Dukinfield. The surroundings are now less industrial, with modern houses and open spaces as far as Guide

Bridge where the canal becomes mixed up with railway lines, one crossing the waterway beneath a road bridge. Then the railway runs alongside on the right and there is Princes Dock, curiously built parallel to the canal with only the towing path between, just long enough for two narrow boats end to end, for the former interchange traffic. The canal shortly runs beside and above the River Tame, until 1974 the boundary between Ashton-under-Lyne, Lancashire, and Dukinfield, Cheshire, into which a deep overflow weir cascades; and at Dukinfield Junction the Peak Forest Canal enters on the right on a fine three-arch aqueduct. Portland Street Basin, opposite the junction, has lost most of its former glory since the very fine warehouse was burned down several years ago. Dating from 1834, only the lower warehouse walls remain into which canal arms enter by three arches. Its cranes were worked by shafts and gearing from an iron high-breast waterwheel which can be seen rusting away in its deep wheelpit, once driven by canal water. The Ashton continues on for another half mile to a messy full stop at Whitelands Bridge where water now enters through a pipe from the Huddersfield Canal on the other side (p. 19). A ginnel takes the towing path through.

The Hollinwood Branch is worth exploring. From Fairfield Junction it is filled in but marked by bridges until the railway line is reached near the site of Droylsden station where an aqueduct has been replaced by a footbridge. Then at Lumb Mill a quarter mile section is in water as a fishery, after which there is more infilling to Daisy Nook. The canal from here has been reclaimed as part of Daisy Nook Country Park which covers 85 acres of the attractive Medlock valley. The main entrance, car park and office are situated on the old canal at Cutler Hill Road, followed by a bridle path along the site of Waterhouses Tunnel, 66 yards long and opened out about 1914. Two short lengths contain shallow water as wildlife habitats. The Waterhouses Aqueduct over the narrow valley and river has a single 40 feet stone arch. Beyond it the Waterhouses Locks have been weired and filled in to a shallow depth to make them safe for children. The first is immediately before a left hand bend, where a wide basin is now a model-boating pool, and this is connected to a second, deeper pool by two staircase locks. The top lock has been completely filled in, but at its head the canal is in water again with the Fairbottom Branch leading off to the right. The branch serves as a wildlife reserve and fishery, and there is an interesting skew aqueduct (now dry) over Knott Lane. At Bardsley Bridge the cast iron arch bears the letters 'M.S. & L.RY.Co. A.C. DEPT. 1868'. Here the Country Park ends but the last 1/8 mile to Fenny Field Bridge, although unnavigable as long ago as 1904, can still be traced. A tramroad ran from its end to Park Bridge Ironworks and a colliery.

Back at the junction the Hollinwood Branch continues towards

Oldham, crossing a narrow lane by an iron trough aqueduct set in a stone arch marked 1859, before reaching Crime Lake, one of the Ashton's three reservoirs. Rowing boats may be hired in the summer and part is a wild fowl refuge. The other two reservoirs were at Audenshaw and Hollinwood (now filled in).

Here the Park ends again and the canal and its bridges are filled in but still traceable to Hollins Road after which new houses have been built on the site of two locks. At Manchester Road bridge there is still a filled-in brick arch on the south side, and close by a playing field marks the site of Hollinwood Reservoir. Canal Street has gone but Wharf Street and **The Navigation** pub are reminders that here were Hollinwood Top Wharf and Basin. On through a housing estate a keen eye is needed to follow the final 3/8 mile to Washbrook, although traces are visible. This section was built by the Werneth Coal Company in 1795, as a private canal to their colliery in Old Lane.

The Bridgewater Canal

THE Bridgewater Canal may not have been the first true canal but it certainly led the way in innovative engineering which made later ones possible. Production at the Duke of Bridgwater's mines at Worsley, five miles west of Manchester, was severely restricted by poor transport. He had seen continental waterways during his Grand Tour and with the help of his agent John Gilbert, an able engineer, he devised a canal of his own from Worsley to Salford for which he obtained an Act in 1759.

There seems little doubt that the credit for the overall planning and construction of the canal must go to the Duke himself and Gilbert. James Brindley was well known to Gilbert, who brought him in as consultant and millwright. He also carried out some of the detailed surveys and gave brilliant Parliamentary evidence, but, as Hugh Malet has pointed out in **Bridgewater, The Canal Duke,** he was rapidly becoming busy with many other projects, including the Trent & Mersey Canal, and during the 13 years in which the full length of the Bridgewater was being built, up to the time of his death in 1772, Brindley was associated with it for only three. His title of 'Father of Inland Navigation' was earned by his concept of a country-wide system, but it was Gilbert who engineered the Bridgewater and pioneered the new technology; Brindley carried some of it out.

Instead of adding a branch to the Irwell, under another Act of 1760 the Duke altered the Salford route to cross the river and run south of it to Manchester. It was Brindley who persuaded Parliament that a water-tight aqueduct could be built by lining the masonry channel with puddled clay, of which he gave a messy but convincing demonstration in the House, and he who was in charge of its construction under Gilbert. In 1761 the great aqueduct was completed with its three arches, 39 feet high - the first to be seen in England. Crowds witnessed the opening and marvelled at 'vessels o'er vessels, water under water'. Two years later the canal reached Manchester where the Duke built extensive wharves and warehouses at Castlefield, at the west end of Deansgate. Coal could now be sold there at less than half the former price.

It now became clear that the Duke's main purpose was to

compete with the Mersey & Irwell Navigation Company (p. 61), which for years had taken advantage of its monopoly between Liverpool and Manchester, and provide cheaper transit free of the hazards of the two rivers. He reached an agreement with the Trent & Mersey Canal to construct a new canal from the Bridgewater at Stretford to a junction with their projected line at Preston Brook, south of Warrington, which would continue thence to fall 87 feet to the Mersey estuary by ten locks at Runcorn, 28½ miles from Manchester. This work was completed in 1776 and would have been finished two years earlier were it not for the delaying tactics of Sir Richard Brook of Norton Priory, against whose refusal to sell land even the powerful Duke for a time was helpless.

The canal took Mersey flats up to 72 feet long with 15 feet beam, carrying up to 80 tons. A flourishing passenger service was also established and at Castlefield the packet station included ticket and parcel offices and waiting rooms. When wind and direction were favourable, sails were used until, with the advent of steam, tugs were used to tow strings of barges. But it was at Worsley Delph that the greatest wonder could be seen, surpassing even Barton Aqueduct. From the canal two tunnels were driven into the cliff, meeting some 500 yards underground. As coal seams were encountered side channels were cut and eventually there was an astonishing and unique underground canal system of no less than 46 miles on four separate levels, one above and two below the original level. The two lower levels were connected to the original level by vertical shafts, and the higher level by a remarkable underground incline on which a boat could be wound on a special carriage on rails at a gradient of 1 in 4 from one level to the other. The boats themselves varied in dimensions up to about 47 feet long and 4½ feet wide, and carried up to twelve iron containers holding 12 hundredweight of coal each, filled from basket sledges dragged from the face. Laden boats were taken out by a slight current created by raising a sluice gate at the entrance and assisted by legging on the roof where it was low; empty boats entered in trains of about twenty, two or three men using hooks which they placed through rings in the roof and then 'walking' the boats forward. The craft were nicknamed 'starvationers', possibly from their exposed internal ribs. Coal boating ceased in 1887 after which the system was used for mine drainage from pits in the Walkden area until the 1960s when it was finally closed.

A 6¼ mile branch canal was opened from Worsley to Leigh in 1799-1800 to meet the Leeds & Liverpool's branch from Wigan, and in 1838 the three shallow Hulme locks were constructed at Castlefield down into the Irwell to provide, at last, a link between the two systems in Manchester. They were replaced by a single twelve feet deep lock in 1962. The Duke died in 1803, whereafter the canal was managed by trustees until 1872. Then, with the

Mersey & Irwell, it was sold and the two concerns became the Bridgewater Navigation Company. This in turn was sold out to the Manchester Ship Canal Company in 1887 (p. 57) to which it still belongs. Today there is little or no commercial traffic, although pleasure boating thrives. British Waterways licences are valid on the Bridgewater Canal for one week and applications for longer periods should be made to the Manager, Preston Brook Marina, Warrington.

Warehouse, Castlefield — Bridgewater Canal

A visit to the Bridgewater should start at Castlefield. Although much has now gone it is still a busy place as the headquarters of the Bridgewater Department, which engages in warehousing and road haulage, and there is still enough left to show how extensive and important it once was to Manchester. The old basin is crossed by the Bridgewater Viaduct connecting Deansgate and Chester Road, from which one can look down on the north west side to the old Castlefield wharves and the sites of the original warehouses of which only the Middle Warehouse and part of the Merchants' Warehouse still remain. Three arms led under the dominating railway viaduct, the widest one, by the entrance to the Rochdale Canal at the end of Castle Street, forming a veritable canal crossroads before splitting into four branches, of which two are left.

Here can be seen a circular weir, the central part of Brindley's original cloverleaf weir which he built to take away surplus water, the idea being to provide maximum outflow over a small area. Water can be taken from the River Medlock under an arch beneath the old section of Chester Road, any excess running out over this weir, through a culvert and back into the river behind Potato Wharf, where it can still be seen. The Medlock itself is taken through a tunnel from sluices behind Chester Road to reappear alongside the weir exit. On the way Brindley ingeniously used it to drive a waterwheel which operated a crane over a vertical shaft up which containers of coal were hoisted from starvationers in a tunnel below, driven into the hillside from the basin.

Another remarkable feature, now long forgotten, was a feeder from Bank Top in the Store Street area near Piccadilly station, to Castlefield. Constructed to bring water to the Medlock, from Shooters Bank, it included a tunnel stated to be 649 yards long, was completed in 1789 and used by boats from Worsley. Presumably navigation ceased when the Ashton and Rochdale Canals were connected to Castlefield in 1800.

Hulme Lock can only be reached by boat; it is barricaded from the Egerton Street entrance but can be seen from the north bank of the Irwell, while the Medlock flows behind Potato Wharf and under Dawson Street before emptying into the Irwell at the foot of the lock. Starting its way westward, the canal is enclosed on one side by the railway viaduct and on the other by factories and warehouses until the railway crosses it. The canal then runs behind Pomona Docks at the beginning of the Ship Canal. The two waterways part company at Trafford Road Bridge, the Bridgewater traversing a dreary area of factories and old railway sidings to the picturesquely mis-named Waters Meeting at Stretford, where the routes to Worsley and Runcorn diverge amidst industrial buildings and a fine selection of graffiti. Turning left, the main line of the canal passes under Longford Bridge on Chester Road to join company with the electrified Altrincham railway line which follows it in a suburban landscape through Sale. There is a boatyard at Stretford and the shallow Mersey valley is crossed by an embankment. Next there is an interesting three-arched aqueduct over a flood channel and Hawthorn Lane, more impressive than the Barfoot Aqueduct further on which spans the Mersey in a deep-cut channel by a single arch, with a significant sag in the middle. The river marks the old county boundary, and there is another long straight stretch before the canal leaves the railway at Timperley to swing westward into the Cheshire countryside on its way to Preston Brook and Runcorn.

Returning to Waters Meeting, the Worsley and Leigh Branch passes through two miles of Trafford Park industrial estate to Barton Swing Aqueduct over the Ship Canal, built in 1893 to replace Brindley's aqueduct (p.59). Near Patricroft station a special pavilion and landing stage were built in 1851 for Queen Victoria, where she transferred from the Royal train to a 'state barge' that took her to Worsley for the night. The boat was built for the Earl of Ellesmere, great-nephew of the Duke, with a saloon, canopy and ornamental bow and stern. It was drawn by two grey horses mounted by postillions. Later it was successively used as the Earl's private barge and as directors' inspection boat, latterly with an engine, until 1938. It was probably built similarly to the famous **Duchess Countess** packet boat that continued in service carrying parcels and cargo—and the occasional passenger—from Manchester to Stockton Heath until 1913 and survived as a henhouse until the 1960s.

From Eccles the water is stained bright orange by iron oxide seeping from Worsley Delph. The two mine entrances are still there, opposite a left hand bend, the Delph itself has been landscaped and an old 'starvationer' is moored on display. Despite its closeness to the M62 motorway Worsley still retains much of the charm of a village with several attractively half-timbered buildings, including an ancient courthouse and the Packet House next to the landing steps leading down to the canal, which itself cuts across the village green and has two warehouses and a boatyard. The canal to Leigh continues through flat country, embanked in places to counteract subsidence, past former collieries at Boothstown and Astley Green which used the canal until quite recently. At Boothstown there was another, smaller underground system about 1½ miles long at Mosley Common colliery. Leigh, with its tall cotton spinning mills prominent across the flat landscape, is eight miles from Waters Meeting. Here an end-on junction is made with the Leeds & Liverpool's branch from Wigan (p. 31).

The Huddersfield Canal

VERY little of the Huddersfield Canal was actually in Lancashire—about a mile in Ashton-under-Lyne and perhaps two miles in Mossley, the section between being in Cheshire and the section beyond in the West Riding of Yorkshire. Now well over half of it is in Greater Manchester metropolitan county and is covered here in order to describe the western part omitted from **Yorkshire Waterways.**

It was the least successful of the cross-Pennine canals and the first to close. Many of its promoters were Ashton Canal proprietors anxious to secure traffic from Yorkshire and fearful that the Rochdale Canal scheme might get in first. Without this incentive it is doubtful that such an unlikely route would have gained support, for it rises 338 feet by 32 locks from the Ashton Canal up the Tame valley to Diggle, passes under Standedge by Britain's longest canal tunnel, 3 miles 418 yards, at a height of 648 feet above sea level, and then drops 493 feet by 42 locks to join the Huddersfield Broad Canal in Huddersfield, all in the distance of 20 miles. Because of its narrow boat dimensions it is known as the Huddersfield Narrow Canal and with Benjamin Outram as engineer 15 miles were completed in five years from the passing of its Act in 1794. But the tunnel was nowhere near completion and money had run out. More capital had to be raised by two more Acts before it was finished and fully opened in 1811, watched by a crowd of 10,000, after seventeen years' work. By then the Rochdale had been open for over six and had cornered much of the traffic. Moreover it could take wide barges, whereas the Huddersfield's narrow boats were too long to pass through the locks on the Broad Canal and the Calder & Hebble so at first transhipment at Huddersfield was necessary. Later special short narrow boats, 57½ feet long, were built for through journeys, but carrying less cargo.

The company's dividend never exceeded 2 per cent and for much of the time it did not pay one. Then in 1844 it sold out and became part of the Huddersfield & Manchester Railway & Canal Company, passing through London & North Western and later London, Midland & Scottish Railway ownership, the latter legally abandoning it in 1944. Since then British Waterways have cascaded the locks with concrete weirs, some filled in to a shallow channel and some roofed over, and parts have been culverted, as the water is still needed to feed the Ashton and the Calder & Hebble from reservoirs above the tunnel. The towing path through Greater Manchester county is part of the Tame Valley Linear Park.

The first lock above the end-on junction with the Ashton Canal at Whitelands Bridge, Ashton (p. 12), is filled in and beyond it the cut is a derelict mess lined by mills. In Stalybridge there is a curious iron trough aqueduct over the Tame—the first of three crossings—with the towing path on a detached stone arch alongside, separated by only a few inches. At Bayley Street the canal is piped under the town centre for nearly three quarters of a mile, parts being built over, although old stone warehouses still stand close to Mottram Road where open water recommences. The disused Friezland Loop railway line joins the canal on the right as the town ends and a Pennine panorama opens up ahead. The canal is broad and deep, but in less than a mile there is another piped section followed by a culverted bridge close to Hartshead power station.

Then the valley closes in, the river flowing through a rocky gorge on the left as the canal cuts through a shoulder of the hillside by the 250 yard Scout Tunnel, now blocked off at both ends although formerly it also took the towing path. Entering Mossley, Egmont Street bridge has a new flat concrete path of navigational height—a welcome sight—and at Micklehurst Road bridge a stream enters on the right. When in flood it flows over the towing path to cascade out on the opposite side into the river. An old stone mill stands alongside the canal, with large doors on to the towing path, and there are more recent mills beyond.

Some of the locks have a narrow stone bridge over the tail, very similar to Outram's work on the Peak Forest Canal, as are the stone road bridges. The valley now broadens again as the canal climbs towards Greenfield, with extensive views but overlooked by high hills on all sides. The Tame is crossed again by an aqueduct with two low arches. At the attractive village of Uppermill the banks have been landscaped close by the local history museum and there are shrubs, trees and ducks, all contributing to a very pleasing environment. In another half-mile the canal doubles under the magnificent, lofty Saddleworth railway viaduct, where the Tame rushes down a side valley from its source above Denshaw. The canal enters a lock beneath the viaduct, the end of the narrow chamber extending across the final aqueduct over the river, a single skew-arched structure known for obvious reasons as 'Old Sag'.

Further on the canal is piped for about 100 yards and then runs alongside a small mill with a basin on the left. A piped bridge takes it beneath the Wool Road, named from the days when packhorses carried wool across the Pennines. A small warehouse, once used for transhipping goods before Standedge Tunnel was completed, is being restored by Saddleworth Historical Society. The railway now hugs the canal on the right through to Diggle, still climbing through numerous locks amidst a wild, moorland landscape more spectacular, even, than the summit of the Rochdale. Diggle, a surprisingly large village for its bleak location, has several mills and a new housing estate on a bare hillside. The low, narrow opening of Standedge Tunnel is entered through a brick 'extension' some 250 yards long, built in 1893 when the quadrupling of the railway entailed the enlargement of Diggle station over the canal. The rest of the tunnel is mainly bare rock with some brick-lined sections, and a trip through in 1961 was a memorable experience, particularly when a steam train roared through one of the three parallel railway tunnels, smoke drifting in through the connecting side adits. The canal tunnel is still important for draining the remaining railway tunnel, and access is not allowed. The boundary between Greater Manchester and West Yorkshire passes over Standedge, and from Marsden at the eastern end the canal starts its steep descent of the Colne valley to Huddersfield.

The Huddersfield Canal Society is aiming to restore the canal, with plans for diverting it along the river at Stalybridge to overcome the problem of the long piped section.

The Lancaster Canal

THE Lancaster Canal is the prettiest canal in the county, its lock-free waters just long enough for a week's leisurely there-and-back cruise through rural North Lancashire, while the more venturesome may easily fit in a trip down the six locks on the branch to Glasson Dock. It is a broad waterway, taking 72 feet boats with 14 feet beam and 7½ feet headroom. For the walker it is equally attractive, with a good towing path and some interesting aqueducts.

The company was incorporated in 1792, the brainchild of Lancaster merchants who saw in a canal from Westhoughton, near Wigan, to Kendal in Westmorland the means of transporting coal cheaply from the south Lancashire pits northwards; furthermore, there was a growing demand for lime as a fertiliser on the Fylde and south Lancashire farmlands that would form ready-made return cargoes from the limestone country north of the Lune. Third, but by no means least, Lancaster regarded a canal as a badly needed fillip to the city's trade, for the port was suffering from the silting of the Lune estuary (p. 49) and severe competition from up-and-coming Liverpool. Supporters in Preston and Kendal were equally enthusiastic for similar reasons.

As originally proposed the canal would have been 75 miles long with aqueducts over the Ribble at Preston and the Lune at Lancaster. Thirty-two locks would have been necessary down to the Ribble Valley and nine further north in Westmorland, but otherwise John Rennie, the canal's first engineer, designed it with three long levels, a remarkable achievement particularly in hilly Westmorland. At the southern end a connection was envisaged with a proposed branch of the Bridgewater Canal, giving access to Manchester and the rapidly-growing network in the Midlands and the South.

By 1797 the first section was open between Preston and a remote spot called Tewitfield, a few miles north of Carnforth where the first of the Westmorland locks was intended, a length of some 43 miles including the Lune Aqueduct. In 1799 12 miles was open south of the Ribble from Bark Hill, near Wigan, to Johnsons Hillock, north of Chorley, by which time the company's capital was spent. A great debate now arose among the shareholders whether to press on to Kendal with what money could be raised—and times were difficult—or to concentrate resources on crossing the Ribble and connecting the two sections. Rennie was now heavily committed on civil engineering work elsewhere and acting more as consultant, but was asked jointly with William Jessop, the pre-eminent engineer of the day to report on a means of crossing the Ribble. They advocated a 40 feet high embankment and a 640 feet long aqueduct over the river valley which, with the help of a short tunnel under Fishergate, would take the canal into Preston on the same level as the North End. Three designs were submitted. Also in their report the two engineers approved the construction of a horse-operated tramroad to temporarily connect the two ends of the canal as suggested by the resident engineer, William Cartwright.

Work on the five mile tramroad commenced immediately, together with an extension of the south end of the canal northward to Walton Summit, involving a 259 yard long tunnel at Whittle Hills. All was complete by 1803 when Walton Summit and Preston Basin became busy transhipment centres to and from the tramroad. Unfortunately the temporary measure became permanent. As money became available other counsels prevailed and first the North End of the canal, as it became officially known beyond Preston, was extended to Kendal by 1819, taking a different route from Rennie's with eight locks at Tewitfield and a 380 yard tunnel at Hincaster. Secondly a branch was opened from Galgate down to Glasson Dock (p. 49) in 1826, 2½ miles long with six locks. Meanwhile in 1816, after much squabbling, agreement had been reached with the Leeds & Liverpool company for the latter to use as part of its own route the South End of the Lancaster from Johnsons Hillock to Bark Hill, Wigan, where junctions were made (p. 32). But the Ribble remained an insuperable barrier, leaving the North End isolated from the South and the rest of the canal system. Likewise, the canal never reached Westhoughton. Although it was not a huge financial success during its independent existence, the company made a modest profit.

With the coming of railways the company foresaw that the tramroad would rapidly become an anachronism and in 1837 they leased it at an annual rental to the Bolton & Preston Railway who had ideas about using its course as an entry into Preston. In the event the railway did not convert the tramroad but was obliged by the agreement to maintain it for the canal company's use and to make sidings alongside Preston Basin, so ensuring that rail-borne coal could still reach the North End of the canal to supply the established trade. Then in 1842 the canal company made a courageous move and, contrary to the prevailing practice, took over on lease the financially ailing Lancaster & Preston Junction

Railway which they operated profitably for six years before being forced by the Board of Trade to hand it back following a serious collision at Bay Horse station. The line formed what became the West Coast route to Scotland and inevitably the railway companies could not countenance control of a vital link in the hands of a rival canal company. Competition eventually forced the canal company in 1864 to lease the North End to the London & North Western Railway and the South End to the Leeds & Liverpool, who subsequently operated it as an integral part of their own canal. The tramroad had long been used only from Walton Summit to Bamber Bridge and it was closed in 1879. The North End of the canal was finally sold outright to the railway in 1885 and the company wound up.

Commercial traffic, latterly mainly coal, continued to Kendal until 1944 and to Lancaster until 1947, since when the canal has been given over entirely to pleasure craft. After 1955 some 5½ miles from Stainton to Kendal were drained, due to persistent leakages, and later about three quarters of a mile at the Preston end. The section above Tewitfield Locks was by this time officially abandoned although still physically navigable, but because pleasure boats rarely ventured up the locks strenuous opposition by the Lancaster Canal Trust failed to prevent five culverts instead of bridges being built under the M6 motorway in 1965. They effectively closed the northern reaches to through navigation, so that today some 42 miles of level canal between Ashton Basin, Preston, and Tewitfield are retained for cruising, with the Glasson Branch. The canal has become so popular that at the last census it accommodated more boats per mile than any other canal outside the immediate area of London.

The Lancaster Canal Trust was formed in 1963 to promote the conservation of the waterway. Its primary aim is still to reopen the northern reaches, as well as to encourage the recreational use of the whole canal, and it has engaged in a number of practical conservation projects.

The South End is described as part of the Leeds & Liverpool (p. 37) and for our purposes we can consider the Lancaster as commencing at the foot of Johnsons Hillock Locks. The first quarter of a mile contains water, after which the canal has been filled in with spoil from the M62 motorway works of 1968. Much of the course is still discernible over the three miles to Walton Summit, including the bridges, embankments and the two Whittle Hills Tunnels, originally one but opened out in 1837 following collapses. The old wharf at Whittle and a limekiln are indications of former activity, together with a thoughtfully transplanted iron milepost on the forecourt of the Lord Nelson pub at Clayton Green. But motorway crossings make continuous walking difficult and the Summit basins have been completely obliterated, while most of the tramroad incline leading down from them is now a new road appropriately called Tramway Lane. An industrial estate is rapidly covering this area. There were two more inclines, at Penwortham down to the Ribble valley and up into Preston at Avenham, all operated by endless chains driven by stationary steam engines.

Despite development some of the tramroad course is still visible through Bamber Bridge and Brownedge to Lower Penwortham, where a low embankment and an avenue of trees mark its route across the valley to the reconstructed Old Tram Bridge over the Ribble. Beyond was the Avenham incline, now in Avenham Park, while further on the line and the tunnel under Fishergate have been covered by late nineteenth century housing and the former Butler Street goods station, apart from a few fragments. The tramroad had a double track with L-section iron rails set on stone sleeper blocks, and horses drew trains of six to eight wagons on flangeless wheels, each carrying about two tons. Contrary to numerous writings, Benjamin Outram had no connection with the tramroad at all, beyond being a partner in Butterley Ironworks where the rails were cast. Repeated assertions that he designed it are completely false.

Toll Office, Preston — Lancaster Canal

Ladywell House and the Harris College now occupy the site of Preston Basin, although a small stone building in Corporation Street, bridge parapets and The Boatman's Arms pub in Marsh Lane, and a bridge next to Canal Foundry in Fylde Road are visual reminders. The canal proper now starts at Aqueduct Street although the name's originator has been demolished. Parts of old limekilns remain in the embankment and alongside the nearby Ashton Basin, where coal and limestone were once unloaded. After Blackpool Road Bridge the canal runs alongside Haslam Park, with a small aqueduct over Savick Brook, and then past new housing at Ingol where the first of the milestones restored by the Trust stands in a private garden. Running due west as far as Salwick, the canal traverses the flat rural landscape of the Fylde in a long loop, including a wooded cutting near the Clifton Arms pub, and then passes the Jolly Roger Boating Haven at Swillbrook Bridge before resuming its northward course at Hollowforth Aqueduct over Barton Brook, preceded by the first of the two swing bridges on the canal and a small boating station. The aqueduct is worth inspecting, taking the brook under the canal by three remarkable elliptical stone 'tubes'.

The buildings at the Jolly Roger originally were stables for horses drawing the swift passenger boats that plied between Preston and Kendal from 1833 to 1842. The boats were specially built, very light and narrow, with two heated cabins in which refreshments were served. The journey time was reduced from ten hours to eight at an average speed of ten miles an hour. Two horses, one mounted by a postillion, hauled the boats at a brisk trot and were changed very smartly, the boats having utmost priority over other craft which risked having their tow lines cut if they did not quickly give way on hearing the postillion's horn. In 1839, following the opening of the railway to Preston from the South, the boats connected with the trains and were included in the railway time-tables. The Lamb & Packet pub in Preston is a reminder of the service.

From Hollowforth there is a fine panorama of the Bowland Fells which provide an eastern backdrop to the canal all the way to Lancaster, in complete contrast with the lush waterside farmlands. After Barton the canal is never more than a mile or two away from the A6 road, the M6 motorway and the main West Coast railway line right through to Tewitfield. Bilsborrow village is close to the canal, with another interesting aqueduct where the River Brock was lowered by means of a weir built upstream. Near Catterall the canal crosses the River Calder by a low stone arch which frequently is under water, and then turns westward to skirt the small, attractive market town of Garstang. It crosses the Wyre by a splendid single arch aqueduct of 34 feet span, again designed by Rennie, with gracefully curved wing walls and a dentilled cornice beneath the parapet. Alongside Garstang Basin, a popular mooring is an eighteenth century tithe barn now used as a restaurant and agricultural museum in which the Lancaster Canal Trust has its own museum and information centre. The canal now wanders on past Winmarleigh, where there was once a waterside tile works—Kilntree Bridge (No. 72) gives a clue—and Forton to pass close to Ellel Grange (1857-59), described as probably the finest Italianate villa left in Lancashire. It was built on the site of an earlier house, and the bridge taking the drive over the canal probably had its balustraded parapet added to match the new house at the same time.

Brock Aqueduct — Lancaster Canal

The next bridge also is worth a look—Double Bridge, so named because it is twice the normal width and carries a third, central parapet dividing the occupation roadway into two halves, one for each landowner on whose boundaries it lies. Just beyond on the left an attractively curved roving bridge takes the towing path over the entrance to the first lock on the Glasson Branch. The six locks are well spaced, the lowest standing beside Thurnham Mill which the canal company bought in 1824 to secure its water rights on the River Conder. It became one of the rare mills to be worked by canal water, and the head and tail races from the canal can still be seen, although it is now powered by electricity. The canal enters the small port of Glasson (p. 49) through a large basin which acts as a reservoir for the dock at low tides. It was quite common for small coastal craft to strike their masts here and be hauled up the canal to Preston and Kendal.

Back on the main canal, after crossing the River Conder on another small stone aqueduct, a marina is passed at Galgate, close to the village with its prominent silk mill of 1792, the oldest in England. The canal now enters the aptly named Ashton Deep Cutting, nearly 1½ miles long, at the lofty arched Brantbeck Bridge (No. 91) and shortly afterwards enters the outskirts of Lancaster. Just past the railway bridge (No. 97) the roofless stone building on the right is the one-time packet boathouse where passenger boats were housed. The upper floor was a workshop into which they were lifted for repairs. Beyond is a group of grey stone buildings forming the canal maintenance workshops, and opposite the old Aldcliffe Basins stands another set of packet horse stables, unfortunately recently damaged by fire. The city council plans to redevelop the wharves for amenity purposes, and next to Penny Street Bridge (No. 99) a paved area with shrubs and seats forms an attractive foretaste.

Running along the back of the town through a little-seen industrial district, the canal is lined with old stone-built mills that it helped to establish by providing water and transport. Near the footbridge (No. 102) an interesting new housing development named Canal Walk takes full advantage of the canal—in contrast to older terraced houses which turn their backs on it—and once past the old dry dock the Ridge Lane Bridge (No. 104) the canal affords a panoramic view of the castle and priory church overlooking the Lune.

Bending left on to a new concrete aqueduct over Bulk Road, A683, the canal crosses the magnificent 600 feet long Lune Aqueduct, 62 feet above the river. Its five stone arches each span 70 feet and took four years to build. It is one of Rennie's finest works and rivals Pontcysyllte on the Llangollen Canal as the most impressive aqueduct in the country. Plaques on each side respectively proclaim 'To Public Prosperity' and (translated from the Latin) 'Old needs are served; far distant sites combined; Rivers by art to bring new wealth are joined. A.D. 1797, J. Rennie, Engineer, A. Stevens & Son, Builders.'

The canal now turns back on itself before resuming its northerly course towards Hest Bank and Bolton-le-Sands from where there are fine views across Morecambe Bay to the Lake District, at one point the beach being within a quarter of a mile. Hatlex Bridge (No. 120), the second swing bridge on the canal, marks the approach to Bolton-le-Sands, a village of character where it groups around the canal, the Packet Boat pub reminding present day boaters that it has been satisfying canal thirsts for a very long time. Bolton Cinder Ovens Bridge (No. 125) also recalls earlier days when small coke ovens were built along the canal in this area for local use. Cinderbarrow Farm just past Tewitfield Locks is another. The canal skirts the edge of Carnforth, primarily a railway junction now well-known for its collection of preserved locomotives at 'Steamtown', and then swings eastward under the M6 motorway along a specially diverted channel to Capernwray where there is a short branch into what were once extensive quarries, but is now a secluded caravan park. It was a busy place in its day, with a row of quarrymen's cottages, demolished a few years ago, and still the remains of loading chutes. The River Keer is crossed here by a graceful lofty arch alongside an old mill, now a private house, but still retaining its wheel and some of the machinery. It was driven by water from the canal which in turn took in water from the river on the upstream side.

After winding past the charming village of Borwick, with its green and Elizabethan hall, another couple of bends bring the canal to an abrupt end at the embankment of the A6070 road where it crosses the M6, the first of the culverts that effectively stop further navigation. There are moorings here and further exploration can only be done on foot or, as far as Stainton, by canoe. It is worth first crossing the motorway bridge to look at a short depression in a field on the west side, marking the preliminary excavation for Rennie's original 1791 route to Kendal, later revised when the canal was extended in 1803.

From this point the towing path is a public right of way to Kendal, although diversions are necessary at some of the motorway crossings. The eight locks ascend 76 feet, spaced out over three quarters of a mile, and have had their gates replaced by concrete weirs. The M6 alongside is noisy, but once past it the canal again enters peaceful country, now out of Lancashire and in Cumbria. Near Burton a high embankment is pierced by two tunnel-like aqueducts taking roads through it; the canal then passes behind Holme Mills, built for flax spinning in 1790 and rebuilt in 1860, now making floor coverings. Rows of mill cottages adjoin. At Holme village a series of seven attractive and closely-spaced limestone bridges span the canal as it approaches the foot of Farleton Knott (801 feet), with another culverted road crossing on the way. Duke's Bridge at Farleton has an unusual small second arch acting as a cattle creep, and there are derelict packet boat stables close by. In the next 1¼ miles to Crooklands two more culverts follow in quick succession, after which the motorway leaves the canal which now enters a delightfully remote stretch winding away among low hills. Crooklands wharf on the right was formerly terminus of a tramroad running from gunpowder mills up the valley at Gatebeck on the River Beela, which acts as a feeder from Killington Reservoir six miles away in the fells near Sedbergh. Later the tramroad was extended across the canal alongside Crooklands Bridge and ran beside the road to Milnthorpe station.

The attractive Field End Bridge has recesses which once contained a pair of double stop gates for sealing off the canal in either direction, a job now done by dropping planks into slots. At Stainton a single arch aqueduct takes Stainton Beck under the canal, the most northerly feeder and the reason for retaining it in water to this point. Just beyond at Stainton Crossings Bridge the canal is sealed off and thereafter the bed is empty.

Hincaster Tunnel, 378 yards long, is isolated from the canal at both ends by the A591 Kendal bypass but is still accessible. Its stone portals belie the brick-lined interior above the water line. There is no towing path, and boats were hauled through by a chain fixed to the wall. It is dangerous to try to penetrate the tunnel as it is deep with mud. Instead a good horsepath goes over the hill, partly in a stone-lined cutting with three miniature canal bridges crossing it, one carrying the railway. At the far end the bypass traverses a length of the canal's course before veering away, leaving a dry bed to run along a delightfully wooded hillside above the gorge of the River Kent at Sedgwick where once there were more gunpowder mills. The pretty village clusters around an embankment which crosses the main street by a fine skew aqueduct, after which the canal merges into the surrounding fields, its course marked only by the footpath and stone bridges standing in grand isolation. From Crow Park Bridge into Kendal the canal, with its bed now completely filled in, passes the site of the gasworks that for so long kept it open, and a rather dismal wasteland enlivened by the ruins of Kendal Castle on its hill to the right. Finally the terminus is reached, part of the basin still marked by edging stones, the remainder covered by an extension to Canal Ironworks which incorporates in its buildings the old warehouse. The two streets leading down to the river are still named Canal Head North and South, from which it is a short step into the attractive town centre.

The Leeds and Liverpool Canal

IF the Lancaster Canal is the prettiest in Lancashire, the Leeds & Liverpool has the greatest variety of scenery. One hundred and twenty seven miles long, it is Britain's longest single canal, reaching a height of 487 feet with 92 broad locks, and was the longest in being built, 46 years. Of the three trans-Pennine canals it was started first, in 1770, and finished last, in 1816, and is the only one still open.

In the mid-eighteenth century communication between Lancashire and Yorkshire was mainly by packhorse but imaginative men, inspired by the success of the Newry, St. Helens and Bridgewater Canals, were thinking of better ways of crossing the Pennines. John Longbottom, a Halifax engineer, convinced a group of Bradford businessmen that it was possible to take a canal from the Aire & Calder Navigation at Leeds up the Aire valley, cross the low watershed between Skipton and Colne and then descend the valleys of the Lancashire Calder and the Ribble, passing near Preston and thence across west Lancashire to Ormskirk and Liverpool. Ready support was forthcoming from Lancashire, particularly Liverpool merchants, and an Act was obtained in 1770, work commencing simultaneously in both counties the same year. By 1774 boats could sail from Liverpool to Wigan, party by means of the River Douglas Navigation, and by 1777 from Leeds to Skipton and Gargrave, a total of 58 miles.

One of the company's first moves in Lancashire was to take over the River Douglas which had been made navigable from the Ribble estuary to Wigan back in 1742 as a means of taking Wigan coal up and down the coast, and could be navigated by Mersey flats. The opening of the canal saw its progressive decline as a navigation, hastened in 1781 by the opening of a branch canal from Newburgh to the tidal Douglas at Tarleton, known as the Rufford Branch. So it is not surprising that by this time financial resources were exhausted and new Acts to raise fresh capital were needed in 1790 and 1794.

Meanwhile internal dissension among the shareholders and intense political activity among rival canal companies bedevilled further progress. The Lancashire proprietors succeeded in altering the original route to pass instead through Burnley, Blackburn and Chorley to join the completed canal at Wigan, a longer line but with prospects of greater revenue from the growing east Lancashire cotton towns. It was completed from Gargrave through to Blackburn by 1810. This decision upset the Lancaster Canal company who were busily building the South End of their canal (p. 22), parallel to the proposed new route, which would also intercept their water supply running down from the moors to the east. The Bridgewater, Rochdale and Manchester, Bolton & Bury companies also saw the Leeds & Liverpool as a threat and for nearly twenty years progress was delayed through intermittent squabbling between them; a classic example of early canal promoters' parochialism.

Common sense prevailed at last when the Leeds & Liverpool agreed to extend their canal from Blackburn to the Lancaster at Johnsons Hillock and construct a flight of locks from their Wigan terminus up to Kirkless, using the Lancaster to link the two sections. The work was finished in 1816 when a grand flotilla of boats sailed from Leeds to Liverpool to celebrate the end of 46 years' work. The branch from Wigan to Leigh, connecting with the Bridgewater and thus opening up a route to the Midlands via the Trent and Mersey, was opened in 1820, but the canal remained unconnected to the Mersey at Liverpool until 1846.

So well established was its commercial influence that the Leeds & Liverpool was not at first affected by railway competition, and in fact was continuously profitable from 1786 to 1919, handsomely so from 1820 to 1850. Then in 1853 the company leased its merchandise revenues to a group of railway companies in return for a guaranteed income for 21 years. The railways priced the traffic off the canal on to their lines, where it was more profitable, so starting a long period of slow decline despite the canal company's efforts at revival after the lease ended. Even so, traffic lasted for another century, the last regular cargoes—coal to Wigan power station—ceasing in 1972.

Most of the canal is designated a cruiseway, and although there is still something of a question mark over the future of the section through Liverpool and the branch to the docks the situation is much brighter than it was, thanks to the campaigning of the Inland Waterways Association and local officials of the British Waterways Board. Cruising is growing in popularity and apart from in Liverpool the towing path is readily accessible. From Liverpool to Lock 85—the second up the Wigan flight—inclusive, and throughout the Leigh Branch the canal takes craft 72 feet by 14 feet, originally to accommodate Mersey flats and Midlands narrow boats, but thereafter and on the Rufford Branch it will only take craft 62 feet long, for which stretches special 'shortboats' were built, a relic of the early rivalry between the Liverpool and Yorkshire shareholders.

Headroom is eight feet.

At Liverpool the canal originally started at Pall Mall where there were extensive warehouses and the company's head office (after removal from Bradford in 1852), all of which were badly damaged in wartime air raids. The canal has since been cut back a quarter of a mile to the first bridge at Chisenhale Street, flanked on both sides by Tate & Lyle's sugar refinery. The towing path is closed as far as Litherland in an attempt to keep children off and permission for access should be obtained from British Waterways at Wigan. Close to Lightbody Street Bridge the four Liverpool Locks fall away to the left, forming a link with the Mersey through Stanley Dock, alongside Jesse Hartley's magnificent tobacco warehouse of 1857, and under Regent Road swing bridge into Collingwood and Salisbury Docks. Users of the locks should give 24 hours notice to the Board's Inspector at Burscough. Near the top of the locks the canal is joined by a line of electricity pylons from Clarence Dock power station, prominently straddling the water as far as Litherland.

For the next two miles the canal lies close to the docks, although they are rarely in sight from the towing path as it passes through Sandhills and Kirkdale. Beside Bankhall Street (Bridge I) there stands a tall three-storey warehouse still bearing the company's name. A canal arm went into the basement and there was a covered wharf adjoining. Passing Bootle wharf the surrounds are still industrial. At Litherland until recently there was an unusual electrically operated bridge (No. 2J) which lifted the deck vertically and, when the canal was busy, was notorious for the long traffic queues it created. It is now replaced by a high level bridge.

The canal traverses a suburban area through Netherton, where it swings in a long eastward loop to cross the River Alt by a single stone arch at Aintree, passing alongside the racecourse and the famous Canal Turn before turning north again. At Aintree the first of the many swing bridges is encountered. Boaters should ensure that they have an appropriate key, obtainable from the Waterways Board. Gradually the surroundings become more rural past Maghull, and after Lydiate the canal enters flat, fen-like country, an area of small farms and market gardens. Near the Ship Inn at Haskayne Bridge (No. 21A) is a boatyard, and then beyond Halsall the lofty tower of Scarisbrick Hall can be seen above the trees. The house, now a school, is a famous Victorian Gothic extravaganza designed in 1837 by A.W.N. Pugin. It is open to the public during summer holidays.

Southport began to develop as a seaside resort in the early 1800s and the Liverpool-Wigan packet boats stopped at Scarisbrick Bridge (No. 27A) to connect with coaches that conveyed passengers the remaining four miles. By 1821 Southport had grown sufficiently to warrant a separate Manchester-Scarisbrick service, in addition to the established Liverpool-Manchester boats that competed with those via the Mersey and the Bridgewater—a longer journey but, as the company's bills pointed out, 'without the risk of the Tideway'.

The canal now swings east to Burscough, where there is a maintenance yard and Inspector's office for the Liverpool length. The entrance to the Rufford Branch is marked by a handsome stone roving bridge dated 1816, a group of canalside cottages and a dry dock that is still used for repair work. It is seven miles and eight locks to the Douglas, the first two locks close to the entrance followed by Runnel Brow, Moss, Germans and Baldwins spaced out over the next 1½ miles. Several still have old 'jack clough' ground paddles comprising a long wooden handle and lever which swivels on the lock wall, peculiar to the Leeds & Liverpool. Rufford Lock is close to Rufford Old Hall, a magnificent half-timbered mediaeval mansion owned by the National Trust, housing a folk museum.

At Sollom (Bridge No. 10), where the towing path ends, there is a gateless lock chamber, once the entrance lock into the Douglas before the river was diverted in 1805 in connection with the draining of adjoining marshlands and the canal extended along the old river bed to Bank Bridge (No. 11), beside another old canal warehouse. Thence it takes a new, straighter course to Tarleton. The canal made Tarleton into a small port where in the early 1850s some 300 vessels a year brought in slate, iron ore and gunpowder and took out coal from Wigan. A large basin has been filled in but there are still extensive moorings and a boat-building yard, where once barges and sailing flats were launched but which is now busy with pleasure cruisers. It was from Tarleton that barges were taken to and from the Lancaster Canal after local boat building ceased, via the Ribble estuary and around the coast to the Lune and Glasson Dock. Craft wishing to navigate between the two canals still have to do the same today.

The Douglas can only be entered from the canal at high water through Tarleton Tide Lock, 62 feet by 18 feet, and about half a mile downstream is a pipe bridge with 20 feet headroom. After another half a mile a swing bridge on the Preston-Southport railway was once a hindrance to sailing craft but since closure it has been removed and only the embankments on each side remain. Between 1882 and 1887 there was a station named River Douglas close to the bridge. It had no road access and seems to have been intended for use in connection with a paddle steamer service which operated on the river about this time, although this particular piece of local history is rather obscure. There was also a branch railway from Hesketh Bank to the canalside at Tarleton from 1880 to 1930, used only for goods traffic except for a very brief passenger service in 1912-13. In another 3½ miles the Douglas enters the navigation channel of the Ribble estuary opposite Freckleton, where there was a wharf served by barges crossing from Tarleton (p.66).

Returning to the main canal, this crosses the River Tawd on a stone arch and then the Douglas on a larger one, whence it follows the river to Wigan. At Parbold there is a windmill tower beside the bridge (No. 37), a much photographed scene, and on the other side stands Ainscoughs' flour mill which once had its own fleet of barges and still retains the loading equipment. Close to Alder Lane Bridge (No. 38) a short arm opposite a sharp right-hand bend was constructed as a starting point for Longbottom's original route towards the Ribble valley, which never got any further. The narrow Douglas valley is a sudden and dramatic change, its entrance commanded by Parbold Hill and Ashurst Beacon, only 500 feet above sea level but appearing higher as they rise abruptly from the plain.

Three Milestones
a   **Lune Aqueduct — Lancaster Canal**
b   **Radburn Wharf — Lancaster Canal [Leeds & Liverpool type]**
c   **Bury — Manchester, Bolton & Bury Canal**

The valley is pleasantly wooded and it is difficult to imagine that the winding little river once took sailing flats to Wigan. There were eighteen locks from Tarleton and it is possible to find the remains of some of them. Appley Locks, the first since leaving Liverpool, comprise a single twelve feet deep lock with two shallower ones alongside, added to speed up traffic when the canal was busy but now lying disused. Along this stretch a number of horse tramroads once ran down to the canal bringing coal and stone. Dean Locks, two side by side with one now disused, are dominated by Gathurst Viaduct on the M6 motorway. Between them and the river are the remains of one of the old Douglas locks on a dry short-cut. Here also is a derelict side cut and lock from the canal down into the river to reach a tramroad at Gathurst wharf that continued in use after the main river navigation ceased. There is some industry at Gathurst but otherwise the valley is secluded for another half a mile to Crooke where it widens out into an old mining area. A short branch on the left, now filled in, ran into underground workings. Crooke Lock gates were removed when subsidence made the lock superfluous. Ell Meadow Locks are another side-by-side pair, followed by the single Pagefield Lock, built in 1904, again to counteract subsidence.

On entering Wigan there are large brick warehouses on the left and, straight ahead, a roofless stone warehouse with arches over the canal. This was the original terminus for 36 years, before Wigan Locks were completed in 1816. The main canal turns sharp right under a roving bridge to the two lowest locks (Nos. 87 and 86) of the great Wigan flight of 23, alongside the workshops and office of British Waterways' Area Engineer. Then the Leigh Branch, seven miles long, turns off to the right.

The branch has been severely affected by subsidence. Originally there was a lock at Poolstock, two at Dover and one at Plank Lane, but now there are only two at Poolstock shortly after leaving the main line, followed by an unbroken level through the Bridgewater Canal to Runcorn, over 43 miles. If one discounts the stop gate at Dutton, on the Trent & Mersey, the level goes as far as Middlewich, over 56 miles. The flat, empty wastelands through Ince and Abram, broken by old railway embankments, are now gradually being reclaimed, including the 'flashes'—the flooded areas of subsidence—where fishing, boating and wildfowling are being encouraged. Eventually there will be little evidence that this was once a thriving colliery district. Bickershaw Colliery, alongside the canal close to Leigh, is still working. Until 1972 it provided the last regular traffic on the canal to Wigan power station. The busy Plank Lane swing bridge is electrically operated during daylight hours by a resident bridge-keeper. Leigh itself was primarily a cotton spinning town, although the tall red brick mills are now mostly occupied for other industries. On the left is a large wharf with a group of typical Leeds & Liverpool warehouses, followed by Leigh Bridge and the end-on junction with the Bridgewater marked by a narrow section, a large notice board and a crane for dropping in stop planks.

Back at Wigan, Westwood power station stands at the junction followed by the impressive flight of 21 locks rising over 200 feet in close succession. They are particularly interesting for their variety of paddle gear. Near the top lock are three canalside pubs, just as necessary now as in the canal age, and immediately beyond it the old South End of the Lancaster Canal is joined (p. 22) by turning left at a T-junction (the right-hand is merely a short arm). On the right beyond Springs Bridge (No. 59A) are the remains of Haigh workshops, a handsome Georgian-style building of 1839 with a cupola. It was built by the 24th Earl of Crawford and Balcarres for his collieries and ironworks, all that is left of a large industrial complex that generated heavy traffic on the Lancaster Canal, of which the Earl was a prominent promoter.

Here there is an extensive view over Wigan before the canal enters a quiet wooded section past Haigh Hall and park, built by the Earl between 1827 and 1840 on the site of a mediaeval house. The estate has a number of attractions and is owned by Wigan Corporation. The canal runs along the 300 feet contour with high moors to the east. After Red Rock Bridge (No. 63) it crosses a disused railway by an iron skew aqueduct and then passes the moated Arley Hall—now Wigan Golf Club. More tramroads once served the canal from long-gone collieries in this area. There is a boatyard at Adlington after which the canal is quiet and wooded again despite the proximity of a main road and railway, before skirting the east side of Chorley, a cotton town that had its wharf at Botany Bay (Bridge No. 78A) just under the M61 motorway bridge.

After Chorley the canal is rural again all the way to Blackburn, winding between low secluded hills with good views. At the foot of the seven Johnsons Hillock Locks the old Lancaster Canal, or Walton Summit Branch, forks leftward (p. 24). The Lancaster company also built the locks, the Leeds & Liverpool proper starting again at the top where there is a lock cottage, Top Lock pub (formerly The Anchor), moorings and another boatyard. Withnell Fold (Bridge No. 88) is an interesting early nineteenth century mill village, built around a square, for the employees of a canalside paper mill, now used for other purposes. Near Riley Green Bridge (No. 91A) is an old boat-building shed and a mile further on a working paper mill at the foot of a steep embankment where the canal curves over a narrow, wooded ravine, before reaching Feniscowles on the outskirts of Blackburn.

The canal crosses the western part of the town on an embankment with a magnificent lofty single arch aqueduct at Ewood over a road and the River Darwen, although the latter is now culverted beneath the road forming a bridge under a bridge. The six Blackburn locks follow, rising 55 feet. Although the town around the canal is dismal the locks themselves have been attractively landscaped and eventually this entire length is intended to form part of an imaginative development scheme aimed at transforming it into a 'base line' from which to improve the urban environment on both sides. At present it comprises derelict open spaces, backs of terraced housing, factories and some fine examples of Victorian mills. There is a large canal depot at Eanam, now let to tenants, with the bay windows of the former manager's house overlooking the water. The group of warehouses, with an iron-framed canopy, includes a large grain warehouse with wooden loading chutes. On the other side a yard separates them from an office building with an interesting semi-circular end. The towing path here is fenced off and the walker has to go through the depot yard.

Once beyond Blackburn the country opens out again. A former boat-building shed at Whitebirk Bridge (No. 104B), now a caravan centre, is followed by the remains of Whitebirk power station to which boats brought coal from Burnley, until the great freeze of 1963. Now the power station itself has been closed. Towards Rishton on the left the cuttings of old tramroads can be seen descending the hillside from hilltop quarries. Rishton itself, a small mill town, is in need of urban renewal along the canal side. Past it the canal swings south in a great loop around the Hyndburn valley to the small industrial town of Church where on a sharp left hand bend there is a wharf and warehouse that once served Accrington one and a half miles away. This short stretch is particularly depressing, but soon there are views across the valley towards Pendle Hill (1,831 feet) that are ample compensation. The hill's long bulk keeps the canal company for the next sixteen miles. After more swing bridges there are warehouses and wharves at Clayton-le-Moors, or Enfield as it was known in canal days, a name now almost disused except by the local cricket club.

Winding along the side of the Calder valley the canal passes Altham, where there was another tramroad from collieries at Read, and chemical works at Hapton, to Rosegrove on the edge of Burnley. There are three River Calders, one in Yorkshire and two in Lancashire. This one runs into the Ribble at Whalley. Dugdales Warehouse still stands alongside Bridge No. 126A, with more old colliery staithes on the right just after Gannow Bridge, before the canal swings into Gannow Tunnel (559 yards), the portals of which bear interesting masons' marks. The horsepath over the top is still called Boathorse Lane. Beyond the tunnel there are mills and another surprising view of Pendle on the left, before the canal is swallowed up in a veritable canyon of mills. Through Burnley the canal is full of such surprises, as the scenery changes abruptly with its twists and turns, from distant vistas to close contact with industry. On the right a collection of mills is due for conservation together with Slater Terrace, a row of weavers' cottages with an iron balcony over the canal. This length includes Burnley Depot which, like Blackburn, has an interesting series of warehouses with a canopy over the canal and a toll office perched up against Manchester Road Bridge.

After half a mile the canal emerges at British Waterways' Finsley Gate maintenance yard, where the restored and landscaped buildings have gained an award, to turn sharp left and stride across the rooftops on the great Burnley Embankment, three quarters of a mile long and 60 feet high. It contains aqueducts over the River Calder and a main street from where one can look down on the town centre. Then comes Burnley's last surprise, a leafy section alongside Thompson Park, at the end of which an aqueduct crosses the River Brun. Here a short arm formerly served Bank Hall colliery, now completely razed and transformed into a public open space.

From Burnley to Nelson the two canal banks provide a complete contrast. On the right are the mills and houses of Reedley and Brierfield, while on the left one looks across the valley of Pendle Water to the hill, soon to be spoilt by a new motorway. Nelson warehouse is one of the last the canal company built, its red brick and railway style frilly-edged canopies markedly different from the older ones seen earlier. The canal now leaves industrial Lancashire and enters a long and attractive rural section with wide views of hills and valleys that last intermittently almost to Leeds. Colne Water is crossed by the low, three-arch Swinden Aqueduct as the seven Barrowford Locks are approached in their picturesque setting. They rise 69 feet and alongside is Barrowford Reservoir which stores excess water from the summit level. There are six other reservoirs, one at Rishton, four close to the summit near Foulridge and the largest at Winterburn, north of Gargrave, that supplies the summit by pipeline. Even these are insufficient in drought conditions and parts of the canal have been closed by water shortages on numerous occasions throughout its history.

An old warehouse and toll office stand above the second lock, at one time the wharf for Colne, and beyond the top lock there are moorings. The canal is now on its summit level and approaching Foulridge Tunnel, 1,640 yards long. The tunnel was the cause of major delay in opening the canal through to Burnley in 1796, having taken five years to build under the supervision of Robert Whitworth, another notable engineer of his day who succeeded Longbottom. Much of it is at a shallow depth and was constructed as a cutting and then covered over. There have been four collapses at various times. Originally craft were 'legged' through by professional leggers whose stone hut can be seen above the western portal. Then from 1880 to 1937 steam tugs were used, by which time horse boats had largely given way to diesels. As well as for the tunnel vessels steam power was extensively used on the Leeds & Liverpool for normal towage and for self-propelled barges from 1880 upward. The company at one time had a fleet of 30 steamers in addition to those operated by private owners, many of them 'flyboats' that worked to a timetable and had priority over other craft. Diesels came into use in the 1920s but the last steamer did not disappear until the 1950s.

The towing path goes over the top of the tunnel along a good track, passing three ventilating shafts, like low stone chimneys, in the fields. Foulridge warehouse and wharf are at the eastern end and beyond are some old stables, all close to the village. The Hole-in-the-Wall pub has a photograph of a cow that was reputed to have fallen in the canal and swum through the tunnel, although one suspects it was probably able to touch bottom most of the way. According to a local boatman this happened on two occasions, the animal being towed out by a passing barge on the second occasion.

The Lancashire-Yorkshire boundary was formerly at County Brook which flows under the canal just past Mill Hill Bridge (No. 149), but as Barnoldswick, two miles further on, is now in Lancashire it forms a good excuse to mention the hidden Rain Hall Rock Branch on the right just short of Long Ing Bridge (No. 153). No sign of it is visible from the towing path as the first few hundred yards have been filled in, but beyond a clump of trees lies a deep rock cutting with two short tunnels and a remarkable lofty three-arch viaduct. This isolated branch still holds water and originally was cut as a long, narrow quarry into which water was let as excavating progressed, so that limestone could be loaded direct into boats and taken out on to the main canal. The new county boundary is just beyond the three Greenberfield Locks, whence the canal starts its long panoramic descent through North Yorkshire to Leeds.

ASHTON CANAL. The two-rise locks on the Hollinwood Branch at Waterhouses, now cascaded and landscaped in Daisy Nook Country Park. The base of an old crane is on the left.

BRIDGEWATER CANAL. Barton Swing Aqueduct, open to the Manchester Ship Canal. (Photo: Waterways World).

LANCASTER CANAL. Barge 'May' and boat family, with a cargo of stone near Garstang, pulled as was customary by two horses. Probably about 1910. (Photo: Lancashire County Record Office, Preston).

LANCASTER CANAL. The Lune Aqueduct in 1953.

BRIDGEWATER CANAL. One of the underground canal entrances at Worsley Delph in 1966 before the area was landscaped.

HUDDERSFIELD CANAL. Climbing up the Tame valley towards Mossley and the Pennines, from Scout Tunnel.

LEEDS & LIVERPOOL CANAL. Pleasure cruiser descending Barrowford Locks in 1965.

LEEDS & LIVERPOOL CANAL. Laden diesel barge 'Farnworth' passes maintenance boat 'Plover' near Scarisbrick in 1960. (Photo: Jack Parkinson).

LEEDS & LIVERPOOL CANAL. 'Midst dark satanic mills'—Blackburn Locks in 1971.

MANCHESTER, BOLTON & BURY CANAL. Looking up Prestolee Locks to the junction in 1920. (Photo: J. H. Denton).

MANCHESTER SHIP CANAL. The motor vessel 'City of Dundee', with masts and funnel demounted, being towed under Irlam viaduct.

MERSEY & IRWELL NAVIGATION. Suspension bridge and warehouses on Howley Quay, Warrington.

ROCHDALE CANAL. The canal slides through the centre of Manchester—looking towards Oxford Road from Deansgate, with Central Station arches on the left, in 1968.

ROCHDALE CANAL. Clegg Hall and mill on the canal bank between Rochdale and Littleborough.

ST. HELENS CANAL. The road bridge lifted at Sankey Bridges to let the barge 'Ellesborough' through.

ST. HELENS CANAL. Hulme Lock and cottage, the only one still reasonably complete, in 1978.

The River Lune

ONLY the tidal section of the Lune up to Skerton weir at Lancaster is navigable. Robert Lawson developed Sunderland Point, on the north side of the estuary where it enters the sea, as a landing place in 1680 and built a jetty about 1700, but as the road was flooded at high tide the hamlet did not grow, although remains of warehouses are still to be seen. Lancaster itself was developing as a port for coastal and overseas trade and in 1749 St. Georges Quay was built below the castle, with its fine stone warehouses which still stand, followed by Richard Gillow's handsome customs house in 1765. Silting of the estuary led in 1767 to the building of New Quay for larger ships, one mile downstream, followed in 1787 by Glasson Dock five miles seaward in a further effort to solve the problem. But navigational difficulties proved insuperable as ships grew in size, a 1799 scheme for a ship canal was abandoned, and by the end of the nineteenth century Lancaster was no longer a port of any significance.

Glasson Dock was used for coastal shipping, including until recently a container service to Ireland, but like the Lune itself is now mainly given over to pleasure craft. The dock, about 500 feet by 200 feet, has a tidal entrance lock and is surrounded by attractive Victorian cottages and pubs and some light industry. A former dry dock has been filled in. Looking out over the river is a lighthouse and a small harbour office. A barge lock and swing bridge lead from the dock into a large basin acting as a reservoir into which runs the Glasson Branch of the Lancaster Canal (p. 27). A five-storey warehouse and storage sheds once stood on what is now a car park.

Glasson is popular with visitors by car and boat alike, and there are ample facilities, including a floating cafe.

The Manchester, Bolton & Bury Canal

THIS is a canal for the industrial archaeologist. Only a few parts contain water, and while much of its course can be walked it is not in attractive country, although for the historically minded there is much of interest.

The idea of a canal from Bolton and Bury to the Irwell at Salford was actively supported by the Mersey & Irwell Navigation Company, an Act was obtained in 1791 and work commenced on a line from Oldfield Road, Salford, up the Irwell valley to Bury, with a branch following the River Croal to Bolton. The new company also had ideas about continuing from Bolton to the Leeds & Liverpool's originally projected line near Horwich, and across the Pennines from Bury, past Littleborough, to Halifax, thus pre-empting the Bridgewater and the proposed Rochdale Canal as the main east-west route. Both parties had Bills before Parliament in 1794; the Rochdale won and the Manchester, Bolton & Bury's was rejected. Another link was envisaged with the Leeds & Liverpool at Church, near Accrington, by a canal from Bury, indirectly supported by the Manchester, Bolton & Bury company and called the Haslingden Canal. An Act was obtained in 1794 for a line climbing some 400 feet with inclined planes instead of locks, and severe restrictions on water supplies. Not surprisingly such an improbable scheme collapsed. Later the agreement with the Leeds & Liverpool fell through as well so the Manchester, Bolton & Bury (M.B. & B.) was left as a T-shaped canal connected with other waterways only at its foot. As such it was moderately prosperous serving the coal and cotton industries of the Irwell valley.

By 1796 the canal was complete except for three eighths of a mile from Oldfield Road to the Irwell. Dithering over whether to join the Irwell or the Rochdale Canal (which in any case would have required an aqueduct over the river) caused more delay until, after pressure was applied by the Mersey & Irwell company which had no desire to see M.B. & B. traffic passing on to the rival Bridgewater Canal, the link was finally made in 1808.

The canal was 12¾ miles long to Bury, the Bolton Branch was three miles, and there were seventeen locks, six of them staircases, all between Salford and the junction at Prestolee near Little Lever.

Maximum length of craft was 68 feet, width 14 feet, and both barges and shortened narrow boats used the canal, the latter carrying coal in containers similar to the Bridgewater system. The containers were bottom-opening and could be lifted out by crane for easy emptying into carts or bunkers. So efficient was the system that coal carriage between waterside collieries and customers' wharves remained competitive until the collieries themselves progressively closed, the last in 1951. Passenger-carrying was also a notable feature from 1796 to 1838, with regular services from Manchester to Bolton and, after 1810, a Bolton-Bury service connecting with the Manchester packets at Prestolee Locks. In 1832 a light swift-boat was introduced, drawn by four horses, and the following year well over 64,000 passengers were carried.

The M.B. & B. was a canal that turned itself into a railway company, called the Manchester, Bolton & Bury Navigation & Railway, empowered by an Act of 1831 to build a railway 'upon or near the line of the ... Canal' and to close such parts as might be needed. Pressure from coal interests forced the company to retain the canal, however, and a new Act in 1832 empowered a separate railway which in some places was built well away from it, and was opened to Bolton in 1838. In 1844 the company amalgamated with the Manchester & Leeds Railway, later becoming part of the Lancashire & Yorkshire and subsequently the London, Midland & Scottish which abandoned nearly seven miles of the canal in 1941. The Prestolee-Bury and Clifton-Irwell sections remained open until 1961, the last traffic being coal from a wharf at Bury to a factory on the opposite bank about 100 yards away, and boiler ash back, carried in an old compartment boat poled across the canal. During its last years colliery subsidence caused several breaches and during the war a half mile section at Clifton was piped in order to avoid flooding in the event of bombing.

In **Canals to Manchester** David Owen quotes an account of the lower section of the canal in 1907 when, despite waterside collieries, mills and factories, parts of the Irwell valley were still sufficiently wooded and attractive to tempt the Agecroft Rowing Club to take to the water, with egg teas and weekend camping amid orchards and gardens near Ringley. They even set sail if the wind was favourable. Now it is difficult to imagine the scene.

The stonework at the Irwell entrance alongside Princes Bridge can still be seen, but thereafter the canal has been filled in. There was a staircase pair of locks at the entrance and a single at Ordsall Lane, closely followed by another staircase pair and a single at Oldfield Road, all within the first three eighths of a mile. Here the canal passed under and then ran alongside the railway out to Clifton. There were extensive wharves and arms at the back of The Crescent, now the site of new buildings. After Broughton Road the channel becomes visible, showing the fine stone lining, although

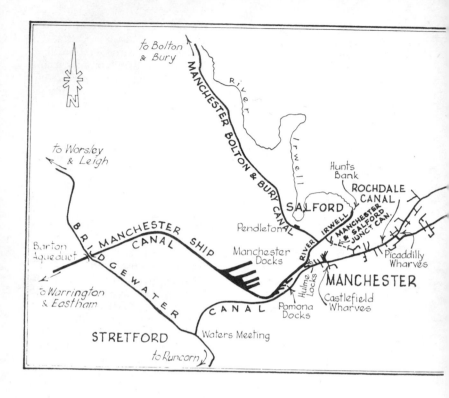

infilling is continuing progressively. Throughout this length the bridges remain, although the arches of some have been filled in. Agecroft power station lies on the right, served by conveyors from the colliery across the canal and railway, and just beyond it the canal veers away behind the Chloride Batteries factory to turn sharp right over the Irwell on the three-arch Clifton Aqueduct and then sharp left, dominated by a disused railway viaduct.

Although filled in here, it is possible to see the site of Fletcher's Canal which carried straight on parallel to the Irwell on the left bank. It was built before the M.B. & B. in 1790 as an extension of a remarkable pumping system at Wet Earth colliery, constructed by James Brindley in 1756. The pumps drained the mine and were operated by a large wheel driven by water taken from the Irwell some 860 yards upstream, through a syphon beneath it and along an open channel to the colliery. The channel was then continued for just over a mile as a navigable canal. Matthew Fletcher operated Wet Earth at this time but did not connect his canal to the M.B. & B. until 1799, by an unusual lozenge-shaped lock large

52

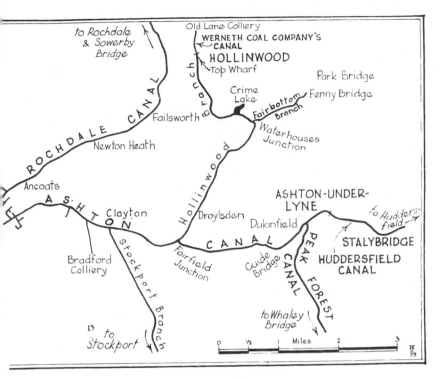

Canals in Manchester

enough to take three narrow boats side by side but with a fall to
the main canal of only eighteen inches. There seem also to have
been underground canals at Wet Earth and at Botany Bay colliery
(close to the present Pilkington Tile Works), on the Worsley
principle. Wet Earth pit closed in 1928 and the last short stretch of
Fletcher's Canal to the tile works in 1935.

The M62 motorway crosses the valley here and for the next two
miles the canal is harder to trace, covered by a sewerage works
where once Rhodes Lock stood. Then, still hugging the north bank
of the river, came the picturesquely named Giant's Seat
locks, and water reappears beyond Ringley village at the
the filled-in pair of Ringley Locks. Past Prestolee village t
water on the fine four-arch aqueduct re-crossing the Irwe
its confluence with the Croal and then, dry once more, the
turns sharp right to ascend the dramatic flight of six Pr
Locks, or Nob End as they were sometimes called, split int
staircases of three. The massive stonework is still well visib
the top there is an acute-angled junction back towards Bolto

Bury line continuing straight on, where one can gain an impressive view back down the locks to the aqueduct below. To the left the canal is in water again, with a stone-sett towing path, old canal workshops, cottages and the former Nob Inn. The water is wide and deep, forming a fishery as, for the next three quarters of a mile, it clings to the side of the Croal valley which has been planted and landscaped here. The water ends in a wide basin at Little Lever where a stone aqueduct over Hall Lane (A6053) has been demolished, but beyond it the line can be traced again for another mile to the site of Darcy Lever Aqueduct that took the canal over the River Tonge and Radcliffe Road on three arches. One more short length can be traced to Bentley Bridge, but on under Burnden railway viaduct the channel is barely discernible and is finally swallowed up by the new relief road that cuts through the centre of Bolton along and over the river. The terminus was at Church Wharf beneath the Croal railway viaduct, the street bearing the same name. Even that now seems to have disappeared.

The towing path has stone edging and walls for the entire distance and at the Salford end much of the offside bank is walled as well. Another notable feature marking it out as a North Country canal is the stone slab boundary walling set upright in the ground and secured by iron ties, similar to parts of the Rochdale Canal. At quarter mile intervals old milestones can be seen too, with a large letter 'M' and the distance from Manchester cut in them. There are several on the eastern branch which is filled in for half a mile from Prestolee, following a breach in 1942. A paper mill warehouse is built on the site at the end of this dry section and then there is water for the rest of the way, the length as far as Radcliffe giving views across the steep-sided valley of the Irwell, although industry and housing mark the skyline. The remains of the Ladyshore colliery arm can still be seen, which provided the last traffic to Bury. At Radcliffe the canal is shallow, reedy and rubbish-strewn, factories and mills line its banks, and at the culverted bridge in the town centre an open space is all that remains of the old wharf. Then follows another open section close to the Manchester-Bury railway line until the Irwell intervenes once more and is alongside the canal for the remaining distance. On the left under the embankment of Elton reservoir is a feeder and the old Farmers Arms pub; opposite is a new overflow weir into the river. The canal now ends at the first of the mills that used to stand alongside it for the last three quarters of a mile into Bury. From here it is filled in under the railway viaduct and partly built over by a large factory. The basins at Irwell Bridge are now an empty waste. A short extension called the Coal Branch ran on under Bolton Road by a 141 yard tunnel, taking only narrow boats to more wharves. It also acted as a feeder for excess water from the river.

The Manchester & Salford Junction Canal

HARDLY seen in the centre of Manchester and only five eighths of a mile long, it is not surprising that this canal, the Manchester & Salford Junction, was so little known. Until 1838 the city was served by two distinct systems: the Mersey & Irwell Navigation and its feeder, the Manchester, Bolton & Bury Canal; and the Bridgewater, linked to the Yorkshire and Midlands canals. For long enough the Mersey & Irwell and the M.B. & B. had desired a connection with the Bridgewater in Manchester, but the Duke was against it as he would lose more trade than he would gain. Finally in 1836 an Act was gained for a canal from the Irwell just above and opposite the M.B. & B's entrance lock to an end-on junction with a branch of the Rochdale at Lower Mosley Street, passing from Atherton Street beneath Deansgate to Watson Street in a 499 yards long tunnel. It rose by four locks, the upper two a staircase, and the tunnel had a towing path and gas lighting. The top lock was six inches above the level of the Rochdale to prevent water being taken from the latter, so water for the locks had to be pumped up from the Irwell by two steam engines.

Opened in 1839 it was not a successful canal, partly from the expanse of pumping but mainly because the Bridgewater, reconciled to the inevitable, had already constructed a much more convenient connection at Hulme Locks at Castlefield (p. 15) in 1838, to which the Mersey & Irwell had acquiesced although still proceeding with their own independent link. When the Mersey & Irwell was taken over by the Bridgewater in 1846 the junction canal lost completely what little value it had as a competitive route, and on the building of Manchester Central station in 1875 the section between Lower Mosley Street and Water Street was filled in. The Irwell end remained in use for access to wharves around Water Street and when the Great Northern Railway's Deansgate goods station was built over the canal tunnel in 1899 lifts were installed for interchange of traffic. Regular use ceased in 1922 and abandonment took place in 1936.

Part of the tunnel is still there beneath the Granada television studios and during the war was used as an air raid shelter. The infilled entrance from the Irwell can still be seen from the opposite bank below Quay Street and at the other end the bridge under Great Bridgewater Street still stands, although the canal has been filled in.

The Manchester Ship Canal

THE Ship Canal is not only Lancashire's but Britain's greatest inland waterway, allowing ocean-going vessels of up to 10,000 tons to reach Manchester, 42 miles inland from Liverpool. The creation of the Port of Manchester is really the culmination of the story of the city's rise from 'cottonpolis' to the commercial and industrial capital of the North West, a story beginning with the Mersey & Irwell Navigation (p. 61), continued by the Bridgewater Canal (p. 14), then the railways and completed by the Ship Canal.

For many years Manchester had suffered from excessive port charges at Liverpool, lack of interest by the Bridgewater Trustees in improving either their own canal or the Mersey & Irwell which they also owned, and high railway rates. Several schemes for a ship canal were suggested but it was Daniel Adamson, a Manchester industrialist, who in 1882 finally got the project started. Plans prepared by Edward Leader Williams, a gifted civil engineer who worked on the River Weaver Navigation and then the Bridgewater, and who designed the Anderton boat lift near Northwich, were selected and against strenuous opposition from Liverpool, the Mersey Docks & Harbour Board and the railway companies an Act was obtained at the third attempt in 1885. The promoters now had to raise £5 million in two years before work could commence under the Act, and also had to find over £1.7 million to purchase the combined Bridgewater and Mersey & Irwell undertakings. Later, as more money was needed because estimates inevitably were exceeded, Manchester Corporation made a large contribution in return for majority representation on the board, which they still have. The total cost on completion was some £15.5 million.

Daniel Adamson, despite his vision and immense drive, was not a financier and he voluntarily retired from the leadership, Lord Egerton taking the chairmanship of the company. Leader Williams was appointed engineer, and in 1887 work began on cutting the 36 miles of canal from Eastham along the Cheshire bank of the Mersey to a site beside the Irwell at Pomona Gardens, Manchester, not far downstream from the Bridgewater's Castlefield wharves. After the three side-by-side tidal locks at Eastham four more pairs were built, rising a total of 60 feet 6 inches. Nineteen bridges were required, nine of them swing type and the rest high level. The minimum width at the bottom is 120 feet except for a few short sections, and, since deepening a few years after opening, the maximum depth on the non-tidal section has been 28 feet. Maximum headroom is 70 feet.

Construction took seven years and at its height employed 16,000 men. It was the first major civil engineering project to use steam power for digging, with 97 excavators and grabs plus numerous steam cranes, but even so there was still heavy reliance on men with spades, including the time-honoured method of using horse-gins and planks for taking barrowloads of spoil up the cutting sides. Work proceeded well for two years and then in the four successive winters 1889 to 1892 severe flooding damaged the workings, that of November, 1890 being particularly bad when fourteen miles from Latchford to Trafford Park were inundated under 40 feet of water. However, despite these and other difficulties the whole remarkable undertaking was opened to traffic on New Year's Day, 1894, and ceremonially opened by Queen Victoria on 21 May. Manchester was no longer a canal port; it was an ocean terminal, and as the Port of Manchester it now comprises the Ship Canal itself, Manchester, Ellesmere Port, Runcorn, Stanlow and Queen Elizabeth II Docks (the latter at Eastham), and the Bridgewater Canal. Over 16 million tons are handled annually. The port also has its own railway system which serves the Manchester Docks and Trafford Park Estate, and until recently ran along the Lancashire bank of the canal as far as Latchford, with a further separate section thence to Runcorn. It has now been cut back to Thelwall.

In order to gain an adequate water supply the Rivers Irwell and Mersey were taken into the canal as far as Rixton where the Mersey resumes its old course through Warrington, and tributaries like the Bollin and the Glaze Brook also feed it. Control of levels is exercised by large sluices at the locks and overflow sluices into the Mersey above Runcorn and opposite the Weaver outflow.

In Manchester the canal is really a continuation of the Irwell although the official commencing point is Woden Street footbridge just below Regent Bridge and Hulme Lock from the Bridgewater. The canal is not easily accessible other than by seeing it from bridges, and the best way to view it is to sail up or down. Public trips on an ex-Mersey ferry steamer are run during summer weekends to and from Pomona Docks and Liverpool by the Co-operative Travel Agency, providing a six-hour cruise full of interest.

Pomona Docks, lying between the Ship Canal and the Bridge-water, are numbered 1 to 4 and see less traffic now than formerly, although still used by 'roll on-roll off' vessels. Then come Trafford Road and the dock railway swing bridges, with the main

Manchester Docks, Nos. 6 to 9 (there is no No. 5) on the right. No. 9 is the largest, used by container ships, and from here runs a twice-weekly service to Montreal and a 12-day service to the Mediterranean. Alongside stands the largest grain elevator in Europe. The whole dock estate covers some 700 acres. Just beyond on the left are three dry docks, immediately followed by Mode Wheel Locks. One is 600 feet long and the other alongside is 350 feet. Both have intermediate gates so that shorter vessels do not require a whole lockful of water, and the fall is 13 feet.

The canal now traverses the northern side of Trafford Park estate, mainly oil tank farms, as far as the remarkable Barton Swing Aqueduct. After the Anderton Lift and the Ship Canal itself, Barton Aqueduct is Leader Williams' third masterpiece of engineering ingenuity. His problem was to replace Brindley's old Bridgewater Canal aqueduct over the Irwell by a structure that would cause no obstruction to the Ship Canal. His solution was to build a 235 feet long by 18 feet wide watertight tank, 7 feet deep, pivoted at the centre, in which water could remain while being swung open to allow ships to pass. Both ends of the tank and the canal were fitted with gates and in order to provide sufficient clearance for swinging a narrow gap was necessary, sealed when closed by hydraulically-operated rubber-shod iron wedges, ensuring a tight fit. The pivot comprises tapered iron rollers running in a circular trough, and much of the 1,450 tons weight of the full tank is taken by a central hydraulic press to reduce friction on the rollers. Nowadays the aqueduct is normally kept open to the Ship Canal and is only swung for Bridgewater traffic. Parts of Brindley's original masonry can still be seen on the north side.

Close by is Barton Road swing bridge, followed by the high level bridge carrying the M63 motorway. On the right a close observer can see part of the original course of the Irwell before it was by-passed by the Mersey & Irwell's Stickings Cut before 1783, and then Barton Locks are reached, of the same dimensions as Mode Wheel with a fall of fifteen feet. The first of the ferries is passed on the approach to Irlam, and then two miles from Barton are Irlam Locks, again similar in dimensions with a sixteen feet fall. Irlam and Cadishead high level railway viaducts follow, between them on the right hand bank lying the site of the old Irlam Steelworks and Partington Coaling Basin, no longer used for bunkering ships although oil can be taken on, and coal as cargo. On the south side immediately after Irlam viaduct the Mersey enters over a weir, while beyond Cadishead the Glaze Brook enters on the right and, a little further on, the Red Brook on the left.

Warburton high level toll bridge replaces an earlier one over the Mersey and a mile further on the River Bollin flows in on the south side at Rixton Junction. Opposite, the Mersey diverges towards Warrington, no longer navigable. Here the Ship Canal cuts across a great loop of the Mersey's old course (p. 64). A mile or so further on after Thelwall viaduct on the M62 motorway another Mersey loop, this time still part of the river, comes alongside the canal immediately beyond Thelwall Pumping Stage where dredgers discharge on to extensive dumping grounds. Latchford Locks, similar to the previous ones but with 16 feet 6 inches fall, have a road running along on the north side and are the easiest of all to reach for watching the passage of a large ship.

The canal now passes the south side of Warrington beneath a series of bridges, starting with Latchford railway viaduct and then four road bridges—Knutsford Road swing, Latchford high level, Northwich Road and Chester Road (both swing), followed by Acton Grange viaduct taking the West Coast main railway line across at an acute angle. Beneath Northwich Road Bridge on the right can be seen the east end of the first section of the Runcorn & Latchford Canal creeping in almost unnoticed at the site of Twenty Steps Lock. It was another of the Mersey & Irwell's short cuts and at this end is dry and partly filled in. A quarter of a mile further on a branch canal leads off on the same side, part of the old river but now an arm to wharves, and just inside the entrance there is another branch through Walton Lock linking with the tidal river and now the only means of access to the upper river at Warrington.

The Ship Canal formerly was the boundary between Lancashire and Cheshire from Irlam as far as Randles Sluices, half way between Warrington and Runcorn, a role inherited from the Mersey. Now Warrington somewhat incongruously forms part of Cheshire. The rest of the Ship Canal onwards through Runcorn to Eastham is therefore dealt with in David Owen's companion volume **Cheshire Waterways.**

Pleasure cruising on the Ship Canal is not encouraged and is restricted to craft of proven seaworthiness under competent command, and is subject to stringent conditions. Application should be made to the Harbour Master, Dock Office, Manchester, M5 2XB.

The River Mersey
and the Mersey & Irwell Navigation

THE tidal Mersey up to Warrington has been used as a commercial navigation since medieval times. At the lowest crossing of the river, the town was a place of consequence for centuries while Liverpool was only a fishing village, the latter's rise to importance dating from 1715 when the first dock was opened. The estuarial Mersey was, and still is, the great highway of trade for the North West, but up to the eighteenth century all goods had to be transhipped at Warrington or up the tidal Weaver above Frodsham, to or from packhorses.

The first record of an attempt to improve the Mersey navigation was in 1698 when fish weirs were removed up to Bank Quay, Warrington, and 2,000 tons of goods a year were moving to and from Liverpool. Sailing barges, or 'flats', were developed over the years for river traffic, small at first carrying only 10 or 15 tons, but by the nineteenth century evolving into craft of 100 tons burden, or 200 on the Weaver, and venturing up and down the coast, to the Isle of Man and to Ireland. Generally they had a gaff fore-and-aft rig for coastal and estuarial sailing, but inland their masts were dismantled and they were hauled by gangs of men or, later, by horses. It was the Mersey flat that dictated the dimensions of the river navigations and canals spreading inland from the Mersey; the furthest point they reached was Sowerby Bridge in Yorkshire at the far end of the Rochdale Canal. The Leeds & Liverpool to Wigan, the Bridgewater and the St. Helens Canals were all built to take flats, together with the earlier Douglas Navigation, from the Ribble to Wigan, and the Lancaster Canal, reached via Glasson Dock.

As early as the 1660s a Bill to make the Rivers Mersey and Irwell navigable to Manchester had been introduced into Parliament in an attempt to avoid transhipment at Warrington, but it failed. Later Thomas Steers, who built Liverpool's first dock, was commissioned in 1712 to survey the two rivers. Nothing was done until, in 1721, an Act incorporated the Mersey & Irwell Navigation Company. Of the 38 promoters, 33 were Manchester men. Eight weirs with locks were authorised to raise the water level, and, after a slow start, navigation was possible to Blackfriars,

Manchester by 1736, and was extended a little further in 1740 to Hunts Bank. Later wharves and warehouses were laid out at Great Sankey, Warrington and in Manchester. Two artificial cuts had been made at Woolston and Howley above Warrington by 1761.

The opening of the Bridgewater Canal to Runcorn in 1776 introduced competition, to the extent that in 1779 the navigation was sold to a group of Liverpool and Manchester men who immediately set about improvements, so that by 1793 there was a total of six short cuts avoiding loops in the river, significantly reducing the distance above Warrington. The really big improvement was the cutting of the Runcorn & Latchford Canal on the Cheshire side in 1804, 7¾ miles long and saving over three miles of tidal water. Then in 1821 the Woolston Cut in turn was superseded by a new one, 1½ miles long, avoiding yet another curve, so that by this time the length of the navigation was reduced to 28¾ miles, not much longer than the rival Bridgewater.

Despite intense competition between the two parallel waterways the rapidly expanding economy provided enough business to earn handsome profits for both, until the opening of the Liverpool & Manchester Railway in 1830. Even then, by a combination of judicious rate cutting and tripartite agreements, all three concerns continued a healthy existence until the Bridgewater Trustees took over the Mersey & Irwell in 1846, although the new owners continued to operate it as a separate concern. In 1872 the Bridgewater Navigation Company was formed under indirect railway ownership, but with a considerable degree of independence so that improvements continued up to the formation of the Manchester Ship Canal Company in 1885 (p. 57). Under their Act they were obliged to purchase both navigations, although it was really the Mersey & Irwell that was wanted in order to construct the Ship Canal along it. As a result the Warrington-Runcorn section of the Latchford Canal was abandoned, together with the various cuts above Rixton Junction, leaving only the original section of navigable river in Manchester, the River Irwell Upper Reach to Hunts Bank, which in effect was an extension of the Ship Canal. Now only a short arm at Warrington stays in use as a dock; the Woolston New Cut and the river via the Butchersfield Cut to the Ship Canal at Rixton were out of use for navigation by the early 1930s; the upper part of the Runcorn & Latchford was no longer used after 1970; but traffic to Warrington from the Ship Canal can still use Walton Lock.

Like the Bridgewater the Mersey & Irwell company operated an extensive passenger service from 1806 well into the railway age in the 1860s. Boats left Manchester for Runcorn from a wharf on the Salford bank near what is now Albert Bridge, where waiting rooms were made under the roadway. They called at Warrington and connections with the Liverpool river steamers were made at

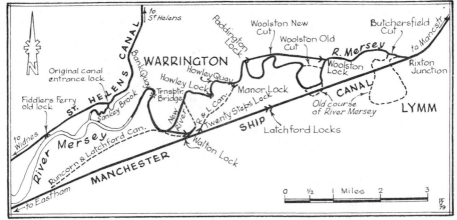

Three generations of waterways at Warrington

Runcorn. Downstream packets took eight hours—an hour less than the competing Bridgewater service—and in the upstream direction boats took the same time as the Bridgewater's.

Starting from Victoria Bridge opposite Manchester Cathedral, the first remains to be seen of the old navigation are the mouldering wooden landing stages whence until comparatively recent times steamers started for pleasure trips to Pomona Gardens. They were also used for landing goods to be stored in arches beneath the road. The river here is generally slow-flowing, held back by the Mode Wheel sluices except in times of flood. Beyond Albert Bridge the large Ralli Building on the right has canopies over the water, beneath which barges used to tie up until the mid 1970s; this is followed on the Manchester bank by some fine old Mersey & Irwell warehouses backing on to Water Street, and the few remains of the Manchester & Salford Junction Canal entrance (p. 55). It was at the busy quays hereabouts that in the early and mid 1800s so much of Manchester's freight was handled, with barges filling the river—a scene difficult to picture today. On the Salford side alongside Princes Bridge the Manchester, Bolton & Bury Canal entered (p. 50). Here a good towing path starts, running under the old Liverpool & Manchester Railway bridges and Regent's Bridge, and crossing an old arm to a Salford Corporation depot with the coat of arms in the ironwork. Hulme Lock, the navigation's connection to the Bridgewater (p. 15), and the mouth of the Medlock can be seen on the opposite bank beneath the railway viaduct; then Woden Street footbridge is reached, the official commencement of the Ship Canal (p. 57). Nearby is moored a former Liverpool ferryboat, now 'Manchester's Only Ship Pub', alongside a Comet airliner, looking somewhat out of place but just another of the attractions. From

63

here to Barton the old river has been completely obliterated; Pomona Gardens and Trafford Park with their fine houses and wooded landscapes have long since been turned into docks and the world's largest industrial estate.

Between Barton and Warrington it is possible in places to see three generations of waterway: the winding courses of the original river and the Mersey & Irwell short cuts, both sliced through by the Ship Canal. Yet some sections still hold water like those immediately below Barton Locks, close to Irlam Ferry and near Irlam Locks. From the high cantilevers of Warburton toll bridge onwards much more can be seen, including remains of the old bridge close to the village and, from Rixton Junction, the course of a great loop southward to Lymm and back, forming almost a complete circle but for a narrow isthmus at the top which was severed by the Mersey & Irwell's Butchersfield Cut. From the junction the river is independent of the Ship Canal, looping past Warrington with most of the cuts intact, forming a somewhat bewildering pattern. Woolston New Cut is mainly in water but low and full of rubbish. Paddington Lock at the lower end is filled in, and the wooden trough that once took water across the river to feed the Latchford Canal has gone, although the channel can still be seen running alongside the river to Manor Lock through which the Warrington & Latchford Canal bears away on the south side. It is now sealed off, although the rotting lock gates remain in position. Rather unexpectedly the fall of the lock was into the river, as the canal level was higher, hence the need for the feeder from Woolston New Cut. The river then bends south at Howley Quay, whose large warehouses on the north bank once served Warrington, and, after passing under a suspension footbridge built in 1912, quickly turns west on a sharp horseshoe bend beside Howley Lock and weir. The lock now only serves to regulate the flow, as from here the river is tidal. At Warrington Bridge the Mersey itself was diverted into the New River when the Ship Canal was built, to avoid a further loop down to Walton, part being retained as an arm and dock off the Ship Canal and part, through Walton Lock, as a connection back into the river above Bank Quay. The river curves sharply again from south to north under the main railway line which it follows to Bank Quay, situated on another horseshoe bend now straddled by Crosfields' Soap Works. Connecting the works on either bank is an unusual private transporter bridge built in 1916, one of only four in the country and the only one carrying rail tracks. It has been out of regular use since 1964.

The river now leaves Warrington and winds its way less tortuously between water meadows and reclaimed land past the giant Fiddlers Ferry power station to Widnes and Runcorn, the Ship Canal lying to the south with the lower course of the Runcorn and Latchford Canal sandwiched between them. The widening estuary briefly narrows at Runcorn Gap where it is spanned by the railway viaduct and the new Runcorn-Widnes high level road bridge that replaced the old transporter, and then rapidly broadens around Hale Head and on to Liverpool and the Irish Sea. The West Docks at Widnes are still used, but above them the river is the home of small pleasure craft. The estuary is controlled by the Port of Manchester as far downstream as Bromborough Dock on the Cheshire shore, which marks the boundary with the Port of Liverpool.

The River Ribble

PRESTON was a port at least as early as 1360, but like the Lune the Ribble estuary, navigable to Penwortham Bridge, was always troubled by sandbanks. A Ribble Navigation Company was formed in 1806 but did little more than reclaim land until a new company, in which Preston Corporation held shares, set about dredging the channel in 1838. The Corporation commenced building Victoria Quay at the foot of Marsh Lane in 1839 and the Victoria Warehouse, which still stands in Strand Road, in 1844. Two years later the quays were reached by the Ribble Branch railway and in addition to imported cargoes from Europe and North America there was a steamer service to Liverpool and Scotland.

Previously, in 1834, a ship canal was proposed from Lytham to take 200 ton vessels but failed to gain support, and then in 1842 a dock was opened at Lytham, served by the railway from 1846. Freckleton, too, at the head of a short creek on the north bank, had warehouses and small industries in the early 1800s, and also enjoyed trade by canal barge from the Leeds & Liverpool at Tarleton on the Douglas opposite (p. 35).

In 1882 Preston Corporation took over the Navigation Company, diverted the river across Penwortham Marsh up to the bridge and constructed the 3,000 feet by 600 feet King Edward VII Dock, opened in 1892. For some years it was the largest in Britain and at last gave Preston just claim to being a true port. Unfortunately at present its future is somewhat uncertain. The estuary is popular for sailing and there is a thriving boat club at Lytham.

The Rochdale Canal

THE Rochdale Canal is a remarkable waterway, which makes it all the more sad that today so much of it is derelict, although its most notable feature—92 locks in 33 miles—probably contributed most to its demise. Indeed, it is even more remarkable that in the face of rail and road competition it lasted so long. The canal is broad, crossing the Pennines to link the Bridgewater Canal at Castlefield, Manchester with the Calder & Hebble Navigation at Sowerby Bridge, so giving access to the Aire & Calder system in Yorkshire, and the Humber. The Rochdale was born out of canal politics, set against rival schemes backed by the Leeds & Liverpool and the Manchester, Bolton & Bury Canals for a shorter and more southerly cross-Pennine route, and the projected Huddersfield Canal (p. 19). There was intense argument about whether the canal should be broad or narrow, the Duke of Bridgewater—who was also busily stirring the pot—favouring narrow so that he could keep the Manchester-Liverpool traffic to his own barges. John Rennie surveyed the route, including a summit tunnel in his scheme, aided by William Crosley senior, and at the third attempt an Act was secured in 1794 for a broad canal with locks of Bridgewater dimensions, 74 feet by 14 feet. Rennie has been credited with construction of the canal, wrongly, for it was William Jessop who was appointed engineer with Crosley as his assistant.

Compared with Brindley, Rennie and Telford, Jessop is barely remembered as an engineer, yet he was responsible for 27 canal schemes in the period 1789 to 1796, all of which, moreover, were built substantially as he designed them, including such major waterways as the Grand Canal of Ireland, the 93 mile Grand Junction Canal from London to Braunston, and the Rochdale. In addition he designed extensive fen drainage schemes, the West India and Bristol docks and numerous other works. In his day he was in great demand as the premier civil engineer in Britain.

Jessop was a great believer in reservoirs for supplying canals with water, rather than relying on a long summit level, and he was not a lover of tunnelling. He maintained that the expense and extra time taken in boring a summit tunnel could be reduced by having more locks, a shorter open summit and reservoirs, thus bringing a canal more quickly into revenue-earning use. He also advocated uniform depth of locks, as far as might be possible, as a further means of saving water. All these principles were successfully put into practice on the Rochdale, cutting out Rennie's proposed 3,000 yard tunnel by adding seven extra locks on each side, constructing adequate reservoirs and endeavouring to build his locks with uniform rises. On the Yorkshire side all but two rise almost exactly 10 feet, while on the Lancashire side above Piccadilly they are all between 7 feet 10 inches and 10 feet 9 inches. Uniformity made gates interchangeable, too. Consequently the Rochdale was an exceedingly well built and trouble-free canal.

It was opened in stages from Sowerby Bridge, reaching Piccadilly in 1804. The length to Castlefield had already been open since 1799. It was the first trans-Pennine canal. Rochdale itself was reached by a half mile branch opened in 1798 and in 1834 a branch was opened to Heywood. There were eventually eight reservoirs, the largest and best known being Hollingworth Lake near Littleborough. Unfortunately the Calder & Hebble' Locks were only 57 feet 6 inches long so while their craft could use the Rochdale Canal, Bridgewater and Rochdale barges had to tranship their cargoes at Sowerby Bridge.

The Rochdale was a successful canal, managing to compete with the railways, and traffic did not seriously decline until the coming of the motor lorry. In the early 1920s regular through traffic ceased

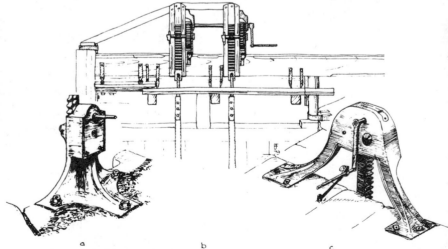

Three Paddle Gears
a   **Ground Paddle, Manchester — Rochdale Canal**
b   **Gate Paddles, Hulme — St. Helens Canal**
c   **Ground Paddle, Galgate — Lancaster Canal**

and in 1923 the reservoirs were sold to local authorities, the company retaining rights to water under certain conditions. The last 'through' working trip was in 1937 and just after the war even short-haul traffic ceased so that the canal was virtually disused as a navigation, for which reason it was not nationalised. In 1952 the company obtained an Act of abandonment for the whole canal except the section between Piccadilly and Castlefield in Manchester.

As part of the Ashton Canal restoration (p. 10) this section of the Rochdale was vital in order to retain the Cheshire Ring. It was known that the company wished to abandon it, so the Inland Waterways Association arranged for a narrow boat to be taken (with great difficulty) through the nine locks to Piccadilly basin. The company then agreed not to abandon the section as long as the Ashton legally remained open, and, following work by volunteers, a rally of boats was held at Piccadilly in 1971. Although in far from perfect condition, the Rochdale Canal in Manchester remains navigable and for the present the Cheshire Ring is safe.

Scenically the Rochdale's climb out of Lancashire is much less attractive than the ascent to the summit from the Yorkshire side. Starting from the entrance lock at Castlefield, cut out of the sandstone, the canal passes alongside the old Cheshire Lines railway viaduct in a rock cutting where three sunken wooden barges lie. Deansgate Tunnel, 78 yards long, has a lock at the end of it and until 1845 was 336 yards long. The canal now climbs through and beneath the heart of Manchester by seven more locks, passing beneath major streets like Oxford Road, Princess Street and Piccadilly, although few people know it is there. At Oxford Road it passes under the well-known St. James House while at Princess Street an iron roving bridge takes the towing path on to the pavement of Canal Street, where the wall coping is smooth from the rubbing of towlines, although these days any towing would be prevented by a row of parking meters. The canalside proper is regained at Minshull Street but the gate is kept locked and the walker has to cross Piccadilly and enter a small door in Dale Street to gain the water again above Dale Street Lock. Rodwell Tower has been built over the lock, creating an eerie place lit by a few electric lights, the concrete columns of the building rising out of the water which rushes in a constant stream over the gates. All the side weirs have been blocked up. In Dale Street itself are the company's offices and an imposing crenellated arch formerly leading to the wharves which have been filled in to make a carpark. Of the great warehouses two remain but are waterless.

The Ashton Canal (p. 9) starts here, leaving the Rochdale on the right. The latter, now unnavigable, continues on under Great Ancoats Street to climb up through Miles Platting and Newton Heath in a generally depressing environment of boarded-up council flats, down at heel industry and empty demolition sites. Like Canal Street part of Redhill Street acts as the towing path and then from New Union Street the path has been asphalted to Varley Street as part of the Ancoats landscaping scheme, with lamps, seats and shrubs. Unfortunately the idea has backfired through severe vandalism, with broken equipment and graffiti galore. While there are derelict and uncared-for buildings around, the canalside is unlikely to be respected. The idea may have been a good one but without education clearly has been impractical.

From Ancoats to the Manchester city boundary the canal has been filled in to a depth of 18 inches and the locks weired, to make it safe, and beyond Varley Street it is mainly a dumping ground. Some bridges have been culverted and at Failsworth, although normal depth is now regained, a large shopping centre and carpark have been built over the canal, the water being piped beneath for some 300 yards; one hopes the pipe never becomes blocked! After Chadderton the canal enters open country with views of the Pennines and it is good to see the bridge at Haigh Lane rebuilt to full height and width instead of the all too familiar culvert. The water is deeper and wider here as it traverses a horseshoe bend to cross the River Irk by a stone skew aqueduct. Some of the locks have retained their upper gates to act as weirs; others have been concreted. Near Castleton the M62 motorway cuts completely across the canal, obliterating the junction with the Heywood Branch which is now filled in, although three bridges remain and a walled open space marks the terminus.

Soon the canal enters the outskirts of Rochdale, here just a trickle of water flowing down a rubbish-filled bed, but beyond the culverted Castleton Bridge things are better and the canal is full again. March Barn Bridge is interesting from an engineering view-point as probably being the first true skew arch to have been built in England with winder courses, a tribute to Jessop's ingenuity and skill. Then a typical row of Rochdale's great red brick spinning mills lines the right hand bank—Arrow, Ensor and Crest. Gorrell's Bridge has disappeared beneath another new road interchange, burrowed by a culvert, and beyond there are more culverts beneath access roads to a housing estate, although the canal is full and has been retained as a feature of the development. Then comes the surprise—from Brook Motors' carpark to Firgrove Bridge there are no more culverts and the two Rochdale Locks are being restored under a job creation scheme to give a one and a half mile cruising length. The locks themselves are being landscaped and the junction with the filled-in Rochdale Branch tidied up. The arm can still be traced into the town centre by its bridges, although the large ware-houses at the basin were demolished a few years ago.

As the canal climbs towards Littleborough and the summit the hills draw closer and Blackstone Edge rises to the north east. The landscape becomes increasingly wild. Between Belfield and Smithy Bridge there is an interesting group of waterside buildings—the derelict seventeenth century Clegg Hall, a row of handloom weavers' cottages, the canal bridge and a small stone-built water-mill with two tailrace openings into the canal. There are more culverted bridges at Smithy Bridge and Littleborough, and a mill extension over the water, before the final locks ascend to the summit cutting, three quarters of a mile long. Then comes the first lock in Yorkshire, starting the steep descent down the dramatic gorge of the Calder valley through Todmorden to Sowerby Bridge.

The Rochdale Canal Society aims to promote restoration of the canal, although the 36 obstructions it has listed, in addition to lock restoration, would seem a formidable deterrent. However, both Greater Manchester and Calderdale councils have agreed in principle to renovation and maintenance of canals for recreational and amenity purposes and to exercise a 'holding' policy to prevent further encroachment. The Rochdale is seen as an important feature in the proposed Pennine Park.

The St. Helens Canal

THE St. Helens Canal was created to satisfy the Cheshire salt manufacturers' need for Lancashire coal. In the seventeenth century they relied on packhorses and ferrying across the Mersey to Frodsham, but by 1732 the situation improved when the River Weaver was made navigable up to Winsford, although there was no comparable development on the Lancashire shore. By this time Liverpool's growing demand for cheaper coal was becoming equally insistent. In 1753 Liverpool Corporation instructed their dock engineer, Henry Berry, to survey the Sankey Brook from the Mersey west of Warrington to pits around St. Helens. Merchants and coalowners promoted a navigation Bill which passed through Parliament without opposition in 1755 and, although the Act clearly authorised the making navigable of 'the River or Brook called Sankey Brook....from the River Mersey near Sankey Bridges', it seems that the promoters knew it was too small and were deliberately relying on a clause empowering 'such new Cuts, Canals.... upon or through Lands or Grounds adjacent.... as they (the proprietors) shall think proper and requisite' to construct an entirely separate canal, using the brook and its tributaries only for a supply of water. Berry commenced work and by 1757 the canal was open from near Broad Oak, St. Helens, running parallel to the brook through what later became Earlestown and Winwick to Sankey Bridges, where it joined the tidal part of the brook about a mile from the Mersey. In 1762 a southerly extension was constructed alongside the river to Fiddlers Ferry, where an entrance lock was built, thus avoiding the lower reaches of the brook. By 1772 the northern end had been progressively extended in three branches to Blackbrook, Gerrards Bridge and Boardmans Bridge, all close to St. Helens, the last being extended again at a later stage to copper and glass works at Ravenhead. Maps of the 1790s show a canal from Thatto Heath collieries to Ravenhead British Plate Glass Works, half a mile long, about which little is known except that it did not connect with the Sankey Brook Navigation.

The canal took Mersey flats, 68 feet by 16 feet 9 inches, and in total was 13 3/8 miles long with ten locks on the main line, the uppermost being a two-rise staircase with another staircase on the

Boardmans Bridge Branch. The bridges were all swing type, so that flats could use their sails whenever possible, carrying up to 75 tons. The canal pre-dated the Bridgewater by three years, but in 1774 competition was felt when Wigan coal could reach Liverpool by the Leeds & Liverpool Canal and the Douglas. Two years later the Duke completed his canal to Runcorn, providing competition from a second source, although most of the Sankey coal went to the Weaver. Such was the demand, though, that the company prospered until 1830 when the rival St. Helens & Runcorn Gap Railway was authorised to provide St. Helens colliery owners with a shorter and quicker route to the Mersey, prompting the Sankey proprietors to extend their canal from Fiddlers Ferry 3½ miles westward to enter the Mersey in deeper water at Runcorn Gap, where they built a dock and twin entrance locks taking craft up to 79 feet by 20 feet, capable of carrying 150 tons. Both canal and railway were completed in 1833, the latter also building a dock, but established trade ensured that canal carriage continued to prosper at the expense of rail until 1845 when the two concerns agreed to amalgamate as the St. Helens Canal & Railway Company. Meanwhile Runcorn Gap had deveoped as the new town of Widnes. New railways were built, some replacing the earlier tramroads that fed the canal branches, and in 1864 the London & North Western Railway absorbed the combined undertaking, later becoming part of the London, Midland & Scottish.

Declining traffic closed half a mile of the Ravenhead arm in 1898 and in 1919 the last craft worked up to St. Helens. Then in 1931 the entire canal beyond Newton Common Lock at Earlestown was closed and retained only as a feeder. Traffic continued to the Sankey Sugar works at Earlestown until 1959, when road transport took over, and the canal was abandoned in 1963.

Throughout the canal most of the bridges have been replaced, culverted or filled in, and only the first six miles from Widnes are easily recognisable, apart from odd sections further on. The two entrance locks are still there, their inner ends filled in, and the canal dock alongside has also been filled in to about four feet and grassed. A large tract of land around the first quarter of a mile between the canal and the Mersey, formerly the railway dock and sidings, is being converted into a park and recreation area by the local authority, although the chemical works still form a backdrop. Except for a trickle of water the broad canal bed is dry, revealing the stout stone walls forming its sides, although it is the intention to fill it again as part of the park scheme. Closely paralleled by the railway on the north side, in two miles Fiddlers Ferry power station is passed on the left after which there is clear, reedy water and the canal assumes a pleasanter appearance. The flat land between it and the Mersey comprises marshes and saltings, and close to Fiddlers Ferry itself on the right is the old entrance lock from the river. Beyond is the Ferry Inn and restaurant, an attractively white-painted low building at the site of one of the old Mersey ferries.

During later years there was an electrically operated, single-span bascule road bridge at Sankey Bridges alongside a railway swing bridge, both now replaced by fixed structures at low level. The Sloop pub nearby recalls former trade. The canal follows the Sankey Brook, skirting Warrington, to the derelict Bewsey Lock where water ends. Beyond this point the brook formerly looped to the east but recently has been diverted through a new channel alongside the canal, which has been filled in with spoil from the excavations. At one point the brook now cuts across the canal bed so that the walker cannot proceed further. The best way is to leave the canal at Bewsey Old Hall and regain it at Dallam where the brook formerly ran under beneath an aqueduct. The old channel can be seen on the right with the remains of a wooden sluice. Hulme Lock at the time of writing (March 1979) is the only one not filled in, its gates rotting but reasonably complete with double paddles, and the lock cottage still occupied, but thereafter the canal has been completely filled in with unsightly waste and only the tops of the gates protruding forlornly from the rubble indicate Winwick Lock.

Notice Board, Winwick — St. Helens Canal

The canal workshops at Winwick Quay retain their attractive outline, with 1841 datestone, and are used by a plant contractor, a far cry from the scene in 1955 when the mayors of Widnes and St. Helens accompanied the Railway & Canal Historical Society on a cruise from Widnes in the Leeds & Liverpool shortboat **Leo,**

74

(afterwards renamed **Shelagh** when she became a trip boat on the Lancaster Canal). The occasion was the celebration of the 200th anniversary of the first canal Act, and the party disembarked at Winwick to view the workshops.

Some three quarters of a mile of canal is in water from Newton Brook near Vulcan village, where a culvert has been replaced by an open channel across the bed and a footbridge. Beyond it the canal is in good shape, wide and clear with a newly restored towing path, although Hey Lock and Bradley Lock, at the termination, have been filled in. Then past the Sankey Sugar works and under Stephenson's impressive Sankey Viaduct on the Liverpool & Manchester Railway the canal is virtually untraceable. The valley becomes more pronounced here and from the site of Newton Common Lock the canal course is a footpath through the Sankey Valley Linear Park, in process of being established with picnic areas and occasional small pools. Close to the A572 road bridge brick arches carry the towing path over an old overflow into the brook.

Approaching St. Helens the walker encounters several short, shallow watered sections with a deep 'flash' alongside, and then close to landscaped colliery tips there is the water-filled chamber of Engine Lock followed by three more ponded sections. Here the Black Brook flowed under the canal but is now diverted along a short part of the bed before joining the Sankey Brook, and stone walling starts on the towing path side. Water flows down the canal bed to this point, and there is a large stone-lined basin that has been restored. Then the cascaded Old Double Lock is reached, the first two-rise staircase and the first staircase lock to be built in the country. At the top the canal divides, left to Gerrards Bridge (now covered by a playing field) and to the right the Blackbrook Branch which is in water. Blackbrook Bridge on the A58 by the Ship Inn was lowered in the 1930s, one of the first results of closure, and beyond it more landscaping is being carried out, including work on a basin on the right, for a stretch of a quarter of a mile to the old terminal basin. The whole valley has been filled in from here, although in places traces of old feeder tramroad and railway embankments may still be discovered.

The Gerrards Bridge Branch can be seen again where it passed beneath Blackbrook Road (A58) nearer St. Helens, as at this point it entered the canalised Rainford Brook which flows out by a side weir. The stone towing path walling is visible for 100 yards but beyond it the brook now has the appearance of an urban watercourse amid much land reclamation. Past Islands Brow there is a deep artificial cutting along the back of Rockware Glassworks to Gerrards Bridge, where only an open space denotes the site of the basin that was the head of the navigation.

Just short of Rockware another cutting leads off the brook to the left, sandwiched between the glassworks and a transport yard, containing the substantial, rubbish-strewn remains of New Double Lock at the entrance to the Boardmans Bridge Branch. Although now severed from the brook itself, some water still runs out through a pipe. The entire site is sordid in the extreme, but above the lock, reached from Standish Street at Pocket Nook, there remains a length alongside the gasworks full of clear water. The bridge has gone but further on again there is another watered stretch beside the railway to Corporation Street Bridge—still complete—after which several hundred yards have been filled in and built upon. Finally, on the other side of Church Street close to the town centre, water reappears for a quarter of a mile length alongside Pilkingtons' Sheet Glassworks which uses the canal for cooling water, resulting in clouds of steam from sprays projecting over it. But the level is wide and deep, and still looks like a canal.

The Ulverston Canal

IN 1793 a group of Furness men obtained an Act to build a ship canal from Morecambe Bay 1 3/8 miles to the market town of Ulverston in order to expedite the growing export of iron ore and slate. John Rennie designed it, 15 feet deep and 66 feet wide, with an entrance lock big enough to take coastal vessels 104 feet by 27 feet carrying up to 120 tons. The canal opened in 1796 and there were ideas about joining it to the Lancaster Canal, which never developed. It was not a financial success, no dividend being paid until 1836, but it helped the expansion of Ulverston. The shifting sands of the bay hindered access and even after a stone pier was built from 1815 to 1820 larger vessels could only enter intermittently on high tides. By 1828 there were regular sailings to London, Liverpool, Scotland and Preston, and in 1835 a passenger service operated to Liverpool for a few years. The rise of Barrow-in-Furness really caused the canal's decline and a new breakwater in 1849 failed to save it. The Furness Railway took it over in 1862, from which it passed in 1923 to the London, Midland & Scottish, although the last vessels used it in 1916 after which Ulverston ceased to be a port. The canal was abandoned in 1945 and is now owned by the neighbouring Glaxo factory.

The canal is still complete. A road runs along its north bank from the basin behind the Canal Tavern on the main road into the town from Lancaster. It passes under a railway viaduct and, on the opposite bank, there is a basin built by the railway company and a former foundry and paper mill. A roller-opening bridge (now fixed) carries the former Conishead Priory branch railway over the water, now a siding to Glaxo which occupies the site of an extensive ironworks on the south side. At Canal Foot the sea lock's inner gates are derelict and the outer ones and a swing bridge have been replaced by concrete. The stone pier is still there, with iron bollards, and there are fine views across Morecambe Bay.

The River Wyre

IN the seventeenth century the Wyre estuary was used by shipping at least as far as Skippool Creek on the Fylde bank, and although little now remains it is recorded that grain was still being discharged there around 1870. On the opposite shore close to Hambledon is Wardleys Creek where more substantial remains of a port can be seen—a stone quay and a warehouse. It could have been used as an anchorage as early as Elizabethan times, and in the eighteenth and early nineteenth centuries flax was imported here for the Kirkham linen mills, to be taken across by the ferry at Shard before the toll bridge was built. Shipbuilding was also undertaken into the middle of the last century.

All this was superseded by the development of Fleetwood at the Wyre's mouth, from the opening of the railway in 1840 onwards. Throughout the century the port expanded, particularly the docks under railway ownership, but after the last war decline set in. The railway progressively closed in the years 1966 to 1970, although a container service operates from the reconstructed landing stage. One can also sail from here to the Isle of Man in summer months. Fleetwood still has a dwindling trawler fleet, but as a port is now a shadow of its former prosperous self. Like the Ribble, the estuary is extensively used by small sailing boats.

ACKNOWLEDGEMENTS

I am indebted to David Owen, John Freeman of British Waterways and the Mersey Docks & Harbour Company for information and assistance.

Photographs are by the author or from his collection, except where otherwise acknowledged.

I am also grateful to Peter Fells for the maps and drawings.

GENERAL INFORMATION

British Waterways Board: Area Engineer's Office, Swan Meadow Road, Wigan.

Manchester Ship Canal Company: Bridgewater Department, Chester Road, Manchester, M15 4NU.

Boat Clubs:
(where an address is not given for a club the current secretary's address is obtainable from the British Waterways Board.)

East Lancs. & West Yorks. Boat Club (Leeds & Liverpool).

Lancaster Canal Boat Club.

Mersey Motor Boat Club (Leeds & Liverpool).

Stretford Boat Club (Bridgewater Canal). Edge Lane, Stretford, Manchester.

Watchhouse Cruising Club (Bridgewater Canal). Canalside, Hawthorn St., Stretford, Manchester.

Wheelton Boat Club (Leeds & Liverpool).

Canal Societies:

Inland Waterways Association, 114 Regents Park Road, London, NW1 8UQ.

(for Manchester, Merseyside and North Lancs. & Cumbria Branches).

Lancaster Canal Trust, 74, Margaret Road, Penwortham, Preston.

Huddersfield Canal Society, 3, Pump Row, High Flatts, Huddersfield, W. Yorks.

Rochdale Canal Society, 24, Passmonds Crescent, Rochdale.

Hire Craft Operators:

Ashton Canal -

Wayfarer Narrow Boats, Portland St. Basin, Ashton-under-Lyne, Greater Manchester.

Masons Cruiser Hire, William St. Moorings, Northcote St., Ashton-under-Lyne, Greater Manchester.

Bridgewater Canal -

Cheshire Plain Hire Cruisers, The Old Boat Yard, Worsley, Manchester.

Egerton Narrow Boats, 7, Barton Road, Worsley, Manchester

Lancaster Canal -

Preston Hire Cruisers, Moons Bridge, Catforth. (4, Beech Avenue, Warton, nr Preston).

Adventure Cruisers, Jolly Roger Boating Haven, Swillbrook Bridge, Catforth, Preston.
Ladyline Ltd., Nor'west Marina, Canal Wharf, Galgate, nr. Lancaster.
Nu-Way Marina, Carnforth, Lancaster.
Leeds & Liverpool Canal -
Canal Boats, Ship Inn, Rosemary Lane, Haskayne, nr. Ormskirk.
L & L Cruisers, Rawlinson Lane, Heath Charnock, nr. Chorley.
H. Lord, 58, Mansfield Crescent, Brierfield, Nelson.
Boatell Cruises, Boat Yard, Kenyon Lane, Wheelton, Chorley.

FURTHER READING

The Industrial Archaeology of Lancashire, Owen Ashmore, David & Charles, 1969.
A History of the Ribble Navigation, James Barron, Preston Corporation, 1938.
Pennine Waterway, a Pictorial History of the Leeds & Liverpool Canal, Gordon Biddle, Dalesman Books, 1977.
Nicholson's Guides to the Waterways, Vol 2, North West, British Waterways Board.
A Pictorial History of the Mersey & Irwell Navigation, John Corbridge, E.J. Morten, 1979.
The Canal Age, Charles Hadfield, David & Charles, 1968.
British Canals, an Illustrated History, Charles Hadfield, David & Charles, 1974.
The Canals of North West England, (2 vols), Charles Hadfield & Gordon Biddle, David & Charles, 1970.
William Jessop, Engineer, Charles Hadfield & A.W. Skempton, David & Charles, 1979.
History of the Manchester Ship Canal, Sir Bosdin Leech, 1907.
Bridgewater, the Canal Duke, Hugh Malet, Manchester University Press, 1977.
Waterways & Railways to Warrington, Peter Norton, Railway & Canal Historical Society, 1974.
Canals to Manchester, David Owen, Manchester University Press, 1977.
Canal & River Navigations, E.W. Paget-Tomlinson, Waine Research Publications, 1978.
Mersey & Weaver Flats, Edward Paget-Tomlinson, Robert Wilson, 1974.